WITHDRAWN

THE PUBLIC FORUM
AND CHRISTIAN ETHICS

This book addresses the question of the communication of Christian ethics in the public forum of liberal, pluralist societies. Drawing on debates in philosophy, theology and sociological theory, it relates the problem of communication to fundamental questions about the nature of liberal societies and the identity of Christian faith and the Christian community. With particular emphasis on Kantian and neo-Kantian ethics, it explores the link between autonomy and community in liberal societies. The theology of *communio*, expressed in revealed Christian traditions, can reconcile autonomy and community. Any Christian attempt to communicate this vision must also reflect on Christianity's own identity, especially the ways in which its own self-consciousness grows in critical interaction with secularity. In this light, Christian ethical communication is both a witness to a distinctive identity, founded in the revelation of the triune God, and a vision of universal human solidarity which can reconcile autonomy and community.

ROBERT GASCOIGNE is Associate Professor of Theology at the Australian Catholic University. He is a member of the Australian Catholic Theological Association, the Australian and New Zealand Society for Theological Studies, and the Catholic Theological Society of America, and his published works include *Freedom and Purpose: An Introduction to Christian Ethics* (1993) and *Religion, Rationality and Community: Sacred and Secular in the Thought of Hegel and his Critics* (1985). He has also written articles for *Religious Studies*, *Colloquium* (Australian and New Zealand Theological Studies), *Pacifica*, and *Australasian Catholic Record*.

NEW STUDIES IN CHRISTIAN ETHICS

General editor
Robin Gill

Editorial board
Stephen R. L. Clark, Stanley Hauerwas, Robin W. Lovin

Christian ethics has increasingly assumed a central place within academic theology. At the same time the growing power and ambiguity of modern science and the rising dissatisfaction within the social sciences about claims to value-neutrality have prompted renewed interest in ethics within the secular academic world. There is, therefore, a need for studies in Christian ethics which, as well as being concerned with the relevance of Christian ethics to the present-day secular debate, are well informed about parallel discussions in recent philosophy, science or social science. New Studies in Christian Ethics aims to provide books that do this at the highest intellectual level and demonstrate that Christian ethics can make a distinctive contribution to this debate – either in moral substance or in terms of underlying moral justifications.

Titles published in the series
1. *Rights and Christian Ethics* Kieran Cronin
2. *Biblical Interpretation and Christian Ethics* Ian McDonald
3. *Power and Christian Ethics* James Mackey
4. *Plurality and Christian Ethics* Ian S. Markham
5. *Moral Action and Christian Ethics* Jean Porter
6. *Responsibility and Christian Ethics* William Schweiker
7. *Justice and Christian Ethics* F. Clinton Gardner
8. *Feminism and Christian Ethics* Susan Parsons
9. *Sex, Gender and Christian Ethics* Lisa Sowle Cahill
10. *The Environment and Christian Ethics* Michael S. Northcott
11. *Concepts of Person and Christian Ethics* Stanley Rudman
12. *Priorities and Christian Ethics* Garth Hallett
13. *Community, Liberalism and Christian Ethics* David Fergusson
14. *The Market Economy and Christian Ethics* Peter Sedgwick
15. *Churchgoing and Christian Ethics* Robin Gill
16. *Inequality and Christian Ethics* Douglas Hicks
17. *Biology and Christian Ethics* Stephen Clark
18. *Altruism and Christian Ethics* Colin Grant
19. *The Public Forum and Christian Ethics* Robert Gascoigne
20. *Evil and Christian Ethics* Gordon Graham

THE PUBLIC FORUM AND CHRISTIAN ETHICS

ROBERT GASCOIGNE

Australian Catholic University, Sydney

CAMBRIDGE UNIVERSITY PRESS

PUBLISHED BY THE PRESS SYNDICATE OF THE UNIVERSITY OF CAMBRIDGE
The Pitt Building, Trumpington Street, Cambridge, United Kingdom

CAMBRIDGE UNIVERSITY PRESS
The Edinburgh Building, Cambridge CB2 2RU, UK   www.cup.cam.ac.uk
40 West 20th Street, New York, NY 10011–4211, USA   www.cup.org
10 Stamford Road, Oakleigh, Melbourne 3166, Australia
Ruiz de Alarcón 13, 28014 Madrid, Spain

© Robert Gascoigne 2001

This book is in copyright. Subject to statutory exception
and to the provisions of relevant collective licensing agreements,
no reproduction of any part may take place without
the written permission of Cambridge University Press.

First published 2001

Printed in the United Kingdom at the University Press, Cambridge

Typeface Baskerville 11/12.5 pt   *System* 3b2   [CE]

A catalogue record for this book is available from the British Library

Library of Congress cataloguing in publication data

Gascoigne, Robert.
The Public Forum and Christian Ethics / Robert Gascoigne.
p.   cm. – (New studies in Christian ethics; 19)
Includes bibliographical references.
ISBN 0 521 79093 X (hardback)
1. Christian ethics – Catholic authors. 2. Social ethics. I. Title. II. Series.
BJ1249.G33 2000
241′.042 – dc21   00–023605

*To
Nicholas,
Michael and
Miriam*

Contents

General editor's preface	page xi
Acknowledgements	xiii
Introduction	1
1 Revelation and reason in liberal societies	11
2 Revelation and a contemporary public ethics	45
3 The theology of revelation and Christian identity	94
4 The communication of Christian ethics in the public forum	163
5 Reconciling autonomy and community	212
Select bibliography	236
Index	246

General editor's preface

This book is the nineteenth in the series New Studies in Christian Ethics. It complements David Fergusson's well received *Community, Liberalism and Christian Ethics*, which appeared earlier in the series. If the latter is written from a Reformed Christian perspective, indebted to Karl Barth, Robert Gascoigne's *The Public Forum and Christian Ethics* is written from an explicitly Catholic perspective, indebted to Karl Rahner. It is a sign of theological ecumenism that their differing theological perspectives complement each other so well. Both also admirably enshrine the two aims of the series, namely to promote monographs in Christian ethics which engage centrally with the present secular moral debate at the highest possible intellectual level and, secondly, to encourage contributors to demonstrate that Christian ethics can make a distinctive contribution to this debate.

In this new monograph Robert Gascoigne makes an impressive argument for the public role of Christian ethics, even in a context of modern, pluralistic societies. Furthermore, he does this using a wide range of philosophical, theological and sociological writers. In the process he offers an extended critique of the influential 'ecclesial ethicists', such as Stanley Hauerwas and John Milbank, who argue that it is paramount to challenge secular society with Christian faith and with the values they believe derive directly from this faith. For them, conversion always takes priority over inclusion. Robert Gascoigne's final position, which he sustains well, is that Christian ethics is able to engage in meaningful dialogue with secular forms of ethics in the public forum provided that it does not become too insular.

In entering such dialogue, Christian ethics, so he argues, can still seek to enrich the secular, exemplify Christian virtues and offer faith in a confused world.

An important feature of this monograph is its defence and critique of autonomy. Robert Gascoigne argues that Christians ought to remember that the modern emphasis upon autonomy and personal freedom resulted from a profound distaste for past ecclesiastical attempts to enforce morality and wars over competing 'Christian' visions of faith and morality. His argument here has many links with James Mackey's contribution to the series, *Power and Christian Ethics*. Yet it is finally not the autonomous self which he believes to be sufficient for an adequate understanding of human beings. Like Stanley Rudman's contribution, *Concepts of Persons and Christian Ethics*, he concludes that it is the self-in-community, and especially the self-in-communion with the Triune God, which is truly adequate.

These are very important topics for Christian ethics, which also have significance for ethics in general. Robert Gascoigne's carefully crafted study of them is very welcome in New Studies in Christian Ethics.

ROBIN GILL

Acknowledgements

This book has developed over many years, and its publication is an occasion for thanks to many people! The research which led to its writing would not have been possible but for the generous support of the Alexander von Humboldt Foundation, which gave me the opportunity to have periods of research in the Universities of Munich and Tübingen. In Munich, at the generous invitation of Professor Eugen Biser, I was supported and encouraged by Gerhold Becker's friendship and interest in my work. In Tübingen, the development of this project benefited greatly from Professor (now Bishop) Walter Kasper's hospitality, the stimulus of his doctoral seminars, and social and intellectual companionship with other members of the Faculty of Theology – especially Leo Hell, Roland Kany and Reinhold Rieger.

Earlier versions of parts of this book were presented at conferences of the Australian Catholic Theological Association and the Australian and New Zealand Society for Theological Studies, and at seminars with my colleagues in theology and philosophy at the Australian Catholic University. These occasions were valuable opportunities for developing and rethinking my ideas, as well as a continuing source of encouragement. I am also grateful for the opportunity to publish earlier versions of some of the book in the following locations: 'God and Objective Moral Values', *Religious Studies* 21 (1986): 531–49; 'Kant's Critique of Revelation – a Review', *Colloquium: Australian and New Zealand Theological Review* 21 (1989): 21–6; 'The Relation between Text and Experience in Narrative Theology of Revelation', *Pacifica* 5 (1992): 43–58; 'Christian Faith and the Public

Forum in a Pluralist Society', *Colloquium* 26 (1994): 116–29; 'Christian Narrative, Ethics and the Public Forum', *Australasian Catholic Record* lxxi (1994): 208–18; 'Evangelization and Catholic Identity', *Australasian Catholic Record* lxxii (1995): 269–79. This work has also been submitted as a doctoral thesis to the Melbourne College of Divinity, and I gratefully acknowledge the help of John Hill, whose support and critical acumen were of great assistance in this regard, and the advice and encouragement of Tony Kelly in the final stages of that project.

Robin Gill's positive and encouraging response to this book, and his suggestions for development, were of great assistance in bringing it to completion. Kevin Taylor, for Cambridge University Press, steered the text towards publication and was a prompt and helpful guide in the process. My thanks also to copyeditor Gillian Maude for her assistance in finalizing the text. The comments of anonymous examiners for the Melbourne College of Divinity, and of an anonymous assessor for Cambridge University Press gave me a number of valuable pointers towards the development of the final version. Much of this final text was written during a period of study leave at the Catholic Institute of Sydney, and I would like to thank the President and Staff of the Institute for their friendly hospitality during that time. I am grateful to the Australian Catholic University for the periods of study leave which have been crucial in the development and completion of this book.

The pursuit of research in foreign lands often entails much stress and sacrifice for a scholar's spouse. My special thanks go to my wife, Yvonne, whose willingness to bear these burdens helped to make this book possible. The book is dedicated to my three children, the youngest of whom, Miriam, our own *Münchner Kindl*, was born when it began.

Introduction

In liberal and pluralist societies, Christians seeking to contribute to public ethical debate are faced with a fundamental question: should they base their contribution on an appeal to arguments and insights which constitute the accepted truths of the public forum, or should they appeal to the sources of their own tradition?

There is much at stake, and much at risk, in the choice between these alternatives. An appeal to a shared public truth has the strength of communicability in a pluralist society, but risks reducing Christian communication to statements of generalities which may have only dubious success in expressing a fragile ethical consensus. In appealing to what is held in common, Christians may be sacrificing what is distinctive to their own identity in favour of notions whose general acceptance is based more on their vacuity and banality than their universal transparency. Yet, by speaking directly from their own tradition, Christians may succeed only in alienating other members of society, who hear no more than a religious group recounting special claims to authority and privileged sources of ethical guidance, rather than a community which genuinely seeks to contribute to a common human task.

In the demands of ethical communication, as in so many other matters, the responses of Christians are motivated by their deepest conceptions of the meaning and shape of Christian identity. The church's mode of communication to the world is, at heart, a question of the nature of evangelization: of our conception of the Gospel itself and of a Christian identity that claims to be rooted in the Gospel. This conception, in turn, is deeply influenced by our understanding of the relationship between the church and the world, between the inherited tradition of the church and the variety of forms of practice and understanding that Christians encounter in the societies of which they are a part. The way this relationship is understood has a crucial influence on our conception of evangelization and on the sense of Christian identity which motivates it.

That there must be some kind of relationship between church and world is given in the nature of the Gospel which the church is missioned to proclaim to all nations. It is the nature of this relationship – and of this proclamation – which is such a challenging and conflict-ridden question today. What is at stake is the relationship between the integrity of the church's tradition and its openness to the multiplicity of meanings and messages that emanate from the many cultures that it interacts with. For some, an uncritical openness to many of these cultural forms is undermining the identity of the church, dissolving the integrity of its tradition and depriving its proclamation of its power and uniqueness. Others are more concerned that a closed mentality will do great harm to the church's evangelizing identity by preventing it from listening to those with whom it must communicate, whose voices can contribute to the church's own growth. These fundamental concerns are both focussed on the church's identity precisely as communicator or proclaimer of the Gospel. Reflection on the church's task of communicating with contemporary society, since it is directly concerned with the nature of the relationship between church and world, is, at the same time, a point of focus on the nature of Christian identity.

This book is specifically concerned with the ways in which the church understands and expresses its identity through ethical communication in liberal societies. Ethical matters are of fundamental concern to the church, since it proclaims the Gospel of created and redeemed humanity, and are, at the same time, fundamental to liberal societies, both as the principles which legitimate structures of order and express rights and obligations, and as the visions of human fulfilment that individuals aspire to. Liberal societies have developed modes and contexts of discourse which allow their members to participate, to a greatly varying extent, in public debate. Such forms of discourse provide ethical procedures which enable citizens to defend their interests and express their concerns. Yet, at the same time, liberal societies seek sources of meaning and value which can broaden and enhance such discourse, lest it become simply a mechanism for the frantic and impatient rehearsing of narrow interest. What are the visions of humanity, the sources of life, which can inspire social discourse to become a genuine forum of civil respect, a community of justice and generosity – even of willingness to sacrifice interests for the sake of the need of others? To ask these questions is to consider a fundamental aspect of the relationship between religion and society: the relationship between disclosure and discourse, between visions of meaning, value and purpose and the procedures of argument and debate that give concrete expression to the rights of members of modern societies.

In Christian theological language, this question concerns the relationship between revelation and ethics. At the heart of Christian faith – and of Christian identity – is a vision of the *communio* of the three-personed God who invites human beings to live in *communio* with the divine life and with each other. This vision can be an extraordinarily powerful inspiration for an ethical discourse of justice, peace and freedom. At the same time, it is evident that in modern societies it is one vision of life among others: Christians seek to communicate it to their fellow citizens in a context of a multiplicity of religious and philosophical world-views. The mode of communication of this vision of ethical *communio*, then, is crucial to the kind of influence it can have and the contribution that it can make. Yet this mode of communication is itself profoundly influenced by different conceptions of the meaning of revelation: what is the identity of Christian revelation, as expressed in and through Christian tradition? What kinds of relationship does it have to those worlds of meaning that are distinguishable from it? Such questions are inseparable from reflection on the task of proclaiming the Gospel in its power and integrity in a way which can be heard as a message of universal life and reconciliation in today's circumstances. Because of this, the question of the meaning of revelation must be addressed in any attempt to understand the relationship between the contemporary problem of Christian identity and the task of Christian ethical communication.

The communication of Christian revelation, of the vision of *communio*, is particularly relevant to a crucial challenge for modern societies, that is, the reconciliation of autonomy and community. A constitutive aspect of freedom in modern societies is freedom from the normative authority of particular traditions of the good, from revealed religious traditions in particular. This freedom to accept or reject any particular understanding of the meaning and purpose of human life is crucial to individual autonomy in modern societies. At the same time, it has long posed the question of the sources of community in a radical form, since community cannot flourish in the absence of some common sources of meaning and value. This situation challenges Christians to communicate their convictions in ways that respect autonomy and, at the same time, give fundamental service to their fellow citizens by witnessing to common sources of life and hope. The reconciliation of autonomy and community must be a key aspect of the contribution that Christian revelation can make to the ethical life of modern societies.

It is the purpose of this book to explore the interrelated questions of Christian identity and Christian communication in relation to the fundamental ethical problem of the reconciliation of autonomy and community in modern societies. The concept of revelation will play a key role in this study, both in its content as a vision of *communio* and in its structure as the source and foundation of Christian faith which develops through tradition in relation to human culture and human reason. This book is written in the Catholic theological tradition, while, at the same time, attempting to tackle these questions in the context of ecumenically Christian debate.

The argument begins with a focus on the historical tension in modern societies between political liberalism and the notion of a revealed tradition. Liberal societies are based on the rejection of the notion that any particular tradition of the good, with its attendant beliefs and practices, should dominate society and have the force of law. This is a form of society that some Christians helped to originate, and others eventually learned to accept as an embodiment of their own belief in freedom of conscience. Yet, if liberal societies are based on freedom of conscience, and on the worth of the individual person who acts in freedom, then political and social liberalism cannot ignore the question of the meaning and ground of the worth of persons. In rightly rejecting the authoritarianism of particular traditions of the good, liberalism can run the risk of losing a sense of the foundations of its own core value. The truth of political liberalism lies not in the falsity or irrelevance of particular traditions of the good, but rather in the fundamental goods of freedom of conscience and mutual respect.

A positive relationship between contemporary liberalism and Christian tradition lies in the inspiration and enrichment that Christian revelation can give to a free society's core value of the worth of persons as a communal reality. In rejecting particular traditions of the good in favour of individual freedom, liberalism rightly questioned social structures which imposed various kinds of communal bonds. In doing so, however, it often produced an understanding of the individual as a free agent with no inherent disposition to community, an agent whose rights were not defined in terms of personal worth or dignity but purely in terms of freedom from unwarranted interference. In the perspective of Christian revelation, in contrast, the freedom of persons is based in their relationship to the infinite God, a relationship which of its nature bonds them to other persons in community.

The second part of chapter 1 develops the historical context of this contemporary problem by considering the relationship of revelation, reason and ethics in post-Enlightenment thought, especially the conceptions of this relationship developed by Kant, Hegel and Vatican I. Kant's ethics was the greatest philosophical statement of the positive ethical and political content of the Enlightenment – yet it could not resolve the Enlightenment's fundamental ambivalence about the meaning of 'reason' once human reason was divorced from ontological realities. The historical development after Kant displayed different alignments of the relationship between revelation, reason and ethics. The thought of Hegel and the teaching of Vatican I affirmed the need for an infinite foundation for human reason and the human good, but at the same time placed hope in metaphysical conceptions of reason that could not, in fact, achieve public consensus. Radical expressions of the Enlightenment reduced 'reason' to historical materialism or the calculus of pleasure and pain. In the Romantic movement, and in our own day, the revival of tradition proposed a new source of substantive ethical life, but once again rendered communicability and universality problematic.

Chapter 2 turns to the contemporary form of the relationship between revelation and ethics, exploring the relationship of an ethics of discourse and universalizability to a conception of revelation as *communio* in the common challenge of constructing a public ethics. Contemporary neo-Kantianism seeks to prescind from the religious and ontological question of the worth of persons, and to ground universal ethical principles in the universalizing character of logic or language. Yet none of these attempts can bridge the gap between the autonomous individual and the community of a 'kingdom of ends'. If the autonomous individual, guided by subjective will, is the sole starting-point, then the recognition of the objective worth of all, however marginal they are to others' goals and desires, cannot be achieved. A universal 'kingdom of ends' can only be achieved by a recognition that all exist in a participatory relationship with the infinite, a divine *communio* that situates the worth of all in universal community and which orients subjective reason to infinite truth. In this sense, a contemporary theology of revelation can overcome the dichotomies of the Enlightenment and exist in a positive relationship to liberal societies, which – at the same time – entails a critical relationship to many expressions of liberal philosophy.

Yet such a picture of the relationship between the theology of revelation and political and social liberalism cannot escape the fundamental questions of identity and communicability. The critique of neo-Kantianism – and of neo-Scholastic and

Hegelian metaphysics – presented in this book expresses aspects of the general post-modern critique of universalist rationality, affirming the need for a *locus* of value in concrete tradition. Yet a claim that human value is rooted in *communio* with the infinite creator God is in profound harmony with the desire for ethical universality, characterized by publicness and communicability, which is the lasting heritage of the Enlightenment. The question concerning both identity and communicability must therefore be asked of the theology of revelation itself. What is the relationship of the particularity of Christian revelation to the universality of human community? To what extent can Christians communicate this vision of ethical community, based in revelation as *communio*?

These questions are considered in chapter 3, which develops a theology of revelation based on mystery and historicity, in the light of a critique of those theologies of revelation which set up a dichotomy between the particularity of narrative text and general human experience as a source of insight into meaning and value. The theology of revelation advocated in this account is a theology of mediation, which understands the historical particularity of Christian revelation as a revelation of infinite mystery, whose richness can only be adequately responded to by the attempt to understand it in relation to all of human history and all reality. This process of understanding is dialectical and interpretive, and includes the challenge of coming to know the full meaning of the Christian mystery by responding to the plurality of meanings and values in the human world of experience. In this sense, Christian identity, the process of coming to know who we truly are, is something that can only be reached by way of the challenge posed by the 'other' who provokes us to a fuller grasp of the meaning of Christ for the world.

These philosophical and theological considerations give a basis for developing an understanding of the contemporary task of the communication of Christian ethics in pluralist societies addressed in chapter 4. This task is essentially one of creatively discerning the possibilities offered by the tension between plurality and consensus. The communication of Christian ethics should be based on an understanding of consensus as the resultant of the influence of historical traditions, which converge on a number of principles which can receive strong community assent. Such 'mediating principles' provide a new means of understanding the ancient concept of natural law. They find their context and support in Christian revelation, but, at the same time, can carry conviction, to limited and varying degrees, in pluralist contexts. These principles have their focus in an emphasis on human fulfilment through relationships of community. A crucial role for Christian ethical communication is to strengthen and reinforce such principles in public debate.

Yet Christian ethical communication cannot be restricted to the reinforcement of general moral principles. It must also seek to give these principles a foundation in a vision of life. This is a crucial task in the continuing social argument about the meaning and purpose of human life. Ethical principles become isolated and vulnerable if they are not supported by a vision of life which gives them coherence and plausibility. The task of advocating ethical principles must be accompanied by an interpretation of human existence that demonstrates their power, relevance and sustainability. For Christians, such an interpretation of human life will be based in the particularity of revelation which discloses the mystery of human existence in relation to the infinite mystery of God.

This interpretation of the task of Christian ethical communication can sit well with a distinction between visionary and normative levels of communication. The communication of a vision of life has its context in the dialectic of world views, of understandings of the human condition, which characterizes both the intellectual and artistic endeavours of a society as well as its political rhetoric and media self-images. In these contexts, Christian communication must engage the task of giving plausibility to fundamental ethical principles which challenge all reductions of human community and human existence to the competitive struggle of subjective and arbitrary will and desire. Yet, in those situations where debate is squarely focussed on the detailed normative implications of fundamental principles,

Christians must use religious language with parsimony, aware that in this context it is specifically ethical argument that is both relevant and respectful of religious plurality.

The concluding chapter of this book seeks to explore the meaning of these approaches in a more concretely sociological context by considering the possibilities for a reconciliation of autonomy and community in the understanding of the modern self. The search for such a reconciliation is a fundamental social and intellectual problem that has been a feature of Western societies since the age of religious war and the birth of societies based on principles of individual freedom of conscience and the secularity of the state. In terms of ethical meaning, the problem can be posed as the search for a meaning that can overcome the potential vacuum of meaning characteristic of autonomous individualism, while, at the same time, avoiding all forms of social union which depend on social control, violence, fear and intimidation. These problems of meaning have a wealth of religious expressions, including the development of a range of religious doctrines and practices which focus on self-realization and self-fulfilment in a transcendental context. While critical of many aspects of modernization, these religious forms share liberalism's emphasis on autonomy, and are in tension with important aspects of Christian life. Drawing on discussions in the sociology of religion and sociology of modernity, and on an interpretation and critique of such contemporary religions of self-realization, chapter 5 argues for an understanding of Christian revelation as a vision of self-giving and self-sacrifice which can inform human personal and communal relationships and which can intensify social solidarity, especially solidarity with suffering and deprivation.

The attempt to understand the task of Christian ethical communication in liberal societies seeks to discern the meaning of witness to the Christian Gospel in ways which serve a created and redeemed world. Such service can only be based on a discernment of and respect for the fruits of the Spirit in the different forms of meaning which characterize our contemporary experience. The experiential meaning of the theological notions of particularity and universality is in the Christian's sense of fidelity to the person of Jesus Christ as the Word of God and in this recognition of the Spirit at work in the world. For Christian faith, all such fruits of the Spirit have their confirmation and transformation in Christ, but it is only with their help that the fullness of his mystery can be displayed. In this light, the task of Christian ethical communication is a form of witness and service which seeks to enlighten and liberate others in a way which recognizes that they can sometimes lead us closer to the heart of our own true identity.

CHAPTER I

Revelation and reason in liberal societies

LIBERALISM AND REVEALED TRADITION

The development of liberal and pluralist societies has offered individuals a range of life styles and a freedom of expression without precedent in the traditional societies of the past. Liberal societies have removed any substantive unitary tradition of values from the public forum, freeing their members to pursue any conception of the good, so long as the freedom of others is not thereby restricted. This freedom from a unitary tradition is also a freedom from the violence which stems from the attempt to assert one tradition as the sole claimant to the status of shared and public conception of the good.

The reaction to the violent assertion of the unity of religious and political allegiance in the post-Reformation conflicts was a crucial historical factor in the genesis of liberal societies. If religious differences led ineluctably to protracted and mortal combat, then religion could no longer form the central focus of meaning and allegiance of any polity. In the aftermath of the wars of religion, many thinkers and statesmen developed theories of the state's legitimacy based not on religion but on the state's own nature as a contract or as a necessity for the preservation of basic human needs.[1] The liberal state's excision

[1] In his *Anthropology in Theological Perspective* (Edinburgh: T. and T. Clark, 1985), W. Pannenberg emphasizes the effects of the wars of religion in the process leading to the abandonment of religion as the unified base for state and society. He argues, however, that the transition to theories of natural law as the basis for the state's legitimacy was itself influenced by religious ideas (168). For a very different interpretation of the significance of the wars of religion, see William T. Cavanaugh, '"A Fire Strong Enough to Consume the House": The Wars of Religion and the Rise of the State',

of an overarching conception of value from the public sphere began as the rejection of religion as the guarantor of legitimacy and meaning – a rejection made imperative by the destructive combination, in a formerly unified cultural realm, of a new religious plurality combined with an ardent and intolerant commitment to particular conceptions of religious truth.

By abolishing religion as the guarantor of political legitimacy and the source of ethical and political values, the liberal tradition prepared the way for the recognition of individual worth and individual rights as a self-sufficient and universal foundation for a free political order. It was not the individual's belief in or allegiance to a religious order of values that gave worth and identity, but simply the individual's natural freedom, which, in free association and contract, was the basis of the state. In releasing the state from the legitimizing power of religious order, the tradition of liberal thought discovered a new foundation in the dignity of individual freedom. This development was hastened by another accompaniment of the new religious plurality: the emphasis by some Protestant religious groups, especially in the American colonies, on freedom of conscience and religious belief.[2] It was the inherent dignity of

---

Modern Theology 11 (1995): no. 4. For Cavanaugh, the wars of religion were caused by the state's rise to power, rather than by conflicts inherent in the sundering of the bond between religious unity and political unity. Cavanaugh rejects the attempts of John Courtney Murray and others to develop understandings of the ways in which Christian communities can contribute to the life of liberal polities, since he argues that the state is intrinsically rapacious, and can be resisted 'not by Church participation and complicity in the "public debate"' (414), but only by the 'counter-discipline' of the church. This account fails to perceive that liberalism and modern Christianity are at one in their fundamental agreement over the importance of freedom of conscience, recognizing how destructive the attempt to violently reimpose the unity of religious and political allegiance was to both church and state in the early modern era. My disagreements with Cavanaugh's general position on relations between church and state will be evident from the argument of this book as a whole.

[2] See, for example, the discussion by W. Kern, in his 'Der Beitrag des Christentums zu einer menschlicheren Welt' in *Handbuch der Fundamentaltheologie*, volume IV (Freiburg im Breisgau: Herder, 1985). Kern emphasizes the crucial importance of the right to religious freedom in the development of political doctrines of human rights in the American revolution (306–7). This represented a particular combination of influences from Protestant traditions and from the American Enlightenment, cf. S. Ahlstrom, *A Religious History of the American People* (New Haven: Yale University Press, 1972), ch. 23: 'The Revolutionary Era'. As John Rawls notes, in pre-liberal Europe 'Intolerance was accepted as a condition of social order and stability. The weakening of that belief

the individual conscience, not its allegiance to what might be deemed to be objective truth, which constituted the individual's claim to be the irreducible and active constituent of any truly legitimate political order.

Destroying this understanding of political legitimacy, and returning to a state publicly founded on the imperatives of a particular religious tradition, is, in the Western world, an option cherished only in the fantasies of eccentric minorities.[3] Major Christian denominations have all accepted the legitimacy of the liberal state, and have come to recognize that its foundation in individual rights is in harmony with Christian faith's own emphasis on freedom of conscience and human dignity.[4] Yet Christian support for the liberal state goes hand in hand with concern for the dilemma that it faces: the freedom that it derives from the abolition of a shared, public tradition of meaning and value, a common conception of the good, can also be an emptiness which weakens the conviction of human worth which is at its own foundation. The liberal state gives freedom to a diverse range of values to flourish by prohibiting domination of public life and consciousness by any one tradition of meaning, but at the same time is threatened by a decline in legitimacy resulting from agnosticism about the sources of those values which are essential to it. If traditions of meaning and value are removed from the public forum, what will continue to vivify the commitment to the value of the individual that informs it? Yet, if such particular traditions are admitted as constitutive sources of public ethical and political consciousness, will they destroy its public character, the impar-

---

helps to clear the way for liberal institutions. Perhaps the doctrine of free faith developed because it is difficult, if not impossible, to believe in the damnation of those with whom we have, with trust and confidence, long and fruitfully co-operated in maintaining a just society,' *Political Liberalism* (New York: Columbia University Press, 1993), xxv.

[3] For fundamentalist critique of the liberal state, see *Fundamentalisms and the State: Remaking Polities, Economies and Militance*, ed. Martin E. Marty and R. Scott Appleby (University of Chicago Press, 1993).

[4] In the Catholic tradition, this came – belatedly – with the promulgation of *Dignitatis Humanae*, the Decree on Religious Liberty, during the final session of the Second Vatican Council in 1965.

tiality of the liberal state to any tradition of meaning and value?

These questions are particularly relevant to a fundamental problem of liberal societies: the reconciliation of autonomy and community. If the worth of persons has no substantive foundation, then individual worth tends to be conceived of purely as freedom from unwarranted interference, rather than as a good which is founded in a commonly shared reality, however this is conceived. Yet a conception of autonomy as freedom from unwarranted interference makes moral community essentially problematic, since it implies that there is nothing intrinsic to personal freedom which seeks community for its own fulfilment. Liberalism is a powerful critique of all social philosophies which threaten or destroy individual freedom by coercive practices based in various unchallengeable doctrines of social union. Yet autonomy and community cannot be reconciled without an attempt to understand our personal value in ways which also illuminate the essentially communal character of our existence. The quest to reconcile autonomy and community raises the ontological question of whether our personal worth is grounded in a reality which also inclines us towards communion of life.

Our conception of the challenges facing liberal societies essentially depends on our understanding of the nature and context of individual worth and individual rights. The evacuation of meaning and value from the public forum constitutes no threat to liberal societies if a strong sense of individual rights is wholly independent of any substantive or metaphysical conception of human value. From this perspective, human liberty is an irreducible given that needs no justification or context in metaphysical conceptions of human worth or dignity. On this account, liberalism can prescind from any conception of the good, since it is based purely on an understanding of the right, the right being that which any association of free individuals would give assent to as a fair system of mutual allocation of benefits. Since its own foundations are independent of any particular conceptions of the good, the liberal state can be impartial to all such conceptions, which remain part of the private sphere of cultural and religious activity, but have no bearing on the legitimacy of public institutions.[5]

The moral and political philosophies of Immanuel Kant and of the neo-Kantian tradition are crucial sources of liberal thought. While Kant made the worth of persons as 'ends in themselves' crucial to his ethics, contemporary deployments of the principle of universalization in ethics are not based on any postulate of the universal worth of persons. In particular, they do not seek to revive the notion of a 'kingdom of ends' by understanding the concept of the worth of persons in the context of an ontology of communion. Such a concept appears to imply an ontological status which contemporary philosophy has no grounds for attributing to all human beings simply because they are human beings. The normative character of a universalist ethics is no longer drawn from an ontology of the human person. It is rather sought in the rationally binding character of certain procedures of universalization and generalization (Hare), in the implications of prudential reasoning in a carefully defined 'original position' (Rawls), in the conditions which define the processes of developing norms in 'domination-free space' (Habermas), or in the transcendental characteristics of communication itself (Apel). These attempts at a contemporary restatement of the essence of Kantian ethics all dispense

[5] In his *Political Liberalism*, Rawls emphasizes that liberal political values are not based on any philosophical 'comprehensive doctrine' but are rather drawn from the public consciousness of a liberal political culture, to which religious traditions may have contributed, and which adherents of religious communities may continue to support as part of the 'overlapping consensus' of the various strands of 'reasonable pluralism'. Yet the political values of 'public reason', once they have developed in a liberal society's history, become 'free standing', and no longer require any grounding or nourishment from 'comprehensive doctrines', since they are publicly accepted reasonable beliefs, whose mutual benefits become clear to us as we are inculcated into them in a 'well-ordered society'. The flaw in Rawls' argument is that the values of public reason are not free standing in the sense of being independent of the comprehensive doctrines which deeply influence the sense of the worth of persons and the meaning of human life in the 'background culture', and which can, in turn, deeply influence the character and scope of public political values. Rawls' argument acknowledges that the values of liberal society receive assent from many people as part of their commitment to religious comprehensive doctrines, but neglects the continuing contribution that religious belief can make to these political values themselves. On the interpretation of Rawls' distinction between 'exclusive' and 'inclusive' understandings of public reason, see chapter 4, note 39.

with metaphysical or ontological notions of the 'worth of persons' and seek the normative character of ethics in logic and language.

The great value of all these attempts is that they give rigorous expression to an ethics of human universality, an ethics which affirms the freedom of human beings to develop themselves in any way compatible with the equal rights of others. Their weakness lies in their unwillingness to consider the ontological foundations of ethical universality, of a 'kingdom of ends', in the universal worth of persons. Because the concept of universal human worth, or dignity, must draw on a substantive understanding of the meaning and value of human existence, it cannot be deployed in ethical theories which limit themselves to premises derived from the most general characteristics of logic and language. For these theories, if ethical reasoning seeks to draw on interpretations of the meaning of human existence, it goes beyond the scope of the minimal presuppositions which make it accessible to all members of pluralist societies.

Such theories, then, have the strength of accessibility in pluralist societies, but they also have the weakness of relinquishing substantive interpretive contexts for appreciating and valuing the worth of persons. Ethics derives from an experience of the value of persons and theories of ethical universalization can be meaningfully deployed only on the basis of a prior affirmation of the universality of this value. This has been emphasized by critics of any system of objective universalist ethics, who note that an amoralist, someone who refuses to attribute value to persons, is not constrained to act morally by logical or linguistic considerations.[6] The strength and weakness of universalist ethical theory mirror the strength and weakness of liberal ethical culture. By denying any public tradition of the good a normative role in the public forum, liberalism affirms the freedom of every individual to seek a particular good and to live by it. Yet, by defining such traditions of the good as

---

[6] For this critique, see especially J. L. Mackie, *Ethics: Inventing Right and Wrong* (Harmondsworth: Penguin, 1977), and R. Rorty, *Contingency, Irony and Solidarity* (Cambridge University Press, 1989), Part 1, ch. 3, 'The Contingency of a Liberal Community'.

irrelevant to the public forum, liberalism also runs the risk of impoverishing the appreciation of the worth of persons, which is essential to its own life. Liberal and pluralist societies cannot and should not tolerate the domination of public life by one tradition of the good, yet they can and do derive profound benefit from the insights into the human condition inherent in the symbols and narratives of such traditions. A key concern of chapter 2 of this study will be to address these issues in greater detail.

This interpretation of our situation can be denied by arguing for individual rights while insisting on agnosticism about their foundation and context.[7] In a cultural climate where the value of the person is taken for granted, this may pose no practical problem. It can be assumed simply that all individuals have rights and that the legitimacy of public institutions is derived from their assent. Yet this conception of all individuals as characterized by equal and inalienable rights is not an irreducible and unchallengeable axiom of nature. It has its coherence within a broader conception of human worth and meaning. It can be interpreted, for example, in terms of the rationality of all individuals – but in order thereby to confer rights on all individuals, this rationality cannot be interpreted in terms of each individual's particular rational powers, but rather functions as a transcendent worth-endowing attribute.[8] It can also

---

[7] In his *Sources of the Self: The Making of the Modern Identity* (Cambridge, Mass.: Harvard University Press, 1989) Charles Taylor argues that we need to recognize that our moral reactions are 'an assent to, an affirmation of, a given ontology of the human' (5), but that there are strong cultural forces which motivate 'suppression of moral ontology among our contemporaries, in part because the pluralist nature of modern society makes it easier to live that way, but also because of the great weight of modern epistemology . . . and, behind this, of the spiritual outlook associated with this epistemology' (10). For Taylor, naturalistic critiques of objective moral values based on the unassimilability of such values to the frameworks of the physical sciences fail to recognize that such values belong to the 'best account' of human life, and that this 'best account' should not be abandoned in favour of epistemologies derived from other sources: 'the terms of our best account will never figure in a physical theory of the universe. But that just means that our human reality cannot be understood in the terms appropriate for this physics' (59).

[8] As Bernard Williams, in his 'The Idea of Equality', in *Moral Concepts*, ed. J. Feinberg (Oxford University Press, 1969), argues in relation to Kant's notion of human worth as based in rational autonomy, Kant's 'detachment of moral worth from all contingencies is achieved only by making man's characteristic as a moral or rational

be denied by those who see no reason to attribute such worth to all individuals, since they judge freedom and rationality to be illusions. The doctrine of individual rights bears the weight of the liberal edifice, yet is itself often quite bereft of support, suspended in a metaphysical vacuum.[9]

The opposition of liberal thinkers to any elucidation of individual rights in an overarching context of meaning seems to derive from fears associated with the genesis of the liberal state itself. If the liberal state is founded on an excision of traditions of religious meaning and value from the public forum, in favour of the datum of individual rights, then a recognition of the context of individual rights in the meanings developed within those traditions threatens to readmit the Beelzebub of religious conflict into the public soul swept bare of demons. This threat looms particularly large in liberal consciousness because its own formative tradition is precisely a tradition of liberation from the domination of religious tradition and sectarian conflict. In order to remove this threat, many liberal thinkers deny any need for religious or metaphysical ideas as enriching, contextualizing or illuminating contributions to conceptions of individual rights. The actions of the public, political order must be founded on truths which are accessible to all, and religion, by long and tragic experience, is not thus accessible.

>agent a transcendental characteristic . . . The ground of the respect owed to each man thus emerges in the Kantian theory as a kind of secular analogue of the Christian conception of the respect owed to all men as equally children of God. Though secular, it is equally metaphysical: in neither case is it anything empirical *about* men that constitutes the ground of equal respect' (158).
>
>[9] In his *Contingency, Irony and Solidarity*, for example, Richard Rorty makes a radical rejection of any transcendental support or context for the values of liberal societies: 'in its ideal form, the culture of liberalism would be one which was enlightened, secular through and through. It would be one in which no trace of divinity remained, either in the form of a divinized world or a divinized self. Such a culture would have no room for the notion that there are nonhuman forces to which human beings should be responsible. It would drop, or drastically reinterpret, not only the idea of holiness but those of "devotion to truth" and of "fulfillment of the deepest needs of the Spirit". The process of de-divinization . . . would, ideally, culminate in our no longer being able to see any use for the notion that finite, mortal, contingently existing human beings might derive the meanings of their lives from anything except other finite, mortal, contingently existing human beings. In such a culture, warnings of "relativism", queries about whether social institutions had become increasingly "rational" in modern times, and doubts about whether the aims of liberal society were "objective moral values" would seem merely quaint' (45).

These ideas are still profoundly influenced by an image of religion as essentially divisive and destructive of individual freedom – an image associated with the wars of religion and with liberalism's own origins. Such an image fails to do justice to an extraordinary range of phenomena in religious history which bears witness to religion's support for social action for justice and freedom. We need only to call to mind – for example – French Catholic liberal thought in the nineteenth century, the contribution of Christian politicians to the stability of Western European democracy after World War II, the various forms of Latin American liberation theology or the Solidarity movement in Poland's recent history to be aware how one-sided this image is.[10] The global phenomenon of religious fundamentalism does indeed show how dangerous some religious forms can be to a free and stable political order, but fundamentalist movements are quite clearly distinguishable from those religious communities which seek both to affirm and to improve liberal polities. Further, some versions of liberal modernity are themselves not free of blame in exacerbating the evacuation of tradition which has been one causative factor in the growth of fundamentalist movements.

For avowedly secular versions of liberal philosophy, only those truths which can be shown to be such by rational argument and empirical evidence can be admitted as the foundations of public order and constraint.[11] This begs the question whether the truth of the notion of individual rights can

[10] As Nicholas Wolterstorff notes, in his 'Why we should Reject what Liberalism tells us about Speaking and Acting in Public for Religious Reasons', in *Religion and Contemporary Liberalism*, ed. P. J. Weithman (University of Notre Dame Press, 1997), most of the violence in the twentieth century has been caused by secular ideologies. 'The common denominator is that human beings tend to kill and brutalize each other for what they care deeply about . . . Liberalism's myopic preoccupation with religious wars is outdated' (167). Further, religion has been a great source of reforms congenial to liberalism: 'even the *free and equal* doctrine, which lies at the very heart of liberalism, had religious roots – in Protestant dissent of the seventeenth century' (168).

[11] Thus Rawls argues that the principles of justice must be formulated 'in the light of true general beliefs about men and their place in society', and that 'there is no necessity to invoke theological or metaphysical doctrines to support its principles' (*A Theory of Justice* (Oxford University Press, 1972), 454). For Hare, in his *Freedom and Reason* (Oxford University Press, 1963) 'the duties which we acknowledge towards people are not derived from the "essence of man" or from any philosophical

be demonstrated in this way. Much of the value of the notion of individual rights can be shown through the empirical evidence of political experience – on the good effects, for example, that it has on the peace and prosperity of a nation. Yet assent to this truth does not depend purely on assent to such evidence, but rather on inculcation into the tradition which embodies it. Endorsement of the freedom and dignity of individuals is not an uncontroversial result of critical argument and clear-cut empirical evidence – as is noted by those whose adoption of a reductionist or determinist world-view admits of no such conceptions. Its evidential power derives from the tradition of which it is a part, through the persuasive power of that tradition for those who give assent to it. The legitimacy of the liberal state is not derived from the excision of all traditions of meaning and value from its public discourse, but rather from the continuing value of that tradition which ascribes rights to individuals in community. A liberal polity is right to deny any particular religion a dominant role in public life and consciousness, to endorse pluralism of world-views, but it should not thereby deny the relevance of traditions of meaning and value to its own constitutive elements.[12] To do so is to rest content with an impoverished notion of individual rights simply as an assumed procedural basis of a political order, rather than a

mystifications of that sort; they are acknowledged because we say "There, but for my good fortune, go I. That man is like me in important respects"' (222).

[12] For Thomas Nagel, in his 'Moral Conflict and Political Legitimacy', in *Philosophy and Public Affairs* 16 (1987): no. 3, 'the distinction between what is needed to justify belief and what is need to justify the employment of political power depends on a higher standard of objectivity, which is ethically based' (229). Religious ideas cannot be made the basis of political power and constraint because they are incapable of strong public justification: the religious person can believe something to be true while accepting that in the public forum it appears simply as my belief (231). Beliefs which can make a claim to be constitutive of political institutions must be based on critical rationality and consideration of evidence, since 'it must be possible to present to others the basis of your own beliefs, so that once you have done so, *they have what you have* [Nagel's italics], and can arrive at a judgement on the same basis' (232). Nagel is right to argue that the controversial character of religious claims in the public forum means that they cannot be made constitutive of the institutions of political power. To argue, however, that the key ethical values of a liberal and pluralist society can be communicated in terms of straightforward empirical and logical argument is to neglect the role that traditions – including religious traditions – have played in developing the power and plausibility of these values.

conception of individual worth which can continue to draw on traditions of meaning and value for the enrichment of freedom and dignity.

This contemporary debate on the relation between traditions of the good and the public forum of liberal societies provides the opportunity for a re-assessment of the relationship between the Christian revealed tradition and ethical reasoning in a pluralist society. Christian revelation can be understood as a narrative tradition founded in particular historical experiences of disclosure, experiences which have the power to enable insight into the meaning and value of the human condition. If ethics can no longer rest content with the universalizing character of logic and language, but must rather draw on symbolic and narrative traditions in order to nourish its commitment to human value, then Christian revelation can offer liberal societies resources which can contribute to a common task. While the public forum of liberal and pluralist societies cannot give a normative role to any particular tradition of the good, including any religious vision of the good, it can benefit from the symbolic and narrative resources of such traditions.

We considered above the objection of liberal thinkers to any public role for religious ideas: that they are essentially particular and divisive. Since – it is argued – Christian religious ideas have their origins in revelation, and the claims of revelation are without public warrant, then these ideas can have no place in the public forum. Further, since religious traditions are particular and mutually exclusive, they cannot form the basis of a unified political consciousness. This argument states the core of a liberal consensus: ideas and values that invoke particular religious traditions in a pluralist society cannot become part of its normative public categories. Religious traditions are varied; they make incompatible claims and, therefore, cannot be the foundation of political union. That foundation must be in a common commitment to individual rights, to the dignity of the person expressed in democratic political processes.

The liberal argument is right in its rejection of any role for particular religious traditions in the political structures of a pluralist society, but wrong in its judgement of the irrelevance of revealed traditions for such a society's continuing vitality. The liberal judgement of revelation tends to derive from the controversies over revelation and reason characteristic of the eighteenth and nineteenth centuries. Revelation is conceived of as a body of recondite propositional truths, based on miracle and prophecy, which compete with empirically or rationally derived propositional truths in the same order of meaning. On this basis, revelation may be tolerated as the basis of private religious communities, but has nothing to contribute to the public realm of value, which is based on truths derived from critical reasoning or empirical evidence.

A crucial flaw in this argument is that it uses a paradigm of revelation that is no longer central to the theological consciousness of the Christian churches. The understanding of revelation as a set of propositions warranted by proofs from miracle and prophecy was an attempt by the churches to answer the rationalistic critique of the Enlightenment in its own terms, and it was marked by the limitations of that debate. Contemporary theology, while affirming the necessity and validity of propositional expressions of the content of revelation, emphasizes the primary significance of its character as disclosure: Christian theology is a tradition which interprets the power of disclosure of particular events. It affirms the historicity of meaning and value, and contends that certain unique events can disclose the meaning of human existence in ways that are of ultimate significance. Revelation discloses the love of God for humanity and the cosmos in the person of Jesus, and at the same time discloses to human persons their transcendent worth as creatures loved by God.

Much liberal thought, of course, would be inclined to reject the relevance of such traditions of disclosure as well, based as they are on the belief that crucial human values are disclosed in narrative, rather than being evident to non-historical rationality. Yet this critique is flawed by its failure to appreciate the historicity of liberal values themselves. It was argued above that these values had their genesis in the early modern crisis of religious conflict, and their continuing validity derives from their power to offer a solution to the problems of public legitimacy in pluralist societies. The liberal values of individual rights and tolerance derive their power and plausibility from the relative success of the polities that have been based on them. They have a narrative character, in the sense that they draw on narratives of national history and tradition which manifest their success and resilience, narratives which include emancipation from religious tutelage. These narratives embody historical experiences which have disclosive significance for liberal traditions – notably the great events of liberal nation-building. The fact that liberal values receive almost universal assent in liberal societies does not mean that they are narrative-free truths of reason: they depend, for their continuing power, on narratives which can sustain conceptions of the worth of persons.

The question of the public role of Christian faith turns, then, on the service its traditions of disclosure can give to a pluralist society – a society that may not, because of its own essential characteristics, give any particular religious tradition public pre-eminence or normative status.[13] What such a society does give normative status to is individual freedom and the rights that flow from this. If, despite what some liberal theorists argue, the value of individual freedom does require continuing enrichment from traditions of meaning, then the traditions of disclosure of Christian faith can be of crucial significance to it. In particular, these traditions of disclosure can contribute to the discursive practices which are essential to a liberal society. Such practices depend on mutual respect and tolerance, on a willingness to recognize a common and shared situation, on a readiness to include all potential and rightful contributors, however marginalized by disability and deprivation. The traditions of disclosure of Christianity, which ground individual worth in an ontological communion of love with God and neighbour, can play a key role in sustaining and energizing such

---

[13] A question central to the concerns of David Tracy's *The Analogical Imagination* (New York: Crossroads, 1981). One of the key achievements of this work was to emphasize that 'disclosure' can have both a public character and a fruitful relationship with 'discourse', that the power of disclosure of the 'classic' made it a 'second candidate for publicness' alongside the received forms of public discourse (134).

discursive practices. Revealed traditions can serve liberal societies not only by enriching and affirming the ethical value of human dignity, but also by fostering the hope that is crucial to any project of communal freedom.

Since, however, such traditions are not the object of common belief in pluralist societies, how are their contents and vision to be communicated in ways which can be of benefit to society as a whole? Can the Christian understanding of the human condition be communicated as a contribution to the public life of a society, not all of whose members are Christian? Does sensitivity to Christian values require a fully explicit Christian faith? These questions concern not only the point and purpose of Christian ethical communication, but also the identity of Christianity itself, since its conception of its own identity is deeply involved with the ways in which it communicates itself to the world as a whole. If Christian revelation proclaims values radically different in kind from those of all other religions and philosophies, then its meaning cannot be communicated to those outside the confines of explicit Christian witness, whose lives remain interpreted by the thought-worlds of those other religions and philosophies. If, however, Christian revelation is characterized by a dialectic of continuity and discontinuity with other faiths and world-views, then communication of its meanings and values can take place in pluralist societies through the difficult but valuable process of dialogue, in the attempt to achieve shared insight into a common human condition.

The concept of revelation has been a crucial area of contention in the relation between Christianity and liberal philosophy, and it is in the understanding of revelation that both the nature of Christian communication and the character of Christian identity are to be found. The purpose of this discussion has been to pose the problem of the relationship between liberal ethical thought and Christian revealed traditions, in the public forum of contemporary liberal societies. To consider these questions more fully, however, it is necessary to consider their development in the history of philosophy and theology in more detail, and to this task we now turn.

REVELATION, REASON AND ETHICS: AN HISTORICAL PERSPECTIVE

Different societies have unique histories and so a positive and fruitful conception of Christian faith's role in the public forum will have a different face in different times and places. Yet there are problems – and attempted solutions – common to Western societies, which have their sources in the post-Reformation religious conflicts and in the Enlightenment. One way to sum up these problems is as the question of the relationship between *revelation, reason and ethics*. If societies do not have a common revealed tradition or a common interpretation of that tradition's role and significance, and if the concept of reason has an institutional and cultural independence from religion, then how is the ethical life of such societies to be understood?

This question is of fundamental importance to this book, which is concerned with the ways in which Christianity, a revealed tradition, should understand and communicate its identity in societies whose key political beliefs are derived from the Enlightenment – societies for which the concept of the rational autonomy of the individual plays a particularly important role. I have argued in the previous section that a critical challenge for contemporary liberal societies is the task of constantly re-founding a sense of the worth of persons in traditions of disclosure, while maintaining an appropriate neutrality in relation to any particular tradition of the good. This challenge depends precisely on an understanding of the appropriate relationship between revelation, reason and ethics.

The complex of problems summed up in the title of this section has one of its roots in the Enlightenment's own ambivalence about the powers of reason. Many of the thinkers of the Enlightenment emphasized the power of reason to develop universally valid norms, a universal basis for human understanding and co-operation – yet others developed the critical potential of the Enlightenment to the point of denying reason this universal power, of reducing human reason and human nature to sub- or irrational drives and instincts. This ambivalence would crucially affect the stability of the claim that reason could replace religion as a ground for ethics. Was reason a substantive source of values, a means of unifying human beings into a common ethical order, or was it merely a critical tool for destroying received opinion and dissolving illusion? The emphasis on reason implied a rejection of revelation, but the reduction of reason to negative critique raised the question of whether reason required an infinite source of meaning as its own ground, a disclosure of meaning which could provide reason with substantive content. We will approach these questions by considering three attempts to resolve the relationship of reason, revelation and ethics in the aftermath of the Enlightenment: in the thought of Kant and Hegel and in the documents and debates of the First Vatican Council.

Kant, Hegel and Vatican I

Kant's philosophy was the greatest attempt to unify religion, reason and ethics on a deistic basis. For Kant, this could only be done by rejecting the claims of revelation, and by developing a conception of religion that was based on ethical reason. I will first consider Kant's conception of reason and ethics, and then examine its implications for his critique of revelation.

Kant believed that the activity of pure practical reason could give ethics a categorical quality. The rational form of the law, expressed in the categorical imperative independently of the specific characteristics of human nature and of the empirical world in general, gives it universality and necessity. The moral law gives the autonomous subject a guide to action which is produced by the powers of her own reason but which can be seen at the same time as a 'universal law of nature'. The human will must always fall short of the demands of these laws, but human reason has in common with angelic and divine reason the power to create a morality of universal necessity. For the existence of such a morality to be possible, pure reason must be capable of determining the will in its own right, without the influence of any subjective motivation apart from the 'rational emotion' of 'respect for the law'. Since the law is free of all empirical and subjective elements it must be its universal *form* alone which can make 'subjective practical principles' into 'universal legislation'.[14]

Kant's theory depends on the claim that the laws of pure reason, as expressed in the categorical imperative, are sufficient to determine the will to moral action, that pure reason can be 'practical' and become 'the law of a possible order of nature, which is not at all empirically perceptible'.[15] Yet he notes that the power of reason to generate ethical norms through the rational form of the categorical imperative alone cannot be demonstrated. It is a property of pure reason which must be intuited, and it alone can act as the foundation of the ethical world of autonomy and freedom of the will: 'The moral law is given at the same time as a fact of pure reason, which we are aware of *a priori* and which is apodictically certain, even if we cannot find any example in experience, where it is precisely followed.'[16]

The rational act of choosing only those subjective maxims which can be universalized and willed without contradiction is the creation of a moral law. It is simply a 'fact of reason' that such laws are able to motivate the will by their logical form alone, without the influence of any motivations derived from man's concrete nature or from the desired results of an action. 'Respect for the law' is the only feeling that enters into a truly moral situation. This respect may be interpreted as a subjec-

[14] *Kritik der praktischen Vernunft (Critique of Practical Reason)* (1788) (Frankfurt: Suhrkamp, 1968), 136. L. W. Beck, in his *A Commentary on Kant's Critique of Practical Reason* (University of Chicago Press, 1960), emphasizes that the union of law and freedom in Kant's moral philosophy derives from the link between *Willkür* (volitional spontaneity, negative freedom, the arbitrary element of the will) and *Wille* (rational will, positive freedom). 'That the will of man – because of the fact that it is not a simple notion and has two distinguishable aspects – can be both obligation-creating and obligation-executing is one of the most dramatic theses in Kant's philosophy, as dramatic as, and analogous to, the Copernican revolution in his theoretical philosophy ... Because Kant discovered the law in the concept of rational will (not abstract perfection or "will in general") and was able to derive its formula from the concept of its source and because this source was an idealization of the will as a faculty of spontaneity in man, Kant did not have to seek any outward motivation for obedience to it' (199). Kant's understanding of law as produced by a rational will expresses in general moral terms the concept of a 'volonté générale' that Rousseau saw as the foundation of a free political union.
[15] Ibid., 159. *(All translations from German texts are the author's, unless an English edition is cited.)*
[16] Ibid., 161.

tive ground of action, a 'constraining of the will', but it is evoked purely by the rational and autonomous character of the law itself. The human condition is to experience this law as a demand, to obey it out of a sense of duty. The sense of duty demonstrates man's freedom to take part in setting up an ideal ethical order. Duty is nothing else than 'personhood, that is, freedom and independence from the mechanism of nature'.[17]

For Kant, the categorical imperative is distinguished from the hypothetical imperative by its necessary character. It is independent of the particular desires of the agent and holds with the same force as a 'universal law of nature'. This unconditional character of the categorical imperative derives from its universal form: a subjective maxim becomes a moral law when it is capable of being willed without contradiction by all rational subjects. Yet, in the *Grundlegung zur Metaphysik der Sitten* (*Foundation of the Metaphysics of Morals*) (1785), Kant also emphasizes that the moral law requires a 'highest practical principle', something of absolute value which will 'be the ground of a possible categorical imperative'.[18] Without such a principle, the content of moral action could not be defined: 'without this nothing of absolute value could be found anywhere; but if all value were limited, and so contingent, then no highest practical principle could be found for reason'.[19] For Kant, rational beings can be attributed an absolute value as 'ends in themselves'. The concept of each rational being as an end in itself cannot be derived from experience, but is rather the a priori foundation of the possibility of moral law. The moral law gives subjective maxims the form of universality, but all action originates in subjective purpose. The subjectivity, or personhood, of each rational being is therefore a condition of the possibility of morality. Those rational subjects who simultaneously create and subject themselves to the universal law make up a 'kingdom of ends', 'a systematic union of rational beings through common objective laws'.[20]

[17] Ibid., 210.
[18] *Grundlegung der Metaphysik der Sitten* (Frankfurt: Suhrkamp, 1968), 59.
[19] Ibid., 60.   [20] Ibid., 66.

Revelation, for Kant, is a matter of dubious propositions transmitted by a fragile historical tradition: it can make no contribution to reason, once reason has come into its own. In his *Kritik der Reinen Vernunft* (*Critique of Pure Reason*) Kant denied that human reason has the power to prove the existence of metaphysical realities, but his call 'sapere aude' (dare to know) in his *Zur Beantwortung der Frage: Was ist Aufklärung?* (*What is Enlightenment?*) (1783) sprang from the conviction that reason was the highest faculty of the human being, and the path to freedom. It was conceived in explicit opposition to the notion of a revelation transmitted by historical tradition.

For Kant, true religion consists in devotion to pure principles of morality, and those who share this religion constitute a universal and invisible church. Moral principles themselves are based on the law-making character of reason – they owe nothing to religious or metaphysical ideas. Yet reflection on these moral principles does give warrant for a practical faith in three religious and metaphysical realities. From our awareness of moral obligation, we can infer the reality of human freedom. From our awareness that moral action aims at a 'highest good', a union of virtue and happiness which is beyond the powers of finite beings, we can infer the existence of a supreme being. Finally, from our awareness that this union of virtue and happiness cannot occur in this terrestrial life, we can infer the immortality of moral beings. These three principles – God, freedom and immortality – together with the moral principles that were their foundation, make up the universal, rational and natural religion, a religion accessible to all by reflection on experience. On the basis of this natural religion, Kant makes a radical critique of revealed religion and of the notion of revelation as such.

The fourth part of Kant's *Die Religion innerhalb der Grenzen der blossen Vernunft* (1793) (*Religion within the bounds of reason alone*) subjects revealed religion to a thoroughgoing critique. While natural religion is universal and can be perceived by anyone by reflection on experience, revealed religion is associated with historical events, and can only be passed on by the memory of those events. This memory involves erudition, sacred writings and a clerical class. Revelation cannot be necessary to authentic religion, since the true worship of God cannot depend on such frail means of support: books can be lost, memories erased and a clerical class can become a source of oppression. A revealed principle, derived from historical knowledge, can never be certain since it is inevitably affected by the limitations of historical knowledge, unless a 'continuing miracle' of revelation is proposed, perpetually protecting it from error.[21] What is revealed should never lead us to act against rational principles of morality, since historical revelation is of its nature doubtful. While revelation may lend an additional confirmation to natural religion, it is strictly inessential, 'since it could with the passage of time be completely forgotten that such a supernatural revelation had ever occurred, without this natural religion losing the slightest part of its intelligibility, its certainty, or its hold over our minds'.[22] Since the true religion is the awareness of God which flows from our rational respect for the moral law, and since the moral law is known universally and supra-historically by reason, historical revelation can add nothing to it.

Any practices which go beyond the bounds of reason and find no justification in it cannot be pleasing to God: once the principle of rationality is abandoned, there is no limit to the arbitrariness of superstition. One expression of this superstition is the illusion that a religious cult can do anything to put human beings in a right relationship with God. While the practices of revealed religion may help to foster the dispositions of authentic moral religion, they have no value in themselves and are positively harmful when seen as of supreme value.[23]

Implicit in Kant's critique is a number of presuppositions concerning revealed religion. Firstly, that revelation is essentially propositional. Secondly, that this propositional revelation is not at the heart of religious consciousness, but is rather taught to the mass of believers by a learned clerical class in a fallible and fragile process of historical transmission. Thirdly, that the propositions of revelation bear no essential relation-

[21] *Die Religion innerhalb der Grenzen der blossen Vernunft* (Stuttgart: Reclam, 1974), 214.
[22] Ibid., 204.   [23] Ibid., 244.

ship to the rational moral principles of natural religion, but rather are arbitrary teachings peculiar to a particular historical tradition. Fourthly, that the arbitrariness of revelation and its association with a clerical caste leads to authoritarianism and obscurantism. Finally, that the rational moral principles of natural religion are certain, universal and knowable by all those who are determined to use their reason unrestricted by traditional authority. Kant believed that revelation was essentially superfluous, since he was convinced that a practical faith in God, freedom and immortality was based on morality alone, and that morality was based on principles of pure practical reason. Revealed traditions were irrelevant to ethics since they offered no more than the insights of reason in inferior dress.

In contrast to Kant, Hegel's philosophy attributed fundamental importance to historical revelation, and was deeply concerned with the contribution that Christian tradition can make to the development of freedom in modern societies. From his youth, Hegel focussed his attention on the relationship between religion and society, particularly on the contribution that religion could make to a society's ethical life. While his youthful writings were critical of Christianity in this regard, Hegel's mature philosophy saw the source of modern freedom and dignity in the Christian doctrine of the incarnation. This mature philosophy had the relationships between philosophy, religion and ethical life at the centre of its concerns. Because of this, Hegel's thought is a key reference point for this study, which seeks to explore the nature of Christian identity in its relationships with the fundamental ethical problems of a free society.

For the mature Hegel, reason is a participation in absolute Spirit: in its highest sense, reason is the activity of self-development and self-knowledge of absolute Spirit. By coming to know this process, human beings participate in the process of divine reason. While Kant believed that human reason could never know the *noumenon*, the *Ding an sich*, Hegel argued that reason and ultimate reality – absolute Spirit – were one. Reason is not simply the human search for knowledge and insight – it is that reality which it sought to know; it is ultimate reality come to self-consciousness.[24]

Reason, then, is not merely a human faculty, but an expression of the objective process of divine self-externalization and self-recovery, of self-knowledge. Reason is therefore based on revelation, since revelation is the objective process by which absolute Spirit unfolds itself in human history. Human reason cannot come to insight into the meaning of absolute Spirit unless this meaning has become reality in the revelatory process. Philosophy therefore presupposes religion – the forms of religious *Vorstellung*, the sensuous image. Philosophy is an explication of the content of Christian revelation in the highest and most fitting terms – the pure rational concept.[25]

In contrast to Kant, Hegel affirmed the importance of religion for the worth of persons in community. For Hegel, the ground of the ethical dignity of persons is in the union of infinite and finite Spirit, of God and the human person, in the experience of worship. It is this union of finite and infinite, realized in the religious community and religious liturgy, that gives the human person an inviolable character.[26] The dignity of persons is not simply based on their powers of reason and freedom, but rather on their union with the infinite source of freedom and reason, with the divine Spirit of history. In response to the French revolutionary 'Terror', which had sprung from the illusions of the 'absolute freedom' of the self-emancipated mind, Hegel sought to re-establish the links between religious faith's bond with the divine and the Enlightenment's deployment of critical reason, between absolute reality and the inquiring mind.[27]

---

[24] See especially *Philosophie des Geistes* (*Philosophy of Spirit*), 373–4, and Hegel's reflections on 'finitude' in *Philosophie der Religion* (*Philosophy of Religion*), vol. I, 151–201, 'Die Notwendigkeit und Vermittlung des religiösen Verhältnisses in der Form des Denkens'. References to Hegel's works are to the *Theorie Werkausgabe*, ed. E. Moldenhauer and K. M. Michel (Frankfurt: Suhrkamp, 1970).

[25] *Philosophie des Geistes*, para. 566.

[26] Positions developed, in particular, in *Philosophie der Religion I*, 202–46, 'Der Kultus', and *Philosophie der Religion II*, 301–32, 'Die Idee im Element der Gemeinde: Das Reich des Geistes', 299–344.

[27] Hegel's reflections on the opposition between 'belief' and 'pure insight', and the culmination of 'absolute freedom' in the Terror are a key source for his conception of

For Hegel, then, a historical process of revelation is the foundation of philosophical reasoning and of human ethical dignity. Philosophy presupposes the historical process of revelation, since philosophy does not itself create meaning, but rather brings an already present meaning to conceptual self-clarification. Human ethical dignity is not based on the subject's own self-rule, but rather on the subject's union with the infinite Spirit, which has given itself to humanity in history.

A further implication of Hegel's philosophy and theology of history is that ethics itself is subject to historical development. Since the sense of human worth derives from the relationship with God, then that sense develops as religious conceptions grow more refined: only with the full development of Christianity does the concept of universal human worth come to fruition.[28] Further, since reason itself is historical, then ethical reason depends on the historical consciousness of the society which it reflects. Ethics is the expression of social values in their historical development. Hegel contrasts *Sittlichkeit* (usually translated as 'ethical life') with Kantian *Moralität*, or abstract morality: ethical life is the concrete and multidimensional ethical practice of a given society, especially in terms of the relationship between the individual, civil society, the family and the state.[29] For Hegel, this is a much richer and more substantial reality than that envisaged in the transcendental and universal norms of Kant's ethics.

With the development of his mature philosophy, Hegel believed that a reconciliation had been achieved between revelation, reason and ethics. Christian revelation was the objective basis for a philosophical comprehension of the absolute. Ethical life had reached the stage of the *Rechtsstaat*, the 'law

the relationship between faith and reason. *Phänomenologie des Geistes* (*Phenomenology of Spirit*), 392–434.

[28] 'This consciousness arose first of all in religion, in the innermost region of the Spirit; but the building of this principle into the being of the world was a further task, whose carrying out and completion required a long and difficult labour,' *Philosophie der Geschichte* (*Philosophy of History*), 31.

[29] The discussion of *Moralität* and *Sittlichkeit* make up the second and third parts of Hegel's *Grundlinien der Philosophie des Rechts*, volume 7 of G. W. F. Hegel, *Werke in zwanzig Bänden* (Frankfurt: Suhrkamp, 1970). E. T.: *Philosophy of Right*, trans. M. Knox (Oxford: Clarendon Press, 1952).

state', based on a recognition of the worth of the individual person. The historical tradition of Christian revelation had borne fruit in a philosophy that reconciled subjective and objective, human and divine, and in a public ethical life that was free of ecclesiastical interference, yet based on the worth of persons which sprang from religious union with the divine: 'The right of the subject's particularity, his right to be satisfied, or in other words the right of subjective freedom, is the pivot and centre of the difference between antiquity and modern times. This right in its infinity is given expression in Christianity and it has become the universal effective principle of a new form of civilization.'[30]

Hegel's philosophy had achieved an insight into the importance of revelation for ethics which far transcended the thought of the Enlightenment. Yet, for all Hegel's emphasis on revelation as the objective, historical foundation of freedom, his 'sublation' (*Aufhebung*) of religion into philosophy, of image into concept, finally robbed revelation of its status and meaning for Christian faith. In Hegel's philosophy, the self-revelation of God is ultimately not a free gift of self-communication to God's creatures, but the dialectical process of absolute Spirit in which the participation of finite, human Spirit is a necessary moment. Hegel's fear of 'positivity', of the stumbling-block of historical arbitrariness, overrode his concern for the historical character of revelation, and there are suggestions in his work that he believed that religion – although crucial in achieving modern freedom – was dispensable for a philosophical elite.[31] To this extent, Hegel made Christianity part of a free and rational

---

[30] *Philosophy of Right*, Knox edition, 84.

[31] This concern for the arbitrariness, or irrationality, of Christianity was expressed at length in Hegel's youthful *Die Positivität der christlichen Religion* (*The Positivity of the Christian Religion*) (1795–6). The philosophical sublation of religion in his mature system was intended to overcome this 'positivity'. In his *Philosophie der Religion*, Hegel suggests that the reconciliation of religion, philosophy and the state remained nevertheless incomplete, and that philosophy had therefore to withdraw itself into an elite consciousness: 'Yet this reconciliation is itself only a partial one, without external universality; in this respect philosophy is an isolated sanctuary and its servants make up a priesthood set apart, that may not mingle with the world and which must guard the treasury of truth. How the temporal, empirical present will find its way out of its dislocation, what form it will take, is for itself to decide and is not the immediate practical concern of philosophy', *Philosophie der Religion II*, 343–4.

society only by depriving it of its identity as a revealed tradition based in historicity and subjugating it to supersession by the philosophy of absolute idealism.[32]

In the Catholic tradition in the nineteenth century, a very different relationship of revelation, reason and ethics prevailed. The official Catholic position on the relationship of reason and revelation was expressed in Vatican I's *Dei Filius* (*On the Catholic Faith*) (1870). For *Dei Filius*, human reason is capable of knowing God, through reflection on creation. Revelation has the purpose of fulfilling, strengthening and correcting rational knowledge of God, and of making known certain supernatural truths which are accepted by faith on the authority of God. A clear implication of this was that ethical truth, conceived as 'natural law' was likewise known by reason, but revelation was necessary to correct and purify reason, and to overcome the distorting effects of sin.[33]

In the Catholic tradition, public ethics was based on natural law, as derived from the synthesis of Thomas Aquinas. It was argued that all those possessed of right reason could know the natural law, although revelation could clarify and reinforce this law and overcome the blindness caused by sin. For this tradition, then, reason and revelation were understood as

[32] The interpretation of Hegel presented here is drawn from my *Religion, Rationality and Community: Sacred and Secular in the Thought of Hegel and his Critics* (The Hague: Martinus Nijhoff, 1985). For other interpretations of the relationship between Hegel's philosophy of religion and political theory see especially C. Taylor, *Hegel* (Cambridge University Press, 1975), and M. Theunissen, *Hegels Lehre vom absoluten Geist als theologisch-politischer Traktat* (Berlin: De Gruyter, 1970).

[33] For discussions of the theology of revelation of *Dei Filius*, see R. Latourelle, *Theology of Revelation* (Cork: Mercier Press, 1968), Part 4, ch. 2; A. Dulles, *Models of Revelation* (Dublin: Gill and Macmillan, 1983), Part 1, ch. 3; P. Eicher, *Offenbarung: Prinzip Neuzeitlicher Theologie* (Munich: Kösel, 1977), Studie 1. In his *Natural Law: A Theological Approach* (Dublin: Gill and Son, 1965), Josef Fuchs notes that 'it is frequently overlooked that the First Vatican Council was already concerned with the question of natural moral knowledge. True, at the time it was not so much the question of *moral* knowledge that the Council was directly concerned with; it was rather the problem of the knowledge of God. Yet the knowledge of God includes knowledge of morality... The documents of the Council show clearly that for the Fathers of the Council the basic knowledge of God thus described is not only a theoretical but also a practical knowledge of God. It includes the knowledge of at least the fundamental principles of morality' (147–8). See also p. 50 for Fuchs' discussion of Vatican I's deliberations on the relationship between nature 'in its present state' and revelation.

complementary.[34] Reason had the power to know the natural law, the expression of the creator's will. Revelation confirmed this law. The natural law, however, was conceived of in a static and unhistorical way, in terms of a given body of truths, rather than as a means of understanding the key features of the human person in a context of historical development. The notion of founding public ethics in the rights of the human subject was also rejected: in the teaching of the nineteenth-century popes, especially of Gregory XVI and Pius IX, culminating in the *Syllabus of Errors* of 1864, the subjective rights of the person and of conscience were subordinated to the objective imperatives of what was judged to be true order. The implications of human dignity in terms of representative institutions were almost completely neglected. Natural law included notions of monarchical legitimacy, linked to conceptions about the rights of the one true church and the proscription of religious freedom. In 1891, with *Rerum Novarum*, Leo XIII began a tradition of thought critical of the excesses of capitalism, and thus of socio-economic hierarchies hitherto usually considered 'natural', although he continued to have a traditionalist view of political structures.

The relationships of revelation, reason and ethics were central to the thought of Kant and Hegel, and to the deliberations of Vatican I. Yet the sheer magnitude and complexity of these questions – and of their social and cultural context – did not permit any comprehensive resolution during a period marked by such conflict between the churches and the thought of the Enlightenment.[35] None of these three conceptions of the

---

[34] See D. Hollenbach's *Claims in Conflict: Retrieving and Renewing the Catholic Human Rights Tradition* (New York: Paulist Press, 1979), 107–18, for a discussion of the neo-Scholastic conception of the relationship between revelation and reason in morality. Hollenbach notes that its conception of the relationship between revelation and reason explains the fact that neo-Scholastic thought 'simultaneously maintained that Christian faith makes a radically important contribution to the moral existence of persons in society, and that the basic claims presented in the tradition can be known without explicit adherence to this faith' (116–17).

[35] As John A. Gallagher makes clear in his *Time Past, Time Future: An Historical Study of Catholic Moral Theology* (Mahwah: Paulist Press, 1990), there were other attempts to come to terms with the Enlightenment in nineteenth-century Catholic thought, but these had scant influence on Vatican I: 'Previous attempts to respond to the Enlightenment from within the Catholic tradition were dismissed. The traditionalists who stressed the role of faith were dismissed because they denied that reason could know

relationship between revelation, reason and ethics was able to resolve the tension between reason and revelation, universality and historicity, in ways that could affirm the ultimate sources of human dignity in revelation and at the same time the freedom of reason to realize the concrete ethical meaning of this dignity in developing historical contexts. Since Kant rejected the notion of revelation as superfluous to 'rational religion', his ethics was deprived of any ground for human dignity in the communion of the human person with God, and could only appeal to a human worth based in subjective reason. Hegel's conception of human dignity was based in revealed tradition, and affirmed a fruitful reciprocal relationship between religious worship and social ethics, but achieved this only by reducing the gratuitous and historical character of revelation to the necessary dialectic of absolute idealism. The theology of Vatican I did affirm both the distinct character and the interrelationships of reason and revelation, but its essentially propositional conception of revelation and unhistorical conception of reason meant that the meaning of revelation as the infinite and mysterious ground for a historically developing ethical reason could not emerge.

Reason in ethics: reductionism, neo-Kantianism and tradition

I have briefly considered three of the most significant attempts, in the aftermath of the Enlightenment and the French Revolution, to develop an answer to the question of how ethics should be understood in a culture where reason and revelation were experienced to be in a problematic relationship. If ethics was to be based on reason alone, would reason be strong and substantive enough to sustain it without recourse to some absolute

> metaphysical first principles; the ontologists' position was rejected because it denied direct knowledge of God; the romantic Tübingen school of Drey and Möhler was to be discarded because its categories, such as the Kingdom of God, were insufficiently inclusive to serve as the basis of a comprehensive, systematic theology' (40). Of these different positions, it was the Tübingen school and Möhler's thought in particular, together with the belated influence of John Henry Newman, that were to have such importance in the genesis of Vatican II's *Dei Verbum* and its conception of revelation and tradition.

ground of reason? If there were an absolute ground of reason, could it be known in conceptual terms, and become the rational basis of public life, as the concept of 'natural law' implied, or could it be known only through a disclosure made possible by historical narrative, a narrative mediated by a particular tradition? What authority would that tradition have in ethics and public life? If revelation and reason did have a complementary relationship, in what sense were they both historical, so that 'natural law' could be understood as a developing potential rather than a set of static data and revelation itself as a historical dynamic rather than a body of supernatural decrees?

The importance of these questions can be seen when we consider the later development of post-Enlightenment ethics. During the late nineteenth and early twentieth centuries, there developed a number of forms of ethics which rejected all religious claims to truth, and which based ethics on varying understandings of human nature. What they had in common was a restriction on the power and scope of reason: reason no longer had the transcendental universality that Kant had attributed to it, nor its power to ground human dignity.

Hegel's synthesis broke apart in the critique of the next generation of thinkers: his attempt to reconcile Christianity and the Enlightenment in a public ethics was rejected by those who focussed on either secular utopias or religious inwardness.[36] The Young Hegelians transformed Hegel's absolute idealism into a radical anthropology, a critique of religion and politics from the point of view of an avowedly secular humanism. Kierkegaard, in contrast, rejected Hegel's attempt to mediate between religious life and the public world, affirming the individual character of faith, as an immediate relationship to Christ, which had nothing to do with historical development, nor with the public ethical implications of revealed truth.

Marx remained Hegelian in the sense of expecting fulfilment from the historical process itself, rather than from any recourse

---

[36] For interpretations of the post-Hegelian development see, for example, K. Löwith, *From Hegel to Nietzsche* (E. T. London: Constable, 1965); J. E. Toews, *Hegelianism: The Path toward Dialectical Humanism 1805–1841* (Cambridge University Press, 1980); and my *Religion, Rationality and Community*.

to transcendent reason. For Marx, a public ethics could only be based on the material development of the historical process, without any appeal to spiritual realities. Marxism returned to the radical Enlightenment's critique of religion, especially as mediated through the thought of the Young Hegelians Bruno Bauer and Ludwig Feuerbach. Reason became a matter of reflecting on the historical process, which had no divine reason at its source, yet would come to fulfilment in a classless society.

Marxism rejected any appeal to transcendent reason to justify ethical stances. Ethical values were not abstract ideals, to be appealed to as a source of moral motivation. Rather, they were realized in a concrete and determined historical process: it was the objective dialectic of history that would overcome class conflict and bring about a classless society. Ethical reason became the rationality of historical materialism, capable of bringing about an ideal result without the providence of God or the influence of transcendent ethical ideals.

In Anglo-Saxon culture, philosophical ethics was dominated by utilitarianism and positivism. Whereas Kant had emphasized reason, the utilitarians emphasized nature. Rejecting notions of rational transcendence and the absolute value of the individual, the utilitarians derived ethics from natural values: natural benevolence and the experiences and dispositions that human beings prefer by nature. Positivism reduced ethics even further, by restricting the scope of reason: in terms of the verification principle, ethical language was judged to be meaningless. In ethical theory, the expression of positivism was emotivism, the theory that ethical utterances were no more than expressions of preference.

All of these forms of ethics were restrictions of the role of reason in ethics in various ways. The Enlightenment's critique of religion and metaphysics had become a critique of reason itself, reducing it to purely analytical and sceptical roles or to goals-rationality. In contrast to Kantianism, the rational faculty was no longer a ground of ethics and of the worth of persons. Ethics was either found in nature, in the hope that natural benevolence or the natural processes of history would be sufficient ground; or else reason and ethics were opposed to each other, in the positivist classification of ethical language as meaningless or purely 'emotivist' and in the existentialist rejection of universal rational norms as impositions on individual subjective authenticity.

In recent decades, in reaction to these trends, new attempts have been made to reconstruct a rational, public ethics. The role of reason in ethics has been reasserted through a revival of Kantianism in a new and more modest form. These neo-Kantian ethical approaches emphasize the universalizing power of reason, and the rationality of norms based on a consensus derived from dialogue. They place great emphasis on individual autonomy and on the value of a free forum for the development of consensus. This revival of public practical philosophy has been allied with political liberalism and social democracy and has been important as one source of a public philosophy of human rights.

Yet this neo-Kantian emphasis on rationality in ethics continues to be challenged by those forms of ethics which see the human person as no more than an item of nature, and which reject the notion that reason gives us any unique ethical dignity. Reason understood as radical critique argues for a complete reduction of any claims associated with human freedom, responsibility and dignity.[37]

On another front, neo-Kantianism is challenged by the reassertion of themes which owe much to Hegel and Aristotle.[38] These critiques of neo-Kantianism argue that the Kantian revival is purely formalistic, that its universality is incapable of conveying anything substantial about human existence. Ethical

---

[37] For two diagnoses of the current state of moral philosophy, see A. MacIntyre, *After Virtue* (London: Duckworth, 1981), ch. 1, and J. Stout, *Ethics after Babel: The Languages of Morals and their Discontents* (Boston: Beacon Press, 1988). For Stout, MacIntyre is too pessimistic in his judgement of contemporary liberalism, neglecting the possibilities for a modest and pragmatic consensus based on a 'bricolage' of moral practices (ch. 12). Yet Stout's rejection of a role for religion – or any other transcendental perspectives – in grounding the values crucial to liberal societies means that his pragmatism is finally simply a sociological statement of the degree to which liberal societies can function, rather than a contribution of new resources from which liberal societies can draw.

[38] In the English-speaking world, it is the Aristotelian source that is especially emphasized, with MacIntyre as its most influential spokesman.

values, for this critique, are rooted in the practices of concrete communities. This critique is the revival of Hegel's critique of Kant, of the notion of *Sittlichkeit* over *Moralität*. Yet the crucial difference is that this new form of Hegelian critique cannot – and does not wish to – claim Hegelian universality. For Hegel, *Sittlichkeit*, the developing ethical life of those societies which inherit Christianity and the Enlightenment, will win through to universality because it has behind it the dynamism of divine reason in history. Without this, however, concrete *Sittlichkeit* may be no more than a highly limited and restrictive form of behaviour, simply the expression of a given human history. If history is not part of the self-development of absolute Spirit, then the products of human history may have no transcendent or universal value. If tradition does not have absolute reason as its source, why should it be invoked in preference to the Kantian appeal to transcendent reason? The appeal to tradition is of its nature the appeal to the particular and limited, unless this tradition has the seeds of universality within it.[39]

What of natural law? Since ancient times, the tension in understandings of natural law has been between 'natural law' as the power of 'right reason' and 'natural law' as given and static structures of nature. It was this latter understanding which tended to dominate in nineteenth- and early twentieth-century neo-Scholasticism, while contemporary interpretations favour 'natural law' as the fruits of rational reflection on the conditions of human existence. How this 'reason' is related to concrete and particular traditions of meaning and value remains controversial.[40] The continuing importance of a notion of 'natural law' is in its emphasis on the universality and commonality of ethical insight, yet this commonality can no longer be understood in a

---

[39] As MacIntyre recognizes in *After Virtue*, an ethical perspective based on virtues, practices, tradition and narrative is inadequate if there is no general answer to the question of the nature of the good life, and no *telos* which transcends the limited goods of practices, since 'the modern self with its criterionless choices apparently reappears in the alien context of what was claimed to be an Aristotelian world' (188).

[40] For discussions of the use of the term 'natural law' in contemporary Catholic theology, see, for example, T. O'Connell, *Principles for a Catholic Morality*, revised edition (New York: Seabury Press, 1990), chs. 13 and 14; R. Gula, *Reason Informed by Faith* (Mahwah: Paulist Press, 1989); and F. Böckle, *Fundamentalmoral* (Munich: Kösel, 1977), Part 2, sect. 2, ch. 1.

static and unhistorical way. Understandings of the human person are formed by historical traditions, so that any commonality must be the result of a dialogue between traditions: a resultant of historical understanding, rather than an unhistorical 'given'. The development of 'natural law' becomes a reflection on concrete traditions of human fulfilment, a way of conceiving reason's task of knowing the world and discerning the goods that call for ethical response. A shared emphasis on ethics as grounded in the worth of the human person, as both a transcendent and a historical reality, means that the 'natural law' and Kantian traditions can have much greater commonality than they could have in the nineteenth century.

For neo-Kantianism, ethics is based on reason. It is rational universality which is the source of ethical obligation, and the individual's freedom and reason is the source of individual ethical autonomy. This is rejected by those who argue that reason does not, of itself, confer any special dignity on human individuals: ethics is thus conceived of as a 'device for counteracting limited sympathies', rather than as a matter of transcendent and universal obligations.[41] The neo-Aristotelian and neo-Hegelian critique makes a very different point: perception of and response to the worth of persons is not universal but particular, founded in concrete communities. Universal reason, divorced from concrete traditions, has no ethical content.

What we witness in contemporary neo-Kantian ethics is an attempt to develop a universalist ethical theory which is denied by two very different understandings of ethical reason: one which is reductionist, arguing that the true heritage of the Enlightenment is a sceptical reduction of all transcendent claims, including ethical claims; another which is particularist, arguing that the universalism of the Enlightenment was fundamentally flawed, since it divorced ethics from concrete narratives and traditions of human fulfilment. These two critiques of ethical universalism have in common the belief that there is no

---

[41] See Mackie's *Ethics: Inventing Right and Wrong* for a discussion of ethics in these terms. A similar approach for a public, secular ethics, based on a conception of ethics as a means of limiting conflict, is taken in H. Tristram Engelhardt's *The Foundations of Bioethics* (New York: Oxford University Press, 1986), 43 – 7.

universal ground in reason or human dignity for universal ethical claims: strong claims for human ethical community can only be made in particular terms, either purely as useful conventions, as the reductionists would argue, or in terms of the defining narrative of particular communities.

The neo-Kantian recognition of human dignity in terms of autonomy is one important foundation of contemporary social and political rights. The fact that it is independent of particular traditions or, at least, that it uses concepts which can lend themselves to a wide variety of contexts, is of crucial importance in a world of intercommunal and ethnic conflict. Both the Kantian and 'natural law' traditions emphasize something crucial to an ethics of contemporary humanity: that is, the possibility of a global community of human dignity and human rights, based in a confidence in reason as a source of universality and commonality.

Yet the two fundamental critiques noted above do put the crucial weaknesses of Kantianism into stark relief: a universalist ethics is based on reason and freedom, but reductionist critiques insist that these attributes do not convey any special ethical dignity. The strength and capacity of the rational faculty varies between persons, and therefore does not confer equal dignity. For these critiques, human freedom and subjective reason have no transcendent character but are radically limited by contextual determinism. The human person is an item of nature, and ethics must grow beyond the transcendental and universalist illusions of Kantianism. The revival of tradition seeks to fill this gap, by giving the worth of the individual a concrete meaning in the context of historical narratives, but it can only do so on a particular basis. To this extent, the appeal to tradition robs ethics of its universalism. Thus the dilemma faced by a universalist ethics is one between reductionism and particularity. By its universality, it risks reductionism, since it takes the individual out of concrete and substantive contexts of meaning, yet, by particularity, which can ground meaning, it risks loss of universality.

The character of this dilemma invites a reconsideration of revelation as the ground of universal ethical reason – a reconsideration that can go beyond the limitations of the nineteenth-century debate over the relationships of revelation, reason and ethics. At the heart of the Christian theological concept of revelation is the union of universal and particular: the manifestation of divine love in the historical particularity of Jesus of Nazareth. One of the critical problems in the relationship between the Enlightenment tradition and the concept of revelation was the notion that revelation was a set of propositions that conflicted with reason in its own sphere. Contemporary conceptions of revelation as primarily a disclosure of meaning and value, which subsequently receives propositional expression, do render this tension less acute. Yet a critical difference between the theology of revelation and the Kantian tradition remains: revelation does spring from historical experience, and carries its particularity. The theology of revelation cannot share the neo-Kantian belief in a universal ethics which is not based in some way on concrete traditions of value.

This chapter has been concerned with the nature of the tension between liberalism and religious conceptions of human dignity, in the light of an historical consideration of the highly problematic relationships between the concepts of revelation, reason and ethics since the Enlightenment. Let us now consider the contemporary state of the question: how can the relationship of revelation and reason be conceived as we face the pressing question of the sources of a public ethics?

CHAPTER 2

Revelation and a contemporary public ethics

In liberal and pluralist societies, it is a widespread belief that the resources for a public ethics should exclude religious traditions. For this perspective, a public ethics must be exclusively based on what can be perceived and known in common, and this cannot include the particular beliefs of religious communities, based as they are on controversial claims to revealed truth. The common bonds that can give pluralist societies ethical solidarity are to be found – it is argued – in various understandings of reason and of nature. Yet, as I have maintained, without nourishment from an ontology of the human, 'reason' and 'nature' are subject to a reductionism which cannot sustain a public ethics. Such an ontology of the human can only be found in those experiences and concepts which disclose the reality of human value. Ultimately, this search raises the question of religion and revelation, whose relevance to a public ethics of human value in community must be raised in a new context, overcoming the limitations of the thought-world of the Enlightenment.

This chapter examines contemporary attempts to develop a basis for a universal and public ethics from human rationality, with particular reference to the neo-Kantian tradition. This tradition seeks to establish links between individual autonomy and universal ethical community – an attempt rejected both by reductionist philosophies and by the revival of ethics based in tradition and narrative. It will be argued that the neo-Kantian attempt to establish universal ethical community cannot succeed: such community can ultimately be based only on a recognition of our common bond with infinite truth, our *communio* in infinite being, which can unify the autonomy of the person and the union of all in an ethical 'kingdom of ends'.

This bond is precisely the content of revelation, as the self-communication of the three-personed God, who calls persons into union with God and each other. In this sense, the concept of revelation can ground the ethical universality that neo-Kantianism does seek to respect and preserve. Yet how is this conviction of a divine ground to be justified and communicated? This question calls to mind the Hegelian project, which saw the ground of human worth in union with the Spirit, a union which could be publicly known and justified in metaphysical terms. A public metaphysics, however, whether of a Hegelian or neo-Scholastic kind, cannot receive universal assent: it is clearly dependent on concrete revealed traditions. At the same time, there are what could be called 'mediating principles' of a metaphysical character, which can have public communicative power. This chapter will be concerned with the meaning and implications of these questions.

There are a number of ethical approaches which seek to express the contemporary force of the Kantian heritage by developing the ethical implications of rationality. By using the methods of logical universalization and rational dialogue, such approaches provide a structure for coming to terms with public ethical questions, which respects individual autonomy. Yet by denying any ontological claims they limit the scope of reason, and at the same time the force and coherence of the ethical claims they make. This discussion will consider whether or not these public conceptions of ethics, which draw on various understandings of reason, need to be enriched or extended by any ontological claims.

The point of this discussion is not to put in question the necessity and validity of rational arguments for a public ethics, since such arguments are indeed a crucial source of common insight. Rather, it is an attempt to indicate the continuing importance of an ontology of the human person as a sustaining ground and context for a rational ethics predicated on rational discourse and subjective autonomy, in particular for the sake of linking autonomy with community in the sense of a universalist ethics. Such ontological claims draw on traditions of disclosure, the sources of a vision of the worth of persons. This vision is, in turn, an informing premise for practices of rational discourse which can reconcile autonomy and community. How Christian traditions of disclosure can make such a contribution within the public forum, without threatening the character of a pluralist society and without sacrificing their own identity, is a central concern of this book.

We saw in the previous chapter that, since the Enlightenment, there have been a number of attempts to understand the relationship between revelation, reason and ethics. For the Kantian tradition, which denied the possibility of metaphysics and judged revelation to be superfluous to rational and ethical insight, reason is fundamentally subjective – it is the power of the rational subject to construct order and meaning. The rational subject constructs ethical meaning through the various forms of the categorical imperative, employing reason's universalizing force. Yet this tradition faces the question of whether reason can have substantive ethical content without making ontological claims.

In the light of these considerations, I will argue that contemporary neo-Kantian ethics can only have substantive and universal content if it includes some form of the Kantian notion of the 'kingdom of ends', that is, if it can build a bridge between the rational subject and ethical community. If it does include the concept of a 'kingdom of ends', however, it must come to terms with the question of whether or not the concept of rational autonomy alone is sufficient to ground it. If not, then the notion of a 'kingdom of ends' can only be grounded in an ontology of the human subject in community, an ontology which relates subjective reason and subjective autonomy to a sustaining metaphysical ground, a ground made manifest in revealed traditions or traditions of disclosure. On this basis, the recognition of ethical universality, which reconciles subjective autonomy with intersubjective respect, has its source in experiences of disclosure of human community, which are themselves the sustaining context of practices of ethical discourse.

PUBLIC ETHICS IN THE KANTIAN AND NEO-KANTIAN TRADITION

In the discussion of Kant's ethics in chapter 1, I argued that there is a tension in his thought between the universality of the categorical imperative, which derives its force purely from its formal character of rational universality, and the search for a 'highest practical principle', which will unite human dignity into a kingdom of ends. The search for a highest practical principle indicates that the purely rational form of the categorical imperative was incapable of fulfilling the role that Kant hoped to give it. On the one hand, Kant characterized the normative quality of objective morality purely through the rational form of the categorical imperative; on the other, he searched for a highest practical principle which could give the categorical imperative content. The affirmation that human existence is of absolute value is not a logical principle but rather a normative assumption.[1] The categorical imperative is given a necessary character only when this normative assumption is made: my actions must be capable of being assented to by all other rational beings because all rational beings are characterized by a subjectivity which is an absolute value. It is precisely this principle which distinguishes the hypothetical from the categorical imperative: while the hypothetical imperative is based on the particular desire of an agent, the categorical imperative is objectively and universally binding because it is

[1] A comparison with contemporary generalization theories of ethics shows the importance of this normative assumption for Kant's ethics. For Kant, the 'highest practical principle' commands us to act so that we 'treat humanity, in your own person as in the person of any other, always also as an end, and never merely as a means' (*Grundlegung zur Metaphysik der Sitten*, 61). While there could be a logically consistent imperative commanding suicide in certain kinds of situations, Kant's ethics forbids it because it treats life itself as a means to happiness, and the ending of life as a means of avoiding pain. For M. Singer, by contrast, in his *Generalization in Ethics* (London: Eyre and Spottiswoode, 1963), there can be no such moral concept as a duty to myself (317). The generalization principle stipulates like action in like circumstances, but has no relevance to any acts which affect solely the agent herself. Since he rejects the 'principle of personality' as a source of ethical laws, Singer can make no sense of Kant's prohibition of treating oneself as a mere means. Moral action is defined by the generalization principle and is restricted to relations between agents: it is a principle of consistency, independent of any normative assumptions

based on the recognition of the subjectivity of every human being. While the hypothetical imperative enjoins action on the condition that certain ends are desired, the categorical imperative enjoins action unconditionally, since its *telos*, the 'kingdom of ends', an ethical order in which all human beings act and will as subjects, is taken to be an absolute value. The distinction between the hypothetical and the categorical imperative lies not in any difference of logical universality but rather in the difference between relative and absolute ends. Universality has a moral, not a logical, superiority to egoism, and this moral superiority is based on the acceptance of the status of all human subjects as 'ends in themselves'. This status, as Kant emphasized, is not expressed in terms of the empirical characteristics of any person, but is true of any person simply as member of the human species. It is the a priori of moral action and therefore unaffected by empirical differences.

In order to motivate the will, then, the logical form of the categorical imperative must be linked to acceptance of the value of each human being as a member of the 'kingdom of ends' which is both the ideal *telos* and the normative presupposition of moral action. The categorical imperative gives this value rational expression by describing the kinds of action which are consistent with it, i.e. actions which conform to a universal law. It is an expression of the moral stance, but its logical form cannot be used to distinguish it from laws stipulating the priorities of technical or strategic action. The categorical imperative expresses the fundamental principle of morality and provides a means of applying and interpreting it, rather than being identical with it. Once the decision is made to accept the principle of respect for every human being as an 'end', then the maxims of our own actions can be subjected to the logic of universalization. The categorical imperative is a way of deploying this 'highest practical principle' in a form calculated to reveal the consequences of an action and to discover whether or not any action is capable of being assented to by every rational subject.

The a priori of Kantian ethics is not, therefore, an a priori of pure reason but a specifically moral and normative a priori of human dignity. If ethics could be based purely on the motivation of the will by reason's universalizing power, then it would not need any normative assumptions concerning human nature. But it is precisely the normative assumption of the absolute value of every human being which is essential to Kant's notion of a 'kingdom of ends': 'treat humanity, in your own person as in the person of any other, always also as an end, and never merely as a means'.[2] This value, for Kant, derives from our rational nature, but it has nothing to do with the specific rational faculty of each individual – it is independent of the differences between individuals and is absolute in every case.

At the foundation of Kant's ethics is the moral conviction that all human beings have the status of rational subjects and that each rational subject must be the creator of the moral law as well as being under its authority. Kant insisted that his ethics is without any presuppositions concerning human nature and destiny, but his 'highest practical principle' is a normative interpretation of human nature which is required to give his ethical theory a truly moral universality. The human being, as well as being a part of empirical nature whose characteristics can be described in a way analogous to other beings and objects, may be characterized normatively. The affirmation of human dignity grants each individual a moral status and the possibility of belonging to a higher world, a 'kingdom of ends'.

Ethical reason – logical universalization or the universality of a 'kingdom of ends'

The relationship between the categorical imperative and the notion of a 'kingdom of ends' is a central problem in Kant's ethics. This problem has been inherited by contemporary liberal societies, which face the problem of reconciling individual autonomy and community. The universalizing rationality of the categorical imperative cannot have substantive ethical content unless it is coupled with the notion of a 'kingdom of

---

[2] *Grundlegung zur Metaphysik der Sitten*, 61.

ends', a moral community. The meaning and context of the notion of a rational being as an ethical 'end' is therefore of crucial importance. Contemporary attempts to express the Kantian heritage display important differences in the role they give to this concept. For some, the structure of ethical reasoning is sought purely in a reformulation of the rational universality of the categorical imperative, giving no role to the notion of a 'kingdom of ends'. For others, the notion of a 'kingdom of ends' is reinterpreted in terms of forms of dialogue or discourse whose rules respect the autonomy of all participants. The various options discussed in this section have been chosen to represent key positions in a broadly neo-Kantian tradition.

These varying approaches attempt to construct a public ethics on the basis of reason. Reason, in terms of the Kantian heritage, is a subjective faculty which is agnostic about metaphysical realities and which confines itself to the recognition of logical or empirical truths. The purpose of these attempts to develop a rational public ethics is to demonstrate that there can be a public ethics which, firstly, requires no premises which go beyond common rationality and which, secondly, has substantive ethical content or implications. The success of such attempts, then, is to be judged in terms of these criteria. Yet the point of any critique of such attempts cannot be to minimize the role of reason in any public ethics, but rather to strengthen it by indicating ways in which it could be situated in an ontological context, nourished by experiences of disclosure.

Logical universalization – R. M. Hare[3]

Some contemporary attempts to found ethics in reason rely on the logical power of universalization. In its most abstract form, requiring minimal premises, rationality in ethics is the rationality of universal logical laws. This form begins in the subjective will, which is free to will anything it wishes. The only constraint on the will is to act in accordance with reason. Yet reason cannot perceive any purposes in the external world. It is

[3] The presentation of Hare's arguments is based on his *Freedom and Reason* (Oxford: Clarendon Press, 1963) and *Moral Thinking: Its Levels, Method and Point* (Oxford: Clarendon Press, 1981).

completely agnostic about any ontological realities, and does not claim to be able to shape the subjective will on the basis of these. The will is free to do anything that it wishes.[4]

Reason, then, cannot know purposes in a way which will constrain the will. Reason's power is a logical one: it recognizes the force of logical propositions. It can discern similarities in situations and make universal descriptions of them, removing proper names from the descriptions of actors. Further, it can discern the consequences of action and note logical contradictions. Reason does not seek to limit the freedom of the will by positing the existence of objective purposes in reality, nor of entities which cannot be verified in strictly empirical or logical terms. It constrains the will purely by the force of logic: if the subjective will contradicts itself, or fails to recognize the force of logical equivalence, then it ceases to be rational.

Thus if the will wills something, then it must do so in ways that judge like situations to be like – it is constrained to do so by logic. It cannot prescribe something in one situation, and then refuse it in identical situations.[5] It must accept that all situations of that type should be considered in the same way, because they have relevantly similar characteristics. This means that particular persons, in particular situations, cannot claim that they should be treated differently from others. In willing something, in a particular situation, we will something that can be described in universal terms. The replacement of one person by another in

---

[4] Hare argues that philosophy in general, and moral philosophy in particular, consists only in rigorous reflection on the relationship between logical and empirical theses. Ontological questions play no role in it (*Moral Thinking*, 5). In his *Existenzphilosophie und Ethik* (Tübingen: J. C. B. Mohr, 1972), H. Fahrenbach highlights the similarities between non-cognitivist or prescriptivist moral theory, such as Hare's, and the stance of existentialist philosophy, since they are at one in the belief that ethical statements do not have a descriptive character or convey knowledge, but are rather universalizable modes of action or orientations to life (204). For Fahrenbach, the history of existentialist ethics shows that the choice of freedom must eventually express itself in a concrete analysis of human needs, a philosophical anthropology, i.e. a kind of naturalism. Human freedom must be realized in a practical philosophy, of which ethics will be a part (181). Hare would reject such a proposal, for fundamentally the same reason as the existentialists: since it threatens the vision of radically open human freedom, constrained only by the logical requirements of universalization.

[5] For Hare, the essential linguistic intuition for moral thinking is that 'if we make different moral judgements about situations which we admit to be identical in their universal descriptive properties, we contradict ourselves' (*Moral Thinking*, 21).

that situation does not change its universal description: logically speaking, it is still the same situation and the same action is prescribed. The constraint of logic on the will, then, is to limit the will to those actions which it will accept both actively and passively, both as agent and as victim. By the force of logic, it must accept that situations are not made different by the insertion of different particular individuals in various roles. This constraint, then, means that the will is limited to those actions whose effects it will accept for itself. If it does not wish such effects for itself, it would contravene logic to wish them on others.

Reason's agnosticism about objective purposes for action gives it an extraordinary simplicity and universality. For this argument, ethics is based on the clarity and force of logical laws: logic constrains us to recognize that if I prescribe something as perpetrator, I must also be prepared to prescribe it were I in the place of the victim. Since few people are prepared to suffer, were they truly in the place of the victim, then an appreciation of the logic of prescriptions and of the true facts of human situations will give them good reasons to desist from prescriptions which cause suffering to others. As we have seen, the publicly accessible character of this argument lies in its eschewing of any claims at all about the purposes of things, claims which cannot be sustained by strictly logical or empirical procedures. It makes no claim about ontological realities, about human dignity and worth, but achieves ethical universality by the power of logical laws.

Yet the logical universality of this theory is bought at the price of emptiness of ethical content. Its argument is that anyone must, by the force of logic, judge like situations to be like irrespective of particular persons. We must judge alike whether or not we figure in a situation as agent or victim, since we must accept general descriptions of situations which are person-neutral. This presupposes, however, that we do consider a situation in which I am agent the same as a situation in which I am victim. Yet there is no logical obstacle to someone asserting that their own importance makes a situation in which they are agent very different from a situation in which they are victim. Like situations become unlike through a particular person's insistence that their own claims must be given greater weight than those of others. Someone who does not accept that others are deserving of the same respect as himself can argue, without breaching the laws of logic, that he need not accept descriptions of situations which bring out their common features: situations in which he is agent and perpetrator are very different from those in which he is a passive victim, even though their other characteristics may be identical.

A purely logical universality, then, cannot provide a basis for ethics. This logical universality can only be effective when it *presupposes* that all persons are deserving of some ethical respect, that like situations do not become unlike simply because particular persons have reversed roles. Yet, in presupposing such ethical respect, it is making claims about other persons: that they have a fundamental equality which calls for such respect. But it has clearly renounced the power to perceive such objective realities which make a claim on our will and give shape and purpose to our actions. These are claims which go far beyond the scope of the strict empirical evidence or logical inference to which it restricted itself.[6]

Self-interest, rational choice and the natural coincidence of self-interest and co-operation – J. Rawls[7]

If a purely logical universality cannot bear the burden of a common public ethics, then the addition of certain significant

---

[6] Hare rejects any objective theory of the good since it implies ethical descriptivism as well as making ontological claims that philosophy cannot sustain. His emphasis on the prescriptive character of moral judgements is intended to do justice both to their action-guiding force and to our freedom to choose moral principles. Hare recognizes, however, that the 'amoralist' can slip through the net of his theory by refusing to use the tool of moral universalization and by making no 'moral judgement except judgements of indifference' (ibid., 183).

[7] This account is based on Rawls' *A Theory of Justice* (Oxford University Press, 1972), Parts 1 and 3. Here, *A Theory of Justice* is considered as a contribution to *moral* philosophy, an attempt to understand the philosophical foundations of justice between persons. In *Political Liberalism*, by contrast, Rawls presents a *political* philosophy, which presupposes that certain moral philosophies – or 'comprehensive doctrines' – coexist in the 'background culture' of society, including perspectives based in religious faith as well as secular theories such as that developed in his own *A Theory of Justice*. Rawls remains committed to the basic argument of *A Theory of Justice*, but argues that the fact of pluralism means that a political philosophy must be based on an 'overlapping consensus' rather than on any single moral philosophy, considered as a 'comprehensive doctrine' (*Political Liberalism*, xv–xvi).

empirical data may be necessary to show that such a public ethics is possible. Certain items of knowledge can be assumed to be publicly accessible, because they are derived from the empirical sciences.[8] If these are inserted into the process, then the universality of ethical bonds can be established with a reasonable degree of force. For this approach, we must still assume that human beings are motivated by subjective will, by their own interest. Yet individuals' own interests cannot be achieved unless they come to terms with each other. They do not (in the long run) have the power simply to assert their own interests. Nor can they predict how much the fulfilment of their own interests will depend on others achieving their goals. They do not enter the process of negotiation out of respect for others. This is because granting respect for others cannot be justified on these minimalist presuppositions. Their entry into the process is dictated by the exigencies of pursuing one's own interests.

If respect for others as characterized by objective worth cannot be included in the argument as an initial premise, since it would appeal to realities which are beyond the reach of the empirical or logical methods used, the crux of this argument will be in the degree to which willing participation in negotiation will coincide with the satisfaction of self-interest. In particular, it will depend on whether the experience of relationship with others in various forms of negotiation or exchange will gradually generate sensibilities which may transform such negotiation into an experience which is satisfying in itself.[9] Social exchange and reciprocity may become a form of self-fulfilment in themselves. If this is so, then the pursuit of self-interest will include motivations which affirm such processes of social exchange and reciprocity. These motivations can be developed without positing any prior need for 'respect for

---

[8] For Rawls, these 'general facts' about human nature, which include the 'Aristotelian principle' of the enjoyment of realized capacities, are best understood in the light of the theory of evolution (*A Theory of Justice*, 431).

[9] 'The recognition that we and those for whom we care are the beneficiaries of an established and enduring just institution tends to engender in us the corresponding sense of justice . . . In due course we come to appreciate the ideal of a just human co-operation' (ibid., 473–4).

persons', to be justified by appeal to an ontological 'worth of persons' which cannot be made evident in public discourse. We should rather simply acknowledge that the natural facts of human existence predispose us to find great satisfaction in various forms of fellowship and reciprocity, satisfaction which can tend to develop a coincidence between the pursuit of self-interest and a readiness to negotiate.

This argument, then, like the argument from logical universality, eschews any appeal to a universal 'worth of persons', because such an appeal is – in a public context – judged to be a mystification.[10] Like the argument from logical universality, it proceeds from the immediate reality of the subjective will and subjective desire, a will which does not recognize any given or objective purposes to human existence. It does, however, claim that certain natural facts about human satisfactions will, in conducive circumstances, incline the will to pursue self-interest in ways that are compatible with a degree of reciprocity. Recognizing that purely logical considerations are insufficient to constrain someone to make universal moral prescriptions, it introduces factual considerations drawn from a study of human nature. These factual considerations give us materials for developing a public ethics of negotiation. They do not include any ontological claims, drawn from metaphysical or religious sources, but are restricted to empirical observations about human goals and human affections.

In inserting these elements into the argument, this approach has gained a significant body of content. It can show why consistent amoralism is a relatively rare and difficult role to play: it can point out that an amoral pursuit of individual desires will usually be unsatisfying, since it will deprive us of the satisfactions of human fellowship, which many people experience as particularly valuable. It is also the case, however, that, by inserting these empirical elements into the argument, this approach sacrifices full universality. It is true that many human beings derive considerable satisfaction from the reciprocity of

---

[10] The principles of justice must be based only on 'true general beliefs about men and their place in society', without the 'necessity to invoke theological or metaphysical doctrines' (ibid., 454).

human fellowship, but the appeal to such facts of human nature does deprive the argument of any logical or rational necessity. The premise of the argument is that we are self-interested individuals, who may derive satisfaction from reciprocity through the gradual inculcation of certain affections and sensibilities. No other premises are admitted, since no other premises are deemed to be publicly evident or uncontroversial. The force of the argument, then, will depend on the actual extent to which the affections of fellowship do become part of perceived self-interest and self-fulfilment in the lives of individuals. If they do not, then there can be no recourse to any appeals to respect the intrinsic value of other persons, since such intrinsic value is not accepted as a publicly meaningful notion.

The gravest limitation on this approach is that the connection between the fulfilment of self-interest and engagement in moral negotiation, or the assumption of a moral perspective, is clear only in relatively circumscribed contexts. Within a well-defined context, it can be made evident that the satisfaction of personal desires, the achievement of personal fulfilment, is dependent on a readiness to negotiate with others and to take their claims seriously. Once we expand this context in various ways, however, whether in terms of space, time, social group, age group, etc., such connections become more and more tenuous. Such a connection could only have a universal force, acknowledging all potential dialogue partners in a circle of discourse, if it were believed that there is some profound ontological connection between self-fulfilment and the recognition of others. But this is clearly a belief that cannot be invoked on the premises that have so far been granted.

The 'kingdom of ends' as a 'community of communication' in the thought of J. Habermas and K.-O. Apel
To overcome this limitation, the process of negotiation can be conceived in a different way. Rather than being seen as something pursued by self-interested individuals, who may be educated in such a way that a degree of fellowship becomes a part of their conception of their own good, it can be conceived as a

process that all enter into with an attitude of respect for others. Dialogue, for this conception, is a social practice marked by certain conventions which betoken respect. Such conventions would include rules which give all involved an opportunity to express their views, to raise objections to the views of others, to co-determine the agenda of discussion, and to speak without fear or favour. In this way, subjective will achieves rationality through a carefully observed process of intersubjectivity. The rational character of dialogue is not simply the logical universality of prescriptions applying to common features of situations, but rather the universality of practices of common discourse, practices which can incorporate the interests of all participants in a shared process. This approach deliberately incorporates an interpretation of Kant's notion of a 'kingdom of ends' as a key premise. It does not seek to construct ethics purely out of the logic of universalization, in conjunction with some empirical data, but rather involves the principle of dialogue between equal subjects from the beginning. Because this approach – as developed in particular in the work of Jürgen Habermas and Karl-Otto Apel – gives such weight to the contemporary meaning of ethical communication and the community of a 'kingdom of ends', which is central to the concerns of this book, it demands more detailed attention.

In their writings, Habermas and Apel have attempted to interpret Kant's notion of a 'kingdom of ends' in ways which will provide a rational foundation for social and political norms. Rather than positing the categorical imperative as an a priori logical basis for ethics, the foundation of moral norms is sought in the fundamental characteristics of a rational dialogue between equal subjects. The logical universality typified by the categorical imperative becomes the universality of rational dialogue. For Habermas, the Enlightenment's understanding of reason combined 'insight and the explicit interest in liberation by means of reflection'.[11] The understanding of nature and the social world was united with the attempt to liberate human beings from irrational institutions and to develop common

[11] J. Habermas, *Theory and Practice* (London: Heinemann, 1974), 254.

values through rational communication. For modern positivism, however, reason cannot formulate values, so the process of moral reasoning can be no more than the examination of the logical consequences of a value-decision, which itself derives purely from the non-rational choice of the individual. The effects of the abolition of the communicative and emancipatory roles of reason have been the dichotomy of sophisticated techniques in the manipulation of nature for the achievement of given quantifiable goals and increasing irrationality in the setting of these goals and the formation of values. Those theories of ethics which concentrate their attention purely on the logic of moral language or on the examination of the consequences of individual decisions, rather than on the reasons for decisions, are unable to give any answer to the question of the legitimacy of moral norms. The abdication of the field of value by positivism means that talk of the legitimacy of social and political institutions cannot be rationally justified.

For Habermas, the claim to legitimacy of a free society must be based on the possibility of a rational justification of its institutions. This justification emerges from a

> communicative community of those concerned, who examine the claim to validity of norms through their involvement in a practical discourse and who, in so far as they accept them with reasons, come to the conviction that under the given circumstances the proposed norms are 'correct'. It is not the irrational acts of will of partners to a contract, but rather the rationally motivated recognition of norms, which may at any time be subjected to critique, which gives norms a claim to validity... the claim to validity of a norm is itself cognitive in the sense of the (counterfactual) imputation that it can be 'cashed' through discourse, that is, be grounded in a consensus of those concerned achieved through argument.[12]

A rational norm is produced by a free discussion between equals in an atmosphere of dialogue where the only force is the force of a good argument. Social norms, on this model, have some hope of being based on a rational consensus rather than being merely a compromise marked out by the clash of interest of different social forces. Norms are given rational grounding in

---

[12] Habermas, *Legitimationskrise im Spätkapitalismus* (Frankfurt: Suhrkamp, 1973), 144.

the intersubjectivity characteristic of a process of dialogue; they are the product of rational discussion by free agents in a socially communicative situation. The characteristics of norm-founding dialogue are intended to make possible a discovery of common interests, the emergence of a consensus in which each participant can recognize his or her own will. The norms which emerge from this dialogue must always be considered open to the critical examination of those affected by them. It is the universalizability of interests made possible by such a freely communicative situation which, for Habermas, can transcend the limits of a decisionistic ethics. Rather than accepting the apparent pluralism of interests as irreducible, such a discursive situation, by giving rational argument scope and freedom, would hope to identify universalizable interests and to distinguish them from those which are genuinely and irreducibly particular.

In a manner analogous to Kant, then, Habermas argues that the characteristics of rational speech itself are sufficient to give moral norms a rational character. While Kant saw the universal form of the categorical imperative as the source of its normative character, Habermas sees the rational character of norms in their source in a dialogic situation. For both Kant and Habermas, the normative character of morality proceeds from rationality itself. A rational subject will follow moral norms because not to do so would involve a contradiction of the will or an abandonment of the ground-rules of rational speech. Yet, while Kant affirmed that the rational character of morality was capable of motivating the will without any other subjective sources of action, Habermas recognizes that personal motivation and social integration have fundamental links with religious and metaphysical world-views, which set out to make the wretched contingencies of life bearable by putting them in the context of deeper meanings. Such world-views have had both a cognitive and a moral role.

With the disintegration of these world-views, while science and technology have given human beings considerable means to cope with the contingencies of nature, the contingencies of social and personal life stubbornly resist the meaning-bestowing insight of social and psychological theory. While Habermas does contend against positivism that a rational foundation can be given to social norms in the context of critical dialogue, he grants that the disappearance of a religious or metaphysical order must deprive any such projected foundation for ethics of ultimate conviction: 'Practical reason can no longer be grounded even in the transcendental subject; communicative ethics can now only appeal to the basic norms of rational speech, to an ultimate "fact of reason". It is, to be sure, difficult to see how this fact, if it is a bare fact, which is no longer capable of explanation, can exercise a normative power, which can organize human self-understanding and orient our action.'[13]

Habermas' model is fundamentally similar to Kant's notion of a 'kingdom of ends': each subject must be capable of perceiving the reasons for a law which he submits himself to; no social goal is rationally justifiable if it sacrifices the freedom of expression of any member of society. Although a given individual may find a law contrary to her interests as an economic agent, she must, at least in theory, be able to be persuaded that such a law is based on rational grounds to which she is able to give assent. But, as Habermas himself admits, it is difficult to see how this solution can be taken to be the foundation of the normative character of ethics. The communicative situation of 'domination-free space', in which no force prevails but the force of a good argument, is a model expressing the ideal of a 'kingdom of ends' in contemporary language, but it is itself already the practice of moral behaviour, rather than presenting reasons for it. There still remains a burden of argument to show that such a communicative model of human relationships is superior, for example, to a model which sees the dynamic will of individual subjects, untainted by the petty restrictions of endless argument and counter-argument with those of lesser talent, as the sole creative force in society. Social excellence, for this alternative model, is not the product of a process in which everyone, however philistine and uninspired, has a contribution

---

[13] Ibid., 165–6.

to make, but rather the creation of those with distinctive gifts. What is crucial for this model is not the subjectivity which the moral point of view sees as characteristic of every individual, but rather the talents which some possess uniquely. The presuppositions for participation in a norm-founding dialogue might be the possession of expert knowledge and outstanding intellectual powers, rather than the mere status of a subject who may be affected by these norms. Finally, the possession of property, a stake in society's wealth, may be judged to be a criterion of such importance as to exclude the mass of those affected.

Such alternatives and others have been characteristic of the political structures of past and present societies. What is common to all of them is that the subjectivity of each individual is not believed to be a relevant qualification for his or her participation in the act of making laws or founding norms. Rather than seeing subjectivity as the fundamental criterion of equality of rights, other characteristics of an individual, her gender, talents, wealth, position, birth and so on, are made crucially constitutive of her right to participate in the norm-creating process. The moral image of the 'kingdom of ends', the Kantian heritage which Habermas reinterprets, presupposes that this subjectivity is the crucial factor, that subjectivity itself, rather than distinctive rational insight or other empirical characteristics, is what gives each individual an inalienable right to be the creator and 'end' of the law, rather than its 'means' and passive object. Basic human rights are thus not affected by the differences between people, but are characteristic of each person precisely as person – there are no criteria which can exclude someone from the 'kingdom of ends' or 'communicative dialogue' except her own refusal to respect the subjectivity of others.

Habermas' model for the rational foundation of social norms offers a philosophical explication of the dialogic practices essential for a genuinely democratic society. Yet it cannot ground norms, and in particular the intersubjective disposition itself, without making assumptions about what human nature really consists in. These assumptions are similar to those made by Kant in constructing the notion of a 'kingdom of ends' made up of rational beings. These philosophical attempts to give ethics a normative foundation in the fundamental characteristics of rationality assume a certain normative understanding of human nature: the attribution of subjectivity and its associated rights to each individual regardless of his or her empirical characteristics. Habermas claims that his model does not need the introduction of a specific principle of universalization or 'transsubjectivity' based on a moral 'act of faith', since it deals with that universalization which naturally emerges from a communicative dialogue.[14] Yet it may be objected that the decision to participate in such a dialogue, to grant each individual the rights of subjectivity, is made on the basis of an act of faith in the dignity of each individual as a subject. An individual's preparedness to submit his own interests to the critical examination of others in dialogue is based on the specifically moral recognition of mutual obligation. The model of rational dialogue is an expression of this recognition, rather than its foundation, just as the categorical imperative is an expression of the substantive 'highest practical principle' of the status of each rational being as an 'end in itself'.

Karl-Otto Apel shares Habermas' commitment to the task of practical philosophy as the development of a rational understanding of ethics capable of grounding the legitimacy of social and political norms. For Apel, too, the rejection of practical reason characteristic of positivism and existentialism is incompatible with the maintenance of a democratic society. The restriction of the scope of ethical values to the inner choice of the individual denies the possibility of a public political order based on the rational assent of its citizens. Allegiance must be derived from the conviction that the norms which define

[14] An understanding of ethics as based on a 'practical basic decision' for 'transsubjectivity' is characteristic of the writings of P. Lorenzen and O. Schwemmer, contributors to the German-language debate on the foundations of practical reasoning. For Schwemmer, at the foundation of all attempts to reach rational agreement about social norms is the decision 'for the character of the other as subject, the decision to treat the goals of the other – before critically examining them – in the same way as one's own' ('Praktische Vernunft und Normenbegründung', in D. Mieth und F. Compagnoni, ed., *Ethik im Kontext des Glaubens*, Freiburg: Universitätsverlag Freiburg, 1978) 153.

political practice are intersubjectively binding. For Apel, the normative claims of ethics must be defended against those theories

which want to ground the intersubjective validity of norms from the point of view of a methodic individualism or solipsism, that is, purely on the basis of the empirical unification or mediation of individual interests or arbitrary decisions. If there is no ethical principle which is normatively binding as well as intersubjective, then ethical responsibility cannot in principle transcend the private sphere. That means not only that, in a formal sense, the fundamental conventions of any democracy have no morally binding character, but also, beyond that, in a concrete sense those moral decisions of individuals which are not expressly settled by agreement (in everyday affairs and in existential limit-situations) have no obligation to take any account of the demand for human solidarity and mutual responsibility.[15]

Apel's attempt to reaffirm the possibility of an intersubjectively valid ethics begins with an examination of the characteristic presuppositions of positivist ethics: since science deals with facts, and facts can never form the logical foundation for a norm, a scientific foundation for a normative ethics is not possible. Since only science is objective, i.e. intersubjectively valid, then an intersubjective foundation for ethics is impossible and the sphere of the ethical must remain one of private decisions, a foundation too weak for a living democracy or for human solidarity and mutual responsibility. Yet, for Apel, positivism's crucial distinction between scientific facts and decisionist values breaks down once the process of discovery of scientific truth itself is examined. Science's own objective status can be shown to rest on a particular kind of moral intersubjectivity: scientific argument cannot be tested unless a community of thinkers or scientists is presupposed, a community capable of intersubjective understanding and consensus. Truth can only emerge through the process of testing which the readiness of an inquirer after truth to submit her ideas and observations to the examination of others makes possible. Following Wittgenstein, Apel argues that an isolated individual cannot give her thinking

---

[15] K.-O. Apel, 'Die *Apriori* der Kommunikationsgemeinschaft und die Grundlagen der Ethik', in *Transformation der Philosophie* (Frankfurt: Suhrkamp, 1973), vol. 2, 375–6.

validity within the framework of a private language: 'even someone thinking alone can explicate and examine his own argumentation only in so far as he is able to internalize the dialogue of a potential community of dialogue in the critical "conversation of the soul with itself" (Plato)'.[16]

Rational arguments can be developed only on the basis of a process of real or simulated dialogue in which all participants are accorded respect and equality. These moral characteristics of dialogue are essential in order to allow all possible arguments and counter-arguments to be presented without fear or hesitation and to be thoroughly tested. The dispassionate search for objective truth, for the facts which constitute the foundation of scientific consensus, presupposes respect for the subjectivity of each participant in a circle of discussion, since to deny this respect is to deny expression to a possibly fruitful alternative view. The understanding of objective truth as emerging from a 'community of communication' means that a certain ethical intersubjectivity is the presupposition of scientific insight. For Apel, the arguments which are made in the dialogic context of the search for truth are speech acts which make a claim on other participants in discussion: this claim can only be made in an atmosphere of communication which presupposes mutual respect and dignity. The ethical foundation of scientific reasoning is the 'recognition of persons as the subjects of logical argument'.[17] From both a cognitive as well as an ethical point of view, the subject enclosed in a private world and a private language is cut off from meaning. The search for truth presupposes the ethical act of overcoming the barrier of 'methodic solipsism', the false belief that truth can be found in the introspection of the isolated subject.

Ethical norms, then, are objective because they are the foundation of the objectivity of science itself, which has no other testing-ground than a dialogue with fundamental ethical characteristics. Apel grants, however, that to speak of ethics as 'grounded' or norms as 'valid' is to presuppose logical norms as the standard of validity. Yet if ethics is to be the dialogical

---

[16] Ibid., 399.   [17] Ibid., 400.

context of logical reasoning itself, then his whole argument can be accused of circularity. Apel insists, however, that a commitment in favour of rational argument and ethical intersubjectivity can be justified without recourse to decisionism. He approaches this problem through an examination of the characteristics of speech acts: anyone who wishes to challenge the laws of logic must accept the rules of language in order to enter into discussion at all, and by accepting these rules he nullifies his initial position. The subject who consistently rejects the laws of logic is incapable of rational communication and is enclosed in a cage of 'methodic solipsism', which would make even his own self-understanding impossible. The choice between rationality and irrationality thus becomes a choice between communication, with its logical as well as ethical implications, and the madness of a totally private language.

Apel's central concern is to develop a transcendental a priori foundation for morality based on the essential characteristics of communication itself. The transcendental character of language lies in its power to communicate. It is the act of communication, rather than the words of language, which is the ultimate ground of human cognitive and ethical norms. An injured person, for example, may retain communicative competence despite having lost linguistic competence through injury. The normative claims of socio-linguistic institutions must find their validity in the characteristics of the 'meta-institution' of communication: 'The task of a transcendental–pragmatic foundation of all norms – especially of ethical norms – is defined by the demand for rational justification or critique of all actually existing institutions and the affirmation that the meta-institution of communication does make available the normative conditions for the possibility of the fulfilment of this demand'.[18]

Anyone who takes part in discussion has at least an implicit knowledge of the normative conditions of reaching the truth through communication and has at least implicitly accepted these conditions. An essential condition of communication is to tell the truth. An individual can break this norm by lying, but

[18] *Sprachpragmatik und Philosophie* (Frankfurt: Suhrkamp, 1976), 103–4.

she cannot deny its validity altogether without making communication impossible. A crucial step in Apel's argument is that someone who makes interpersonal communication impossible will also lose self-understanding: someone who is no longer aware when he is lying and when not, has lost her orientation to reality. The person who breaks the norm of communicating truth must retain internal awareness of the distinction between truth and falsity, internal recognition of the norm of truth, in order to preserve her own sanity:

> Indeed, the person who loses internal performative control over his own lying – reflexive control in the sense of the linguistically paradoxical phrase: 'I am hereby lying' – is already on the way to mental illness, even though there are empirically harmless transitional stages of self-deception. The true nihilist – as Dostoyevsky saw – is really only conceivable as a determined suicide, that is, a destroyer of his own identity, an identity with and difference from others mediated through communication.[19]

When we communicate, we presuppose an implicit knowledge of the rules of communication in ourselves and in any possible partner. These rules have a transcendental status since they are the a priori condition for any argumentative discourse. The function of rules of promising and similar regulative speech acts, such as to allow, forbid, refuse, accept, etc., is to make the a priori conditions of communication explicit. Thus Apel endorses Habermas' model of grounding norms in an ideal 'community of communication' (*Kommunikationsgemeinschaft*), but he insists that the rational necessity of such a community can only be established through transcendental reflection on the conditions for the possibility of any communicative discourse. Without this final grounding, Habermas' principle would only have the status of a theoretical axiom and could not be used as the basis of all norms. For Apel, 'ethics cannot be grounded in a universal reconstructive theory of the social sciences – that would only be a contemporary form of that "naturalistic fallacy" which has been linked with the self-understanding of every rising empirical discipline'.[20] We cannot merely appeal to the fact that ethical norms can be grounded in the consensus of

[19] Ibid., 118.   [20] Ibid., 121.

a 'community of communication'. We must rather show that the a priori conditions of communication are constitutive of our rationality as such, and therefore give the ethical principles that flow from argumentative dialogue a normative character. Thus, ethics is not a decisionistic supplement to our rational faculty; rather, both ethics and rationality are grounded in the transcendental conditions of communication.

What, however, is the substantial content of the 'principle of reason as the basic norm of an ethics of an unrestricted community of communication'? From Apel's transcendental–pragmatic argumentation, it follows that its content is the 'inescapable obligation of all those who are involved in argument to the principle of the discursive substantiation of all normative claims, according to the measure of the intersubjective universalizability of the interests that those claims represent'.[21] The moral norms implied by a 'community of communication' have a categorical character, Apel argues, since they are necessarily associated with the possibility of rational communication, regardless of empirical conditions. They are not empirical facts, irrelevant to the derivation of value – rather, like Kant's 'fact of reason', they act as the basis for any rational judgement and for the emergence of any verifiable facts. If the search for truth is an imperative, then the ethical norms associated with it can be justifiably called a categorical imperative with an a priori status associated with the a priori status of the laws of logic. The basic characteristics of the Kantian 'kingdom of ends' are already implied in the rational search for truth. If an individual does not wish to retreat into the darkness of 'methodic solipsism', if she wishes to know the truth about herself and the world, she must be prepared to grant those she interacts with a minimum of recognition, and this recognition is an implicit acknowledgement of the subjectivity, the personhood, of the other. Apel intends his argument for the objectivity of norms to be presuppositionless in a way similar to Kant's: it is derived from the characteristics of rational speech alone, and the individual who

---

[21] Ibid., 126.

wishes to reject these will be forced to forgo any form of genuine communication and, finally, the possibility of self-understanding itself.

Apel's demonstration of the relationship between the search for objective truth and fundamental ethical attitudes does succeed in overcoming any positivist bifurcation of scientific fact and irrational value. If the touchstone of scientific truth is the consensus of all those who seek it arrived at through critical dialogue in a broad scholarly community, then certain ethical attitudes are the presuppositions of the search for scientific truth. Yet Apel's attribution of the status of a 'categorical imperative' to such ethical dispositions is valid only if the search for objective scientific truth is itself an imperative. The normative character of mutual respect depends on the normative character of the dispassionate search for truth. This means, however, that, for those who reject the search for a truth which is independent of their particular interests, the ethical attitudes which are related to it are not dictated by rationality itself. To insist that the possession of objective truth is a higher good for an individual than the pursuit of her particular interest, is to set up a norm in the same sense as a moral exhortation to her to situate her own interest in the context of a 'kingdom of ends'.

The determination to seek only that knowledge which is useful for an individual's own life style or desire to dominate others can be called irrational only if rationality is identified with action according to universal norms. Yet action in accordance with a hypothetical imperative related to strictly particular desires is not *ipso facto* irrational. The knowledge necessary for strategic action according to a hypothetical imperative can be acquired without commitment to the maintenance of a 'community of communication'. The fact of rational speech itself does not imply the respect proper to communication, since such speech may be directed towards realizing particular interests in a strategically manipulative way, rather than calling for shared insight into truth as a common goal. Apel's demonstration of the links between objective truth and ethical intersubjectivity does show that the search for truth is based on values, but does not succeed in showing that the search for facts which are irrelevant to particular interests is a rational imperative. The attempt to develop the moral implications of rationality from its cognitive role without the interpolation of a moral decision or commitment fails because of the coherence of the notion of a rational and immoral hypothetical imperative. 'Methodic solipsism' in a moral sense is a possible strategy, just as the 'community of communication' may be restricted to a particular group in the furtherance of interests, avoiding any universal ethical consequences.

In his 'Discursive Ethics – Notes on a Programme for Foundations',[22] Habermas reflects on the results of attempts at establishing a rational foundation for ethics, in the context of his broader concern for the role of emancipatory and communicative rationality in society. For Habermas, there is a need for philosophy to return to an awareness of the reality of moral feelings. Despite the contemporary tendency to reduce values rationality to goals rationality, human beings do have an involvement in a world of moral feelings that they cannot permanently absent themselves from. Theoretical arguments are incapable of persuading us to ignore this bedrock of moral feelings, the affective ground of morality which cannot be reduced to prudence or self-interested rationality.[23] For Habermas, what is common to all non-cognitive theories (that of Hare in particular) is that they devalue this intuitive everyday understanding of moral terms based on irreducibly moral feelings.

Habermas' attempt to develop a moral theory which will do justice to these feelings at a conceptual level begins with his fundamental distinction between communicative and strategic action. Communicative action involves the co-ordination of plans of action, so that the resulting mutual understanding is rationally motivated, based on a recognition of the different claims involved achieved through discourse. Strategic action, in contrast, uses various kinds of power to achieve a goal which has been set in advance by the agent, without consultation with

---

[22] 'Diskursethik – Notizen zu einem Begründungsprogramm', in *Moralbewusstsein und kommunikatives Handeln* (Frankfurt: Suhrkamp, 1983).
[23] Ibid., 58.

those who may be affected by the attempt at realization of that goal.[24]

Moral norms require, in the long run, to be based on reasons, to have a basis in communicative action. In the sphere of morality, we cannot look for proofs of a strictly deductive or empirical kind. What moral theory needs is to develop a moral principle 'which as a rule of argument plays an equivalent role to the principle of induction in the discourse of the empirical sciences'.[25] For all attempts at grounding a rational or cognitivist ethics which can do justice to the reality of moral feelings, such a principle has its source in 'that intuition which Kant expressed in the categorical imperative'.[26] This is the intuition, that 'only those norms can be accepted as valid which express a universal will' in the sense that they are recognized as norms by all those affected.

For Habermas, Apel's arguments do show that – if we engage in argumentative discourse – there is no escaping the dialogic and communicative implications of the principle of universalization, since one must accept the universalizing rules of discursive communication in the very act of challenging them. Yet he does not believe that the rational necessity of engaging in argumentative discourse itself is thereby demonstrated. Those involved clearly recognize these rules as a 'fact of reason' simply through the fact of their participation in argument, but this does not give these rules an ultimate logical foundation. It simply shows that there is no alternative to them if we wish to engage in argumentative discourse.[27] Significantly, Habermas does not accept Apel's claim that transcendental–pragmatic argumentation can give a final and compelling demonstration of the necessary union of logic and ethics. While Apel considers such a demonstration to be essential for the claims of ethical rationality in a democratic society, Habermas gives everyday moral intuitions the role of final court of appeal. We do not need to claim any final logical demonstration for the sake of supporting morality's claims in everyday life: 'Everyday moral intuitions do not need to be enlightened by philosophers.'[28]

[24] Ibid., 68.　　[25] Ibid., 73.　　[26] Ibid., 73.
[27] Ibid., 105.　　[28] Ibid., 108.

What are the alternatives to this discursive ethics in contemporary life? Habermas focuses on two very different options: the first is the sceptic, the second the accusation of empty formalism made against discursive ethics by 'the front of neo-Hegelians and neo-Aristotelians, revived from political motives'. The sceptic can refuse to argue at all and 'relate to his own culture like an ethnologist, who observes philosophical argumentation with a shake of the head as the unintelligible rite of a strange tribe'.[29] The proponent of discursive ethics must accept that there is a final decisionist remainder even when the force of Apel's arguments is granted: a readiness to argue, to participate in discussion, must be presupposed. To that extent, the sceptic can reject morality without sacrificing cognitive and strategic rationality. Yet, although he may reject morality, the sceptic remains within the context of a concrete ethical environment (*Sittlichkeit*). She cannot completely withdraw from the world of communicative action without suicide or psychosis. The moral sceptic cannot restrict herself to strategic action, since the culture to which she belongs, and which she utilizes for the sake of her goals, has developed its characteristic language and symbols through the processes of communicative action. Strategic action cannot be a total programme, since it is essentially parasitic on a context of communicative action which gives it the linguistic and other tools which it needs. Since the characteristics of communicative action are essentially similar to the presuppositions of argumentation, the sceptical refusal to accept these presuppositions must be judged to be possible only on a partial basis or in the short run.

In answer to the accusation of formalism, Habermas emphasizes that the theory of discursive ethics is intended to be a method, a process: substantive moral content can emerge only from its enactment. The problems of any concrete society can be approached through putting this process into action. Habermas accepts that the principle of universalization which is presupposed by discursive ethics can deal only with the question of the right, not that of the good. Discursive ethics is concerned

[29] Ibid., 108.

'not with preference for values, but with the normative status of norms of action'.[30] Cultural values do make a claim to intersubjective validity, but they are too closely bound up with a particular form of life to make a claim to be normatively binding. Habermas grants that the concrete application of the rules of argument and discourse requires virtues of prudence and discernment which are developed in concrete historical traditions. To this extent, a particular historical tradition is prior to and presupposed by a rational and universalist ethics. But this does not mean that rational ethical discourse loses its objective reference. Parliamentary conventions, for example, are particular cultural phenomena, but they do not deprive parliamentary debate of its potential to develop social norms with a rational claim to validity.[31]

Although discursive ethics must clearly distinguish between questions of the right and the good, in practice there is an important complementary relationship between the two: practical normative judgements receive concrete focus and motivating strength from the traditions of the good life rooted in a culture. At the level of universal moral principles, however, morality can no longer depend on the support of particular forms of life: it loses crucial motivational and affective support. Because of this, a universalist morality needs its own form of life which will allow it to be put into practice: 'Only those forms of life, which in this sense "accommodate" universalist morality, provide the necessary conditions for making up for the abstract character inherent in the de-contextualization and de-motivation of universalist morality.'[32]

Religion may be such a form of life, since 'even viewed from outside, it could turn out that monotheistic traditions have at

---

[30] Ibid., 114.   [31] Ibid., 102, 114.
[32] Ibid., 119. In his 'The Church as a Community of Interpretation: Political Theology between Discourse Ethics and Hermeneutical Reconstruction', in *Habermas, Modernity and Public Theology*, ed. D. S. Browning and F. S. Fiorenza (New York: Crossroad, 1992), F. Schüssler-Fiorenza takes up this theme, contending that Habermas' 'interpretation of modernity raises the question of the *locus* of public discourse about issues of justice, right and good in view of the increasing colonization of the public sphere of the lifeworld' (78). Fiorenza argues that the churches can be such an institutional *locus*, engaging in a hermeneutic of the publicly normative potential of their traditions (79).

their disposal language whose semantic potential is not yet exhausted, that shows itself to be superior in its power to disclose the world and to form identity'.[33] Yet Habermas does not accept that discourse ethics needs any ultimate or transcendent context, that it is 'so entangled in limit questions that it finds itself in need of a theological foundation'.[34] Human beings are capable of a 'transcendence from within' which can enable them to transcend the provinciality of particular historical viewpoints. Although such a 'transcendence from within' is limited by death, and cannot restore life and dignity to the annihilated victims of history, this does not 'enable us to ascertain the countermovement of a compensating transcendence from beyond . . . since the circumstance that penultimate arguments inspire no real confidence is not enough for the grounding of a hope that can be kept alive only in religious language.'[35]

In Habermas' ethical project, dialogue is premised on the assumption that all dialogue partners are worthy of respect, a respect which has its concrete form in the common observation of shared discursive practices. His conception of discursive ethics does not attempt to demonstrate that all participants are worthy of this respect, and makes no link to a likely fulfilment of self-interest: it rather assumes that this respect will be shown, in order to give its own processes universality, the universality

---

[33] J. Habermas, 'Transcendence from Within, Transcendence in this World', in *Habermas, Modernity and Public Theology*, ed. D. S. Browning and F. S. Fiorenza 229. David Tracy, in his 'Theology, Critical Social Theory, and the Public Realm', in the same volume, applauds Habermas' contribution to the understanding of modernity through his emphasis on communicative reason (29), but argues that Habermas neglects the power of disclosure of art and religion, running the risk of damaging the life-world – whose integrity he seeks to protect – by the marginalization of religion and reduction of art to individual sincerity and authenticity (38–9).

[34] Ibid., 237.

[35] Ibid., 238, 239. Earlier, in his *Legitimationskrise*, Habermas had argued that a universalist and communicative understanding of human nature could be most coherently associated with certain – in his view unorthodox – interpretations of religious tradition, although this is for him no more than an abstract possibility. Rather than understanding communication as a factual characteristic of speech, which can imply no obligation on those who refuse to communicate or to engage in dialogue, communication is seen as constitutive of true humanity, grounded in God's creative will and purpose: 'God becomes the name of a communicative structure, which compels human beings, at the penalty of the loss of their humanity, to overcome their contingent and empirical nature' (167).

which treats all members of the process as equally entitled to take advantage of the rules of dialogue. The circle of dialogue can be defined in terms as large as necessary: potentially, all humanity can be included, in so far as some fundamental practices of dialogue could be adopted on a global basis.

This dialogic process, however, is still based on the fundamental premise that rationality is subjective. The universality of dialogue is not the universality of objectivity but the universality of intersubjectivity. Our reason cannot be constrained by claimed objective purposes in reality, nor can we introduce such claims into the process of dialogue. The only foundation of ethics is our rationality itself. This means that the respect we grant to others, and which is the crucial presupposition of our process of dialogue, must be a respect for their rationality itself, for their rational subjectivity. It cannot be grounded on a perception of ontological realities, or of a worth of persons grounded in such realities.

It is the rationality of others which calls for our respect, in particular their rational autonomy. We recognize others as deserving of respect because they are capable of choosing goals for themselves or of giving assent to goals recommended by others. The autonomy of rational beings enables them to reflect on their own wishes and desires, and to choose courses of actions which will fulfil them. It enables them to consider whether the prescriptions of others are compatible with their own purposes. This autonomy entitles all rational individuals to participate in the dialogic process. Since autonomy is linked to publicly visible processes of reasoning and reflection, it is a feature of human beings which can be appealed to as a crucial part of the foundation of a public ethics.

The notion of rational autonomy is a powerful source of public ethics. It is a means of interpreting and justifying the respect granted to all participants in a potentially universal circle of discourse. It expresses in contemporary language the Kantian notion of the 'kingdom of ends', and is crucial to contemporary democratic processes. In the Kantian tradition, however, as we have seen, autonomy is derived purely from the human characteristics of subjective will and rationality. It rejects all claims that a full understanding of human autonomy depends on objective ontological beliefs. In particular, it rejects the claim that experiences of disclosure, the source of ontological beliefs, are crucial to our sense of the worth of persons within a 'kingdom of ends'.

What is it, however, that we respect when we respect the autonomy of others? Is it the subjective will as such, and the ability to judge whether or not certain prescriptions conform to our desires? Or is it rather the ability to know the truth? When we respect autonomy, we do not simply respect subjective will, or a means–ends rationality which can achieve the purposes of subjective will. What we respect is the potential of human reason to know the truth. In particular, what we value about a process of dialogue is its potential for arriving at a shared truth.

This link between ethical respect and the search for truth is fundamental to Apel's reformulation of the Kantian heritage. We grasp the union of respect for others and insight into truth when we realize that such insight is achieved by a process of dialogue. We have our best chance of finding the truth by engaging in a process of critical dialogue, open to all possible objections, contributions and points of view. The search for truth is best conducted in the broadest possible republic of letters or of science. This means that truth and ethical respect cannot be separated: we can hope to come to insight only by granting respect to all possible participants in dialogue. The greater and more all-encompassing our search for truth, the greater this circle of dialogue must be. From this perspective, ethical autonomy is the guarantee that the search for truth will not be circumvented by arbitrary limitations on the circle of dialogue – if all are autonomous, and all have the right to contribute to debate, then knowledge will be based on the most rigorous and comprehensive process of critique and debate.

Apel's arguments do succeed in demonstrating the links between the search for truth and ethical respect. If I wish to find the truth, I must be prepared to acknowledge the contributions that others can make – otherwise I am condemned to the limitations of my own perspective, which cannot even become aware of its limitations without the spur of critique. Yet, because Apel's neo-Kantian perspective is agnostic about metaphysical truth, it is limited to a hypothetical argument: if I wish to search for truth, then I need to show some respect to those whose critique can assist me in finding it. If there is no ultimate truth, then there can be no objective necessity to engage in a search for such ultimacy, a search which must include the widest possible circle of dialogue, and be informed by the deepest respect for others.

The search for truth may be a search for a very limited truth, or simply for knowledge which serves self-interest. Limited truths can be found with the aid of a very limited circle of dialogue. The knowledge which serves self-interest can be found through engagement in dialogue in the circles of various kinds of technical elites, excluding all those whose limitations – whether social, economic or intellectual – prevent them from contributing to the fulfilment of my search for strategically useful knowledge. My circle of discourse will include all possible members, and be rid of all taint of strategic self-interest, only if it is a search for a truth whose ultimacy can embrace the true interests of all. The connection between ethical respect and the search for truth can only be made if my search for truth is ethically disinterested: in this sense, it does not ground ethical norms but assumes them. This critical appreciation of Apel's contribution leads us to consider the relationship between autonomy and participation in infinite truth, and to go beyond the neo-Kantian tradition.

REVELATION AND THE INFINITE GROUND OF ETHICAL COMMUNITY

Autonomy and participation in infinite truth

The crucial problem of neo-Kantian ethics is the relationship between subjective autonomy and ethical community. If the human individual is defined as a subjective rational will, what constitutive bonds does this individual have with others? This problem is not soluble, in terms of universal ethical community, if certain kinds of ontological claims about human communion are ruled out in advance. On the contrary, only an affirmation of the commonality of human beings in their relationship to truth, a relationship that is a common participation in the infinite, can ground an ethics of universal community.[36]

If autonomy had no links with truth, then what we would value about it would be the fact that human beings have the freedom to pursue their subjective purposes, whatever these may be. This freedom is a fundamental good, whether or not it is successfully employed in the search for truth. The human ability to reason is a good, whether or not it discovers truth. Human subjectivity, and the autonomy that is its corollary, can be prized simply for the freedom and rationality they express. Yet the nature of human subjectivity does give rise to a fundamental question: do human freedom and rationality have a fundamental orientation to the truth, even though they may not find it? Is subjectivity intrinsically oriented to the objectivity of truth? Does the practice of discourse simply reflect a need for autonomous human beings to negotiate their interests in communicative ways, or does it express a common orientation to truth?

If the notion of autonomy were to be stripped of all orientation to the truth, then it would remain simply the acknowledgement that human beings have desires which they wish to satisfy and that they are capable of reflecting on how to achieve this satisfaction. The rationality that constitutes their autonomy

[36] For Helmut Peukert, in his *Science, Action and Fundamental Theology: Towards a Theology of Communicative Action* (Cambridge, Mass.: MIT Press, 1984), the aporia of neo-Kantian arguments for an unlimited 'community of communication' springs from the 'paradox of anamnestic solidarity', the fact that the living enjoy a solidarity which they owe to those who died innocently for their sake. Since the living cannot repay this debt to the dead, they must deny a basic dimension of the very solidarity they enjoy, and thus live in self-contradiction (209, 215). Peukert's argument is a powerful demonstration of the limitations of neo-Kantian arguments in terms of the inclusion of the dead in the 'community of communication'. In my own argument, however, the limitations of the neo-Kantian argument can be found also in its conception of the dialogue of the living, in so far as this dialogue is not grounded in a common participation in truth. For another discussion of the meaning of solidarity with the dead, see Michael J. Himes and Kenneth R. Himes, *Fullness of Faith: The Public Significance of Theology* (Mahwah, N.J.: Paulist Press, 1993), ch. 7, 'The Communion of Saints and an Ethic of Solidarity'. The chapter includes a striking contrast between Jefferson's sense of each age as belonging only to the living, and Lincoln's powerful evocation of the 'mystic chords of memory' in his First Inaugural Address (159–62).

would be defined purely as a means–ends, or technical, rationality. Yet this gives no means of developing a concept of a 'kingdom of ends' or a community of respect and discourse. There are no bases for understanding the fulfilment of self-interest in communal terms if there are no shared truths. If all are defined as individual agents, seeking the fulfilment of individual desires by appropriate means, then the only basis for a social ethic is a negative form of the social contract: for the sake of the avoidance of conflict between self-interested agents, certain procedures of negotiation are agreed on. These procedures constitute the ground-rules of social relationships, and their maintenance is in the interests of all, since, in general, all benefit from the avoidance of conflict. This 'in general' is, however, a very fragile condition, since there is always the possibility that certain kinds of conflict will bring considerable benefit to particular individuals or groups. There is no objective reason why such conflict should not be risked if it does bring these benefits, because, *per definitionem*, it does not run counter to any general truths about human existence.

It is its orientation to truth, then, which gives autonomy a character which demands ethical respect. The notion of a universal realm of dialogue can have much greater strength from an understanding of rational autonomy which prizes it precisely because it represents the orientation of freedom and reason to the truth. In this case, the contributions of all participants in discourse are valued not only because they are the contributions of individuals capable of subjective will and rational self-interest, but also because they are contributions towards a common search for truth. It is the freedom of rationality which enables it to find truth, but it is truth which it seeks. If rational autonomy is stripped of all reference to truth, then dialogic processes are limited to the negotiation of self-interest or of individual perceptions which can make no truth-claims. This radically limits the potential to evoke respect for all participants.

Respect for autonomy is fundamentally akin to respect for individual conscience. Respect is due to conscience whether or not conscience knows or assents to objective truth. The dignity of conscience is the dignity of subjectivity, of the subjective orientation to truth. Yet that dignity is linked to the truth in a crucial sense: if there were no truth at all, if objective truth were completely chimerical, then conscience would be aimless. Conscience's work of seeking and giving assent to what it subjectively perceives to be truth would be pointless if there were no truth to seek. The nature of subjectivity, and the concepts of autonomy and conscience which express it, are oriented to objectivity, the truth which the subject seeks in freedom and reason.

To relate the dignity of human subjectivity, the meaning of conscience and autonomy, to truth in this way is radically different from the pre-modern conception that individuals have rights only when they in fact give allegiance to what is deemed to be objective truth. For that conception, it was this allegiance, this professed relationship to objective truth, which gave the individual dignity. In contrast to that, a modern attempt to affirm the sources of human autonomy in infinite truth emphasizes the dignity of subjectivity in so far as it is oriented to the truth, not in so far as it has found it or publicly professes it.[37] In this way, subjectivity is neither a freedom we are 'saddled with' in an absurd world nor something we are credited with only if we affirm our affiliation to particular truths, but rather a dynamic orientation to truth which is informed by the belief that there is a truth to be found. This conception can give a ground and purpose to freedom, rather than denying it by asserting that it must be coupled with some particular truth.

The recognition of a common orientation to truth is a

---

[37] This was, of course, a crucial point for Vatican II's *Dignitatis Humanae* (1965), which avoided indifferentism by affirming the objectivity of truth, but at the same time emphasized the subjective rights of conscience in the search for truth. In this way, *Dignitatis Humanae* made a decisive break from conceptions of the objectivity of truth at the expense of subjective freedom which had characterized the nineteenth-century papacy and had its most extreme form in the Syllabus of Errors. See especially *Dignitatis Humanae*, 2. On the meaning of conscience, and the relationship between subjective and objective truth, *Gaudium et Spes* 16 was of particular importance. In his *Church, State, Morality and Law* (Dublin: Gill and Macmillan, 1992), Patrick Hannon offers a detailed and illuminating discussion of the implications of Vatican II's teaching for the relationships between Christian morality, conscience and the law in the context of liberal societies.

powerful source of respect in a circle of discourse. It is a recognition that our partners in discourse are capable not only of pursuing their self-interest, but also of finding and affirming what is in the interests of all. If all participants in discourse are recognized as standing in a relationship with truth, as subjects oriented to truth, then a radical equality is implied. The rational faculties and powers of argument of different participants in discourse may vary, but all stand in a subjective relationship to truth, all – whether actually or potentially – can recognize the truth in their own freedom. In this sense, the truth is not something that must be attained by the limited and particular powers of each participant's reason – it is rather something that all have a prior subjective relationship to, a relationship that is the premise of their participation in genuine discourse. Participants in discourse – whatever their personal powers of argument happen to be – do not have to prove their capacity to grasp the truth: rather, the hallmark of inclusive discourse is that all participants are assumed to stand in a relationship to truth, by virtue of their subjective freedom and their willingness to respect the subjectivity of others.

Since this relationship to truth is a fundamental orientation of our subjectivity, rather than something that we must strive to attain, it is primarily a form of participation. A relationship to truth that all possess, independently of their particular rational powers and education, is a participation in truth that is the basis and ground of our subjectivity – a ground that may be rationally reflected on and articulated, but which is prior to and independent of such reflection.[38] We can be sustained by this

---

[38] For J. B. Metz, in his *Glaube in Geschichte und Gesellschaft* (Mainz: Matthias Grünewald, 1977), Habermas' and Apel's theories have the weakness of assuming the rationality of the subject and imply 'reciprocal recognition'. Because of this, as a general tendency, they give the projected community of communication the character of an 'exchange relationship' (208), which Metz interprets as implying the exclusion of the dispossessed, who have nothing to 'exchange'. Yet this critique neglects the fact that both Habermas and Apel emphasize that all those affected by concrete norms should be involved in their development through discursive processes. As Seyla Benhabib notes, in her *Situating the Self: Gender, Community and Postmodernism in Contemporary Ethics* (Cambridge: Polity Press, 1992), Habermas seeks to 'overcome the problems of modern societies by extending the principle of modernity, namely the unlimited and universally accessible participation of all in the consensual generation of the principles to govern public life' (81). Habermas and Apel do conceive this process in

participatory relationship, without being consciously aware of it or able to articulate it. As participatory, this relationship to truth is not to the abstraction of concepts, but to a ground of being, a source of life which sustains and energizes.

If our respect for persons is linked to our conception of them as related to, and participating in, truth, then that respect is intensified in strength and broadened in scope the greater we conceive this truth to be. In particular, if we are committed to a genuine universality of dialogue, then this relationship must be to a truth which can embrace the whole of humanity, in which all of humanity participates. If this relationship is to a truth that is infinite, that is beyond human powers to abolish or degrade, then this gives human autonomy, or human value, a depth which no human institution can challenge. If the human person participates in an infinite truth, then the subjectivity of all, however marginalized, is enshrined in fundamental equality. If all human beings exist in relationship to an infinite truth, then the differences between them are insignificant compared to their common relationship to a truth whose reality infinitely transcends all human differences.

This relationship to infinite truth, which springs from a common participation in infinite being, is a transcendent and ontological basis for a union of ethical autonomy and community. The theological concept of revelation is intended to express precisely this conviction that human beings do exist in such a participatory relationship to infinite being. For Christian faith, the revelation of God is an invitation to live in communion with the triune divine communion.[39] This participation in the divine

terms of mutual respect, rather than as an 'exchange relationship': what their conception lacks is an ontological ground for such mutual respect, a truth in which all participate, including – as Metz powerfully argues – the dead, with whom the living must remain in solidarity ('God of the Living and the Dead', 72–3).

[39] For Vatican II's *Dei Verbum*, (1965) the meaning of revelation is that 'the invisible God, from the fullness of his love, addresses men and women as his friends and lives among them, in order to invite and receive them into his own company' (2). *Vatican Council II: The Basic Sixteen Documents*, ed. A. Flannery, OP (Dublin: Dominican Publications, 1996), 98. For a discussion of the different dimensions of *communio* theology in the documents of Vatican II, see Walter Kasper, 'The Church as Communion: Reflections on the Guiding Ecclesiological Idea of the Second Vatican Council', in *Theology and Church* (New York: Crossroad, 1989). Significantly, the Latin *communio* is a translation of the Greek *koinonia*, whose original meaning, Kasper

communion is the foundation of human existence, and makes possible those forms of human communion which reflect and express the love of God. Universal ethical communion has its ontological ground in the participation in the divine communion, which is possible because of the prior act of God, calling God's human creatures into existence and sustaining them in love.

The concept of revelation affirms that all human beings exist in a participatory relationship to God. In relation to ethical discourse, it grounds the subjectivity of all in a participatory relationship to truth. Yet the concept of revelation is not merely a theoretical assertion of such a relationship, a *deus ex machina* which confers a formally infinite status on the scope of dialogue and respect. It derives rather from concrete experiences of disclosure, which have become enshrined in Christian tradition as revelatory, as disclosing the infinite love of God for the world. Christian revelation is an affirmation of the worth of all, despite the radical inequalities and injustices of the world, which is inspired by the praxis of Jesus and grounded in his death and resurrection. In this death and resurrection, the love of God for all was disclosed in an ultimate and definitive way: our communion with God and each other is based in the divine solidarity with humanity revealed in the life, death and resurrection of Jesus.

Since Christian revelation itself springs from experience of disclosure, it not only affirms the worth of all in conceptual terms, but also can sustain and inspire the mutual respect that is the premise of ethical discourse. Even more, the story of divine solidarity with humanity in Christ can inspire that solidarity which is the life-blood of a discourse which goes beyond argument to communion, a sharing of life and destiny. Both theologically and ethically, the reality of communion, of mutual

---

emphasizes, is 'participation', not 'community' (154). Kasper's 'The Church as a Universal Sacrament of Salvation', in the same volume, develops a key emphasis of Vatican II which was affirmed at the very beginning of *Lumen Gentium*: that 'the church, in Christ, is a sacrament – a sign and instrument, that is, of communion with God and of the unity of the entire human race' (*Lumen Gentium* ch. 1:1, Flannery edition, 1).

participation, is based in solidarity, a readiness to identify with others and share their suffering.[40]

This understanding of revelation can enable a new conception of the relationship between revelation, reason and ethics, which overcomes some of the crucial antinomies of nineteenth-century thought.[41] In contrast to Kant's understanding of revelation as authoritarian dicta which were at best superfluous to rational ethics, revelation can be understood as the affirmation of the sustaining ground of human subjectivity and ethical community. The acceptance of the value of every human being as a 'subject' is not a logical insight but an interpretation of experience, the experience of mystery. The values which guide thought and motivate action in the great religious and moral traditions of humankind derive from such primordial experiences. These experiences are essentially historical: the insights

[40] The unity of humanity and universal solidarity are brought together with the theological concept of communion in Part V (especially paragraphs 39 and 40) of John Paul II's *Sollicitudo Rei Socialis* (1987). The concept of solidarity came into Catholic theology through its adoption from the labour movement by Catholic social theorists, with its first explicit entrance in *Quadragesimo Anno*, written by O. Nell-Breuning, SJ. See M. Lamb, 'Solidarity', in *New Dictionary of Catholic Social Thought*, ed. J. A. Dwyer (Collegeville: Liturgical Press, Michael Glazier, 1994). 'Solidarity' like 'communio' is a concept which conveys unity without obliterating difference. For a discussion of the recognition of 'difference' in solidarity, see M. Shawn Copeland's 'Toward a Critical Christian Feminist Theology of Solidarity', in *Women and Theology*, ed. M. A. Hinsdale and P. H. Kaminski (Maryknoll, N.Y.: Orbis Books and College Theology Society, 1995).

[41] One effect of the renewed understanding of revelation is to break down the opposition between 'revelation' and 'enlightenment'. In his 'Zur Interdependenz von Aufklärung und Offenbarung', in *Tübinger Theologische Quartalschrift* 165 (1985): 161–73, M. Seckler notes the semantic and historical connections of the concepts of Enlightenment and revelation. Both refer to sight and illumination, and each has historically defined itself in relation to the other. It was the conflict with the Enlightenment that developed the Christian community's awareness that revelation was a key concept in its own theoretical self-determination (166–7). The positive contribution of the Enlightenment to the understanding of the meaning of revelation was to show the inadequacy of what Seckler calls the 'instruktionstheoretisch' model of revelation, a model of revelation as divine instruction which had begun in the medieval period and which culminated in *Dei Filius*. The theology of revelation expressed in *Dei Verbum* shows that fundamental conflict between revelation and Enlightenment is unnecessary. Through the theology of revelation as divine self-communication in *Dei Verbum*, 'an understanding of revelation has come to the fore, that has little more than the name in common with the notion of revelation the Enlightenment attacked' (172). See also Seckler's 'Der Begriff der Offenbarung', in *Handbuch der Fundamentaltheologie*, vol. II, ed. W. Kern, H. J. Pottmeyer and M. Seckler (Freiburg im Breisgau: Herder, 1985).

which derive from them are not retrievable in abstraction from a historical tradition, but rather maintained by the memory, life and practices of an historical community. Further, the insights and values which derive from these experiences are not compelling in a logical sense: perception and response are inextricably fused. The experience and the values that derive from it have an objective character, but the reception, interpretation and perception of the experience depends on the committed subjectivity of persons in concrete situations. This understanding of revelation proposes that the horizons of human feeling, consciousness and action are expanded by privileged or primordial experiences which have a particular historical *locus*. They cannot be anticipated by reasoning or known by reflection on universal experience, but rather emerge as new, liberating and life-giving relationships with mystery.[42]

Such an understanding of revelation provokes some fundamental questions concerning the relationship between revelation, reason and ethics. Can Christian revelation be understood as a narrative tradition with a particular origin but universalist dynamic, a tradition that gives the worth of persons an infinite ground, and ethical discourse a foundation in human community which participates in the communion of the divine persons? Can revelation, reason and ethics be integrated in ways which respect the character of modern liberal societies, the historical character of ethical reason, and the open and narrative character of revelation itself? Neo-Kantianism provides crucial tools for ethical universality and personal autonomy, but does so in ways which leave it open to reductionism. While not necessarily anti-religious, it gives no place to revealed traditions, to narratives of disclosure. In what ways can the relationship between revelation, reason and ethics be reconceived to affirm the contributions of neo-Kantianism while relating ethics to a

---

[42] For a perceptive discussion of the relationship between pre-existing moral horizons and the revelation of new perspectives, see Basil Mitchell's discussion of Kant's famous passage 'Even the Holy One of the Gospels must first be compared with our ideal of ethical perfection . . .', *Grundlegung der Metaphysik der Sitten*, 36, in his *Morality: Religious and Secular* (Oxford: Clarendon Press, 1980), 154.

renewed understanding of revelation as the disclosure of the infinite ground of human value?

Infinite being and public ethics: a public metaphysics?

Our common participation in infinite being, expressed in the concept of revelation, sustains the process of dialogue and gives a basis to the premise of respect for persons that is at its heart. It gives a metaphysical foundation to respect for persons. In doing so, however, it must necessarily transcend the limits of neo-Kantianism. It affirms rational autonomy, but does so in a way which grounds that autonomy in an infinite reality. Yet does it militate against a public ethics by introducing claims that can have no public warrant? The neo-Kantian project was to develop a dialogic public rationality based on respect for rational autonomy. If that respect is strengthened and given an infinite ontological context by a participation in an infinite truth, can this make any contribution to a public ethics?

This raises the question of the possibility of a public metaphysics, and harks back to the nineteenth-century attempts – considered in chapter 1 – to link metaphysics and ethics. Such a notion is characteristic of some versions of the 'natural law' tradition, as well as of the Hegelian tradition, affirming that a public ethics is based on certain metaphysical claims which are publicly shared and which can be publicly demonstrated. For Kant and for neo-Kantianism, clearly no such metaphysical claims can be substantiated, and they would, in any case, lead to a heteronomous foundation for ethics. Hegel revived such claims after Kant, arguing that the subjective finite will on its own was radically insufficient as a basis for a public ethics. For Hegel, a public ethics had to be based on a sense of the worth of persons in relation to God, and all of this could be retrieved philosophically and expressed conceptually. Similarly, the Catholic natural law tradition had confidence in the power of reason – conceived of in classical rather than historical terms – to affirm the existence of metaphysical realities, especially the relationship between God, the rational soul and the moral law. Natural law referred to those realities which could be known by reason, and which were the foundation of a public ethics.

Yet both of these forms of public metaphysics have lost general allegiance in Western societies as the basis of a public ethics. While the Catholic metaphysical tradition, in its Scholastic expression, had dominant and centuries-long cultural influence in the Middle Ages, its nineteenth-century revival was restricted to Catholic circles, and gave way to a new pluralism in philosophy and theology after Vatican II. Hegel's religious metaphysics was rejected immediately after his death by the Young Hegelians: the metaphysically oriented Old Hegelians and the later British Hegelians had only limited and short-lived influence. Neither traditional Catholic metaphysics nor Hegelianism enjoy widespread public acceptance. In particular, their claims to compelling rationality have been rejected. They have been perceived as understandings of the world which are rationally optional, rather than capable of winning over all thinking people by their persuasive force. Whatever their power, they have not achieved a public status, because the truth-claims they make are not shared.

This has different implications for the two traditions. For the Hegelian tradition, it has the implication that its overcoming of religion in the philosophical concept is unsuccessful. The philosophical concept has proved to be as controversial as the religion it was derived from. It has also challenged Hegelianism at the root, in so far as the sublation (*Aufhebung*) of religious image and narrative in the philosophical concept is crucial to Hegelianism. For the natural law tradition, it has the implication that a public metaphysics is less distinct from revealed tradition than it was conceived to be. The neo-Scholastic interpretation of the natural law tradition argued that what could be known by reason was distinct from the truths given in revelation. The truths known by reason could be known in common by all those committed to rationality. Yet the content of a natural law metaphysic is seen more and more to be the philosophical transcription of the implications of the revealed tradition with which it is associated. The metaphysic stands or falls with the perspective nourished by the revealed tradition from which it springs. Rather than being an addition to natural law, as Vatican I conceived it, revelation plays a fundamental role in terms of affirming the universality of human community which is the fundamental premise of a discursive ethics. The insights of a revealed tradition interpenetrate and inform the insights of reason.

Further, an ethics based purely on a metaphysical description of reality would fall foul of the dangers of 'descriptivism' which Hare has drawn attention to.[43] How can a description of reality, however metaphysical, motivate action and excite desire? For Hare, the solution to this problem is to deny that ethics is linked to any ontological realities, and to ground it in subjective desire, constrained by logic. But if logic is incapable of achieving this task, subjective desire is all that is left. If ethics is to have an ontological ground, if the worth of persons is to be understood as grounded in their participation in a metaphysical reality, then it is insufficient merely to describe and conceptualize that reality in metaphysical terms. Rather, that reality must be present as the life which unites and inspires, as the Spirit which is the unseen other in the relationships of persons in community. It must, that is, be present as revelation, as the experience of infinite communion, rather than as a metaphysical description of reality.

This does not mean that metaphysical ideas no longer have an important role in ethical communication – it means rather that their profound links to revealed traditions need to be acknowledged. In many contexts, certain metaphysical ideas can indeed play a powerful role in communicating foundational ethical beliefs. Such ideas, which might be called 'mediating principles', drawn from a philosophical or theological anthropology, would include such notions as the sanctity of life, the freedom and responsibility of the human person and the universal destination of the goods of the earth. These ideas can have a communicative power outside the confines of particular traditions. Such principles form the basis of a post-modern conception of natural law, aware of the indebtedness of funda-

---

[43] See Hare, *Freedom and Reason*, Part I, and *Moral Thinking*, Part I.

mental moral principles to traditions of disclosure. The importance and meaning of these mediating principles from a philosophical anthropology will be further discussed in chapters 3 and 4.

This conception of mediating principles, based in revealed traditions, achieving a degree of communicability and 'translatability' in pluralist societies, can derive support from MacIntyre's notion of 'tradition-constituted enquiry', although the general perspective on the Enlightenment and liberal societies advocated in this book would be unpalatable to him.[44] For MacIntyre, the rationality of traditions presents an authentic alternative to the apparently ineluctable choice between liberalism and relativism. The rationality of a tradition-constituted inquiry is essentially a 'matter of the kind of progress which it makes through a number of well-defined types of stage'.[45] Such an inquiry begins with a 'condition of pure historical contingency', a choice, for particular historical reasons, of 'certain texts and certain voices' upon which a community confers authority. From an original unquestioning stage, the tradition passes through a second stage where questioning arises through the encounter with differing cultures, and may reach a third stage in which the response to inadequacies has resulted in new formulations.[46] The first principles of a tradition, then, are not Cartesian, but have a contingent origin. These principles are justified in a dialectical and historical manner: they are retained if they have survived the challenge of questioning over time,

---

[44] Especially as it is developed in his *Whose Justice? Which Rationality?* (University of Notre Dame Press, 1988), chs. 18 and 19. As noted in chapter 1 (note 13), my approach is also heavily indebted to David Tracy's discussion in *The Analogical Imagination*. Although MacIntyre's general perspectives on these questions are much less sanguine about the possibilities for a public ethical culture than those of Tracy, I share David Hollenbach's judgement in his 'A Communitarian Reconstruction of Human Rights: Contributions from Catholic Tradition', in *Catholicism and Liberalism: Contributions to American Public Philosophy*, ed. R. Bruce Douglass and D. Hollenbach (Cambridge University Press, 1994), that MacIntyre's approach lends itself well to an ecumenical and dialogic ethics. As Hollenbach notes, 'it is on grounds very much like those that shape MacIntyre's book that recent Catholic teachings have joined a strong sensitivity to the role of tradition, community, and practical rationality with an unambiguous affirmation of the human rights to freedom of speech, religion, association and assembly' (144).

[45] *Whose Justice? Which Rationality*, 354.   [46] Ibid., 355–8.

and proved themselves superior to their historical predecessors. Just as their contingent origin distinguishes them from Cartesian first principles, so their historical character distinguishes them from Hegelian principles claiming absolute knowledge.

The answer to relativism, MacIntyre contends, can be seen in the way a tradition responds to what he calls epistemological crisis. The challenge of epistemological crises, of situations which cannot be assimilated by a given tradition, is to develop a new form of the tradition which can assimilate such a new situation. The success of a new form of a tradition consists in its power to explain why this situation was inassimilable for the older form of the tradition, and at the same time to show that the new form of the tradition is in essential continuity with the old.[47] The new form of the tradition will not be predictable from the vantage point of the old – there will be imaginative conceptual innovation.

The relativist critique of tradition does not realize that a tradition in a state of epistemological crisis may find that another tradition has the answers to its problems, answers which are judged to be right by the original tradition's criteria. It also does not realize that a tradition can be found wanting in the face of a new challenge even by its own standards, and can acknowledge that another tradition can respond to a new situation better than itself. Traditions can die because of their failure to respond to such crises. Thus the relativist charge, that traditions are self-contained organisms which permit no genuine interaction and no challenge by a reality which is other than themselves, applies only against those traditions which are not developed to the point where epistemological crises are a real possibility.[48] Further, the relativist critique of tradition itself must be made from within a tradition, which is self-defeating, or outside tradition altogether. The latter alternative is rejected by MacIntyre since 'the person outside all traditions lacks sufficient rational resources for enquiry and *a fortiori* for enquiry into what tradition is to be rationally preferred'.[49]

The rationality of traditions consists of a claim to truth made

[47] Ibid., 362.   [48] Ibid., 365–6.   [49] Ibid., 367.

on the basis of the historical experience of that tradition, with a simultaneous readiness to accept that it may encounter another tradition, in the context of epistemological crisis, which better answers its own fundamental questions than it itself does. When it encounters an alien tradition, any tradition must 'allow for the possibility that in one or more areas the other may be rationally superior to it in respect precisely of that in the alien tradition which it cannot as yet comprehend'.[50] A tradition's commitment to the truth of its own beliefs entails a denial of this happening, 'but it is the possibility of this nonetheless happening which gives point to the assertion of truth and provides assertions of truth and falsity with a content'.[51] A tradition can only make a claim to truth if at the same time it accepts the possibility of error. A mature tradition makes such a claim: it is originally grounded in concrete and contingent circumstances, but this does not mean that it accepts that its comprehension of reality is thereby limited to assertions which have validity only in a limited and highly specific historical realm.[52] To use David Tracy's terms, the disclosures at the origin of traditions claim publicness, a publicness which goes hand in hand with the intensity and truthfulness of their particular origin.[53] They give traditions a dynamic which can include a progressively broader interpretation of reality and a challenging encounter with other traditions. Such a perspective gives coherence to the notion of ethical mediating principles

---

[50] Ibid., 388.   [51] Ibid.
[52] In his *Plurality and Christian Ethics*, (New Studies in Christian Ethics, Cambridge University Press, 1994) Ian Markham generally endorses MacIntyre's notion of 'tradition-centred enquiry' but argues that he 'appears unable to justify' it, and offers 'the Thomist cosmological argument as a way of providing a basis for a traditioned-rationality' in a society characterized by plurality (146). Although Markham acknowledges that the point of such proofs for the existence of God is not to be above the Christian tradition but to point out the explanatory power of the tradition (149, 155), the notion that use of such a proof can be made as 'a basis for a traditioned rationality' appears to give it a role that, as MacIntyre argues, should only be given to 'certain texts and certain voices', or, theologically speaking, to the events of disclosure of revelation.
[53] As Tracy argues, the 'classic' figures of experience of disclosure, 'the artist, the thinker, the hero, the saint – who are they finally, but the finite self radicalized and intensified?' *The Analogical Imagination*, 125.

which originate in traditions but which can achieve a public, communicable status.

The outcome of this discussion of revelation and a public ethics is, in one sense, Hegelian. Uniquely in nineteenth-century thought, Hegel showed an awareness of the profound links between historical revelation and the development of ethical reason, between the meaning of the incarnation and the depths of human dignity and ethical community. In this sense, any project which attempts to explore the meaning of Christian revelation for a contemporary public ethics owes a great debt to Hegel. A contribution of Christian tradition to public ethical reasoning today would revive Hegel's sense of the relationship between revelation and human dignity. It would argue that the gap in the Kantian ethical project can be filled by an understanding of the universal worth of persons as grounded in relationship with God. This is a realm of meaning within which personal value has a coherent context. It is derived from a particular narrative, but has a universal reference, because it speaks of God incarnate, the *universale concretum*.

Yet, at the same time, any contemporary project must be deeply critical of Hegel's sublation of religion in absolute knowledge and the implications of this for the identity of Christianity and the Christian community. As has been noted, Hegel's metaphysical claims were unsubstantiated: there can be no rationally *compelling* public proofs of the absolute character of Christian revelation, or of any philosophical, conceptual expression of it. This means a number of things: firstly, that the contribution that Christian revelation makes to ethics will be in a pluralist context, in a world where no one universal meaning becomes the foundation of public reasoning, but where traditions of reasoning can engage with each other in a recognition that the arguments and answers of one can be challenging and illuminating for others; secondly, it means that Christian revelation always retains its narrative character – it can never be sublated into a set of philosophical doctrines. It is a narrative whose relationship to public argument and practical reasoning is complex and polyvalent, and characterized by a surplus of meaning. Further, it cannot be a revival of Hegel's claim that ethics is primarily about *Sittlichkeit* rather than *Moralität*, about given ethical traditions rather than moral ideals, a claim linked to Hegel's highly immanentist theology of history. A more balanced theology of the Spirit's immanence and transcendence would recognize that, while much of ethics is an appeal to the reason inherent in traditional practices, it must often appeal to values and insights which transcend the given state of general social consciousness. Finally, it would emphasize the irreducible distinctiveness of the role of the church and Christian proclamation, in ways that would avoid any Hegelian claim that the content of the Gospel and of the life of the church can be realized in philosophy and the state.

This last point highlights once again the importance of the consideration of Christian identity in ethical communication. If revelation relates to ethical discourse in the way that has been argued, as the infinite ground of a universal community of communication, what conception of Christian identity does this imply? Hegel's philosophy developed an understanding of the relationship between revealed tradition and public ethical life that continues to be a powerful source of insight. Yet his reduction of Christian revelation to the philosophy of absolute idealism deprived the church and Christian proclamation of crucial aspects of their authentic identity. A contemporary attempt to explore the implications of revelation for a public ethics must affirm universality while at the same time doing justice to the particularity of the church and the Gospel. Only in this way can the character of Christian revelation, as the revelation of the infinite God in the particularity of Jesus of Nazareth, be expressed. This exploration into the links between revelation and ethics, between Christian communication and Christian identity, must now lead to a focus on the theology of revelation itself, in order to consider how this union of universality and particularity can be achieved.

CHAPTER 3

The theology of revelation and Christian identity

We concluded the previous chapter with the argument that the concept of revelation gives an ultimate context to the worth of persons as members of a 'kingdom of ends'. The meaning of revelation is precisely an invitation to share in the life of the divine *communio*, in the life of the three-personed God. Through the union of the love of God and love of neighbour, this sharing in the divine life is also a *communio* with others, an infinite foundation to the 'kingdom of ends' of mutual respect and solidarity. The esteem of all is founded in the infinitude of divine regard, the worth of all nourished by the infinitude of divine love.

The concept of revelation as divine self-communication, as a sharing in the divine *communio*, is a necessary complement to the foundation and full development of notions of the 'kingdom of ends' which conceptualize discursive ethical processes marked by mutual respect. Yet, as we saw in chapter 1, the concept of revelation remains highly controversial in the ethical discourse of liberal and pluralist societies, redolent as it still is for many of sectarian conflict and of the conflict between the liberal state and religion.

In the present context, of course, the character of the debate has changed markedly. Until relatively recently, the debate was often conceived of as the tension between particular religious traditions, with their particular truth-claims, and a universalist Enlightenment tradition based in freedom and reason. Present debate emphasizes the post-modern character of contemporary culture, in so far as the universalist claims of the Enlightenment are themselves subject to suspicion as claims to power of a cultural or technocratic kind.

To conceive of contemporary culture as 'post-modern' is to argue that cultural values do have their *locus* in particularity, in the symbols, values and languages generated by concrete traditions. It is to reject the claim that all such concrete traditions are superseded by a universal rationality, that is itself free of particular interest, bias and prejudice. Yet the recognition of contemporary culture as, in this sense, 'post-modern' faces a fundamental and fateful decision: is 'post-modernity' to mean the acceptance of the inevitable dissolution of universalist ideals in a morass of relativism, a welter of particular and conflicting traditions, or can it tame the reductionist rationalism of the Enlightenment in a way which nevertheless retains its positive and benign universalism, its struggle for global ethical community?[1]

It is a major concern of this book to argue for the latter understanding of post-modernity, for an understanding of traditions not as a conflict of particularities sowing the seeds of relativism and nihilism, but rather as bearers of meaning and value which have a dynamism towards human community, which carry the resources for understanding human existence in terms which are hospitable to the positive ethical universalism of the Enlightenment.[2] In particular, I will argue for an

---

[1] For an illuminating discussion of the tension between modernity and post-modernity in ethics, see Zygmunt Bauman, *Postmodern Ethics* (Oxford: Blackwell, 1993). For Bauman, post-modernity 'is the result of the modern age reaching its self-critical, often self-denigrating and in many ways self-dismantling stage' (2), and 'postmodernity, one may say, is *modernity without illusions*' (32). For Bauman, 'deprived now of its past grounding in the "civilizing mission" of the "culturally advanced" or "most developed" nation-states, the idea of universal morality, if it is to survive at all, may only fall back on the innate, pre-social moral impulses common to humankind . . . or on the equally common elementary structure of human-being-in-the-world' (43). Yet the critique of imposed 'universalisms' should not deny that universalism is possible in a fruitful relationship between the world religions and the heritage of the Enlightenment, a far richer and more powerful source of human commonality than 'pre-social moral impulses'.

[2] In his *Postmodernity: Christian Identity in a Fragmented Age* (Minneapolis: Fortress Press, 1997), Paul Lakeland distinguishes three understandings of the post-modern world: the first, a 'radical historicist perspective', to be found in the thought of such thinkers as Foucault, Derrida and Rorty; the second 'the postmodernism of nostalgia', associated with such critics of modern culture as Heidegger, Adorno and Allan Bloom; and the third, denoted 'late modernism', including such figures as Habermas and Charles Taylor, 'who choose to remain consciously in the tradition of reason and subjectivity, but who nevertheless realize that the post-Enlightenment developments

understanding of the concept of revelation which is rooted in the concrete particularity of historical epiphany, yet whose divine content is of its very nature a proclamation of universal peace and communion. In ethical terms, this implies a distinctive vision of the worth of persons grounded in the divine communion, which can at the same time contribute to the vigour of public values of justice and freedom. This is crucial to any attempt to understand a process of Christian ethical communication which retains Christian identity while at the same time fostering an openness to the work of the Spirit in the world. The purpose of the present chapter is to argue that the Christian concept of revelation is indeed of this character.

THE IDENTITY OF CHRISTIAN REVELATION: PARTICULARITY AND UNIVERSALITY

An important part of any consideration of identity is a consideration of the kinds of relationship the reality in question has to other realities. How does it understand its own distinctiveness, and the ways in which this distinctiveness is maintained? At the same time, how does it achieve a sense of universality, so that this distinctiveness is not a denial of the value of all other realities? Since the Christian faith is based on a distinctive Gospel which is fundamentally committed to the universality of God's love, any conception of Christian identity must address both its distinctiveness and its universality. Any conception of revelation must address the distinctive power of the Gospel it proclaims and its universal scope and intention. More concretely, it must consider how the content of that Gospel relates to the content of general culture.

The question of identity – and of loss of identity – touches both on the concern that an excessive sense of distinctiveness may cripple and distort the Gospel that Christians are committed to proclaim, and on the concern that an uncritical

---

have enormously complicated the question of what the subject is and how, if at all, notions of universal reason can still be maintained' (16–17). My own argument attempts to be a contribution to this last interpretation of the meaning of postmodernity.

openness may dissolve all that is irreplaceably valuable about it. In particular, in the context of the communication of Christian ethics in modern liberal societies, the question of identity concerns the balance to be achieved between affirming the distinctiveness and integrity of the proclamation of the Gospel and a willing and open engagement with the pressing concerns of contemporary culture.

In the light of these general questions, we can identify three principal conceptions of Christian identity in contemporary theology, understandings which take up different positions in this fundamental debate over the specificity of Christianity and its relationship to other realms of meaning and belief: firstly, Christian identity as a praxis based in and inspired by a particular narrative; secondly, Christian identity as an interpretation of universal meaning, based in a theology of mediation; thirdly, Christian identity as a self-contained tradition. Although these conceptions have very important aspects in common, they do focus on different relationships between the Gospel and general culture, and this difference of focus is the source of considerable tension in contemporary Christian life. Each approach has different priorities and implications in terms of the method and content of the communication of Christian ethics.

The argument of the previous chapter linked revelation with ethics through the concept of *communio*. Any Christian theology of revelation will have the gift of participation in the divine *communio*, and its meaning for human community, at its core. As far as the concept and reality of *communio* is concerned, the difference between these different conceptions of Christian identity is not in their affirmation of this most fundamental content of Christian faith, but in the ways in which its implications for human community, in particular the relationship between church and 'world', are understood. The theological concept of *communio* moves from the *communio* of the divine life to the *communio* of the church to the *communio* of humanity. The differences between these different conceptions of Christian identity are in the ways in which the relationship between the church as *communio* and the universal human community are understood: in what sense does the church distinguish itself as a community of faith, and in what sense is its relationship with the 'world' a constitutive part of its nature and mission? Clearly, the understanding of this relationship deeply affects both conceptions of Christian identity and the nature of communication between church and 'world', between communities formed by Christian traditions and other human communities which share the same historical world. This, in turn, affects the degree of importance attached to ethical communication between the Christian churches and the public forum of pluralist societies, as well as the conception and mode of that communication.

For the first conception, Christian identity is formed by a narrative and expressed in praxis. It begins with ethical praxis, in the sense that it is the experience of certain human situations that makes us able to understand and re-live the meaning of the Gospel narrative. If we are able to identify ourselves with human suffering and human need, then we will hear the Gospel not as an abstract message demanding an effort of intellectual understanding, but as the good news of liberation. If we are immersed in human situations which are analogous to the setting for Jesus' ministry, then the Gospel narrative acquires a forceful and contemporary meaning. If we are predisposed to hear the Gospel by ethical praxis, by identifying ourselves with those in need, it is the words of the Gospel, in turn, which shape and inspire our praxis, convincing us that the needs of humanity cannot remain unfulfilled, that justice must be done. Praxis is both the context of our response to the Gospel, and the primary means of witnessing to it.

Since praxis is rooted in the experience of suffering and injustice, and is expressed in the struggle to overcome them, it understands the Christian life as a life lived in tension with a world in which the wicked prosper. Since the Gospel narrative is a word of protest against such a world, and a word which inspires ethical action to overcome it, it is crucial that the Gospel's own native immediacy be respected and retained. The Gospel is fundamentally narrative, a story rooted in historical events, capturing the immediacy of the life of one who confronted injustice and was crucified by it. For this approach, attempts to mediate between the Gospel and other systems of religious or metaphysical meaning are fraught with the dangers of blunting its critical edge by lessening its distinctiveness, and of depriving it of its liberating power by treating it as a key to a theoretical interpretation of reality rather than as an inspiration to ethical praxis.

These emphases on the narrative and practical character of the Gospel, and of Christian identity, are shared by Christian theologians who have different conceptions of what Christian praxis should consist in. For Johann Baptist Metz, Christian narrative and Christian memory are an inspiration to transformative social action, oriented to a critical dissolution of the social structures of injustice.[3] A similar emphasis is characteristic of most Catholic liberation theologians. For Stanley Hauerwas, in contrast, Christian praxis is not a praxis oriented towards transforming the injustices of society at large, but rather the praxis of a distinct community which can give the world an example of a community of peace. For Hauerwas, the contrast between church and world is fundamentally a contrast between peace and violence.[4] Despite these differences, this understanding of Christian identity has a common emphasis on the need for Christians to confront the stark differences between the praxis of Jesus and the ways of this world, and to hear his words as an inspiration to a form of discipleship that radically negates the forces and interests that dominate society.

I have called the second conception an interpretation of universal meaning, based in a theology of mediation. This approach emphasizes that the Christian Gospel cannot be a revelation of God unless it is capable of such universality: if the Gospel, which originates in historical particularity, has no reference to universal reality, then it cannot speak of the God who is the creator of this universal reality. Further, because the Gospel speaks of a God whose Spirit speaks to the hearts of all human beings, then Christians are called to reflect on the relationship between the Gospel to which they witness and the

---

[3] *Glaube in Geschichte und Gesellschaft* (Mainz: Matthias Grünewald), Part 2.

[4] See, for example, Hauerwas' *The Peaceable Kingdom: A Primer in Christian Ethics* (University of Notre Dame Press, 1983).

experience of the Spirit which they recognize in the lives of their fellow human beings. Because we are recipients of the divine gift of reason and hearers of and believers in the Gospel, we seek to understand its relationship to other conceptions of meaning, to develop an understanding of reality as a whole which sees the Gospel as a revelation of absolute truth which does not deny the truth within other religious and philosophical traditions.

For this conception, then, the Gospel is an ultimate truth which encourages us to understand the meaning of all human attempts to know and respond to God, a truth which motivates us to acknowledge and enhance community with other human beings. For Karl Rahner, the Christian Gospel is the final and definitive form of humanity's historical attempt to give categorical or explicit shape to its experience of transcendental revelation, of the grace of God.[5] The universal intention of the Gospel gives us grounds for interpreting and illuminating all of human existence in its light. All human religion, however primitive and distorted, is a response to that experience of the self-communication of God which constitutes our specifically human creatureliness. It is the Gospel, and only the Gospel, which enables us to interpret human existence in this way – without it we would have no ultimate assurance of the nearness and friendliness of God. Yet, in the light of the Gospel, we can reflect on the ways in which other religions and philosophies express aspects of ultimate truth.

Wolfhart Pannenberg, while sharing Rahner's commitment to understanding the universal meaning of the Gospel, is critical of some aspects of the transcendental method.[6] Pannenberg seeks the universal meaning of the Gospel in history. In the history of Israel, the ultimate revelation of God was conceived in apocalyptic terms. For Greek philosophy, by contrast, ulti-

---

[5] See, for example, Rahner's *Grundkurs des Glaubens* (E.T.: *Foundations of Christian Faith*) (Freiburg im Breisgau: Herder, 1976), Part 5, 'Heils- und Offenbarungsgeschichte'.

[6] Pannenberg affirms Rahner's anthropology of openness to transcendence, yet is critical of some of Rahner's terminology. He notes, for example, that 'for a feeling for language schooled by Kant, the notion of "transcendental experience" sounds like a wooden iron', *Systematische Theologie*, vol. 1 (Göttingen: Vandenhoeck and Ruprecht, 1988), 128.

mate meaning was expressed metaphysically. In the resurrection of Jesus, the eschatological destiny of all humanity – and of all creation – was revealed. Because it was the revelation of an ultimate meaning, it could do justice to the questions of Greek culture, converting metaphysical order into eschatological future without denying the scope and importance of the metaphysical quest.[7]

David Tracy's attempt to understand the universal reference of Christianity has been developed in the light of a more explicitly pluralist context and consciousness. Tracy relates his conviction of the Gospel's public scope to the power inherent in any classic to give expression to the intensity of particularity in ways which have wide and long-lasting appeal. Tracy does not construct a general theory of the relationship of the Gospel to universal human experience; rather, he situates it within the conversation of a pluralist culture, as a classic 'disclosure of the whole by the power of the whole', a classic whose interpretive power is at the service of our common humanity. This concern for the public realm is motivated, indeed dictated, by the character of revelation itself: 'the insight into the universal character of the divine reality that is the always-present object of the Christian's trust and loyalty is what ultimately impels every theology to attempt publicness'.[8]

The universality of this second approach is achieved by linking the Gospel with other projects of meaning, on the basis of an appeal to the dialogic potential of rationality. This contrasts with the universality conceived of by the third approach, founded in self-contained tradition. For this conception, universality is to be achieved not by the dialogic mediation of meaning with other traditions, nor by the development of transcendental conceptions of the human person, but rather by the devoted and contemplative unfolding of the universality inherent in Christian narrative and Christian tradition them-

---

[7] For Pannenberg's theology of revelation see especially *Systematische Theologie*, vol. 1, ch. 4, and the earlier statements of his position in *Offenbarung als Geschichte* (1961), E.T.: *Revelation as History* (London: Macmillan, 1968) and 'Die Offenbarung Gottes in Jesu von Nazareth', in *Theologie als Geschichte* (Zurich: Zwingli Verlag, 1967).

[8] *The Analogical Imagination* (New York: Crossroad, 1981), 51.

selves. Religious truth is not to be found through the dialogue with culture, but rather in the abounding richness of a tradition which offers culture a cure for its ills. In Christian tradition, we come face to face with divine love, a love which casts a completely new light on all our experience. This tradition has a complexity and many-sidedness which offers a satisfying and internally fulfilled portrait of human existence in relation to the gift of salvation.

This conception has both Protestant and Catholic forms. For George Lindbeck, Christian narrative is a language that encapsulates a unique world of meaning. There is no religious *lingua franca* that can sustain the project of universalist dialogue. Christian identity consists in becoming one with the biblical world of meaning, and interpreting our lives in its light.[9] John Milbank, in his *Theology and Social Theory*, develops a theology of revelation which portrays Christian tradition as a self-contained community of peace, an *altera civitas*, in the Augustinian political tradition.[10] Joseph Ratzinger places great stress on the comprehensive and integrated character of tradition, and on the richness of its resources for addressing what he judges to be the crises of contemporary Western society. For Ratzinger, it is of great importance that the fullness of tradition, in all its interrelationships, is transmitted. This emphasis is expressed in his essay on catechetics, based on addresses given in Paris and Lyons in 1983.[11] For Ratzinger, too much of contemporary catechesis is based on questions emerging from human experience and from a reading of the Bible in terms of the historical–critical method. Catechesis should, in contrast, be an induction into tradition which places fundamental emphasis on the four 'master elements' of tradition: the Apostles' Creed, the Our

---

[9] See especially Lindbeck's *The Nature of Doctrine: Religion and Theology in a Post-liberal Age* (Philadelphia: Westminster Press, 1984), chs. 1–3.

[10] *Theology and Social Theory* (Oxford: Blackwell, 1990). Milbank's work will be discussed in more detail later in this chapter.

[11] J. Ratzinger, 'Sources and Transmission of the Faith', *Communio* 10 (1983): no. 1, based on addresses given at Lyons and Paris 15–16 January 1983, cf. *The Tablet*, 29 January, 1983. These addresses were given at a time of controversy in France over the text *Pierres Vivantes* and catechetical matters in general. For a discussion of the situation at that time, see O. de Dinechin, 'Catechesis in France', *Lumen Vitae* 34 (1984): no. 2, 226–30.

Father, the Ten Commandments and the Sacraments. This emphasis on the fullness of tradition is also expressed in his critique of the contention that a Catholic theology of legitimate and constructive dissent could be based on the distinction between infallible and non-infallible teaching, between the assent of faith and *religiosum obsequium*.[12] For Ratzinger, such an approach would make Christian faith a skeletal assemblage of dogmas, rather than an organic and interpenetrative whole: Christian faith is a willing response to the wholeness and richness of a tradition which manifests the superabundance of divine love.[13]

Each of these conceptions of Christian identity, and of the meaning of evangelization, has characteristic criticisms to make of the others. For the first approach, focussing on narrative and praxis, the second, or universalist, approach is inadequate because it seeks a universal meaning which must be chimerical as long as so much of humanity lives in an oppressed and marginalized state. No project of universal meaning can have validity unless it can confront the deprivations that induce fear, apathy and despair. Metz, for example, argues that the universalist theological projects of Rahner and Pannenberg run the risk of overlegitimizing Christianity in the face of contemporary threats to its identity, an overlegitimization that moves all too easily from the reality and givenness of redemption to the postulation of universal meaning.[14] For the theologians of

---

[12] Interview with the Milan journal *30 Giorni*, May 1986, quoted in R. A. McCormick, *The Critical Calling* (Georgetown: Washington, 1989), 'L'Affaire Curran', 125–6.

[13] The perspectives of Ratzinger and Lindbeck are linked together by Richard John Neuhaus in his *The Catholic Moment: The Paradox of the Church in the Postmodern World* (San Francisco: Harper and Row, 1987), 150.

[14] *Glaube in Geschichte und Gesellschaft*, 141. P. Eicher, in his *Offenbarung: Prinzip Neuzeitlicher Theologie* (Munich: Kösel, 1977) notes that the theologies of revelation of Rahner and Pannenberg attempt consistently to mediate between faith and thought, to overcome the Enlightenment in the process of acknowledging its insights (557). For Eicher, however, neither Rahner nor Pannenberg succeed in this attempt. Although Rahner's union of transcendental and categorial revelation is made from the perspective of faith, of received revelation, it threatens to deprive the Christ event of its concrete facticity and the explicit faith of the Christian community of its significance. The difference between Rahner's theology of revelation as the categorization of transcendental experience and Feuerbach's philosophy of religion as the projection of human self-consciousness as a species-being is, for Eicher, not as clear as it should be (418–420). Pannenberg's theology of revelation as anticipation of the future finally

praxis, the intellectual task of coming to terms with Western secularity and atheism is not the most critical need: the greatest obstacle to faith is the practical problem of evil, exacerbated by human inhumanity. It is the living of the Gospel in the face of such inhumanity which will give concrete witness to the reality of God, and give credibility to Christian claims of the power of divine love.

For the praxis theologians, while they share its anti-idealist emphasis on the particularity of Christian identity, the emphasis on self-contained tradition is excessively contemplative and authoritarian in character. It does not give sufficient emphasis to the ground in praxis within which the truth of the Christian story is experienced and enacted, and its insistence on the totality of the Christian tradition is linked to an authoritarian unwillingness to focus on what is truly fundamental to the Gospel.

For the universalist conception, both the praxis approach and the emphasis on self-contained tradition lack mediation between Christian narrative and human experience. Both are centred on the concrete sources of Christian life – the biblical narrative or the body of tradition – but neither gives sufficient emphasis to the ways in which these sources need to be integrated with all the other projects of meaning which claim a hearing in our common human world. In reference to the emphasis on praxis, for example, a theology of mediation raises the question of the character and distinctiveness of Christian ethics in relation to other understandings of ethics. If Christian identity is based on praxis, what distinguishes this praxis from the praxis characteristic of secular humanism or other world religions? How does the Gospel inform specific ethical decisions?[15] In reference to the theology of self-contained tradition,

> neglects the revelatory power of the present, because in this theology present and concrete history has meaning only in the light of this future (463). For the present author, the critiques of Metz and Eicher, while highlighting the concrete character of Christian revelation, do not show that Pannenberg and Rahner have neglected it: their theologies remain seminal attempts in contemporary Christian thought to do justice both to the universality of the concept of God, a universality concretely expressed in the universality of God's salvific will and of the Kingdom, and the irreducible concreteness of revelation in Jesus of Nazareth.
>
> [15] The problem of the relationship between narrative theology and normative judge-

a theology of mediation raises critical questions about the history and development of that tradition in the context of its relations to other cultural and religious forms. The present reality of tradition is something that has developed through interactions with culture – some of them giving the tradition new scope and energy, others resulting in a straitened and unbalanced vision. If this is so, then a theological self-consciousness about the tradition's reciprocal relations with culture must be integral to theology's contemporary task.

For those who see the heart of Christian identity in the fullness of a self-contained and integrated tradition, both the praxis and mediating approaches give an excessive role to secularity and to cultural phenomena which have sources other than Christian. According to this critique, the praxis approach dislocates the fundamental Christian response from attentive listening and contemplation to human action, from the self-sufficiency of divine revelation to the efficacy of our struggles for earthly justice. The emphasis on mediation, in turn, risks

ments has been incisively discussed by P. Lauritzen in 'Is "Narrative" Really a Panacea? The use of "Narrative" in the Works of Metz and Hauerwas', *Journal of Religion* 67 (1987), no. 3. Lauritzen argues that Metz and Hauerwas have in common an 'essentially pragmatist account of the truthfulness of Christian convictions': the truth of a narrative is in the praxis that it generates (335). Both argue against any abstract foundationalist epistemology: those claims of Christian faith are true which generate a signficant praxis. Although they have this fundamental stance in common, it generates two very different specific outcomes in their reflections on concrete *praxis*. While Metz advocates radical social action oriented to large-scale socio-economic structures, Hauerwas represents 'a sort of sectarian pacifist witness'. For Lauritzen, 'whatever similarities the two exhibit in discussing the importance of narrative as an epistemological category of Christian thought, when it comes to recommendations for practical action, the category of narrative by itself appears to play almost no role at all. Indeed, it neither helps to explain nor to justify the normative position of either Metz or Hauerwas. It fails to explain their positions because there is no substantive moral position entailed merely by appeal to the category of narrative. Yet there appears to be no way to argue for this substantive content since, on the terms set out by Metz and Hauerwas, the only argument available is one based on the practical consequences themselves, and these will, of course, depend on the substantive content that we are trying to justify' (338). For an extended critique of the use of narrative in ethics, see P. Nelson, *Narrative and Morality: A Theological Inquiry* (University Park and London: Pennsylvania State University Press, 1987). For Nelson, 'while the plurality of readings is not infinite – at least where the church and a confessional interpretive tradition are accorded authority – it is ineradicable. Thus, narrative cannot be expected to overcome the diversity of judgments in theological ethics' (147).

repeating the history of liberal Protestantism within Catholic theology, taking the criteria of secular modernity as a governing principle, rather than the internal norms of tradition itself.

REVELATION, NARRATIVE AND THE CRITIQUE OF ANTHROPOLOGY

At the heart of the tension between these three conceptions of revelation and Christian identity is the question of the relationship between the specificity of narrative and tradition and general human experience. The first and third conceptions have in common an emphasis on the concreteness of Christian faith as a self-contained world of narrative or tradition. The second conception, in contrast, argues that the identity of Christianity is bound up with the mediation of meaning between given forms of Christian tradition and the meanings and values present in other traditions. This significant and critical difference of emphasis is bound up with the general cultural debate about the interpretation of the relationship between modernity and post-modernity. For the two conceptions based in the concreteness of narrative and tradition, the 'theology of mediation' continues to perpetuate the illusions of modernity, projecting a 'general human experience', a false universality which risks the dissolution of Christian identity. For the 'theology of mediation', in contrast, those conceptions based exclusively in narrative and concrete tradition risk incurring the pernicious effects of relativist post-modernity, abandoning the struggle for human community across the boundaries of traditions.

Clearly, this critical debate over models of revelation and Christian identity has fundamental consequences for the understanding of the nature of the communication between Christian tradition and liberal societies. For the models which give pre-eminence to the concreteness and self-sufficiency of narrative and tradition, such communication is to be understood most of all in terms of the example that realized Christian virtue can give to the world, or in the incorporation of new members into an established and integrated tradition. For the theology of mediation, in contrast, this exemplary character of Christian life must be seen in the context of a dialectical process of communication between Christian tradition and the various projects of meaning in a pluralist world.

The emphasis on narrative in contemporary theology focusses on a strongly interrelated complex of themes: on experience, tradition, community and identity. It is an emphasis on the power of the concrete to root and to bind together, on the pre-reflective resonance of story as the unifying force of individual and community life. In relation to ethical values, the emphasis on narrative is an affirmation that our values do not flow from the application of logical patterns of universalization to human interactions, but rather from the experience in concrete situations of other human beings as beings of value: the power and mystery of such situations can be evoked only through narratives that expressively re-create these situations and make them available for an ethical tradition.

This complex of narrative themes bears striking resemblance to the concerns of the early nineteenth-century Romantic movement. For the Romantics, it was the particularity of things and persons that was of prime value – a particularity expressed in terms of tradition, identity and concrete community. This particularity was to be evoked by works of art which delighted in mystery and imagination, and by the artistic manifestos of the awakening nations of post-Napoleonic Europe. Particularity was opposed to the universality of the Enlightenment, to its contempt for concrete histories and native traditions, its preference for reason over image and symbol.

In our own day, the resurgence of narrative reflects the tension between particular ethical and religious identity and the pluralism of values that exists in Western societies, and is a key aspect of the debate over the meaning of the transition from modernity to post-modernity. neo-Kantian ethical theory inherits from the Enlightenment an emphasis on the universal character of reason as the foundation of ethics. Narrative theologies of revelation, and narrative ethics, highlight in contrast the particularity of primordial disclosures as the source of identity and motivation.

For the present author, the historical character of revelation means that narrative – the narrative of a lived history – must play a fundamental role for Christian theology and Christian ethics. It is narrative, above all the narrative of the Gospels, that records, interprets and expresses for all generations the saving and revealing event of Christ. At the same time, however, if revelation is revelation of God as creator and universal Lord, then the concrete events of revelation have universal scope and significance. They can be the foundation of universal concepts, and enter into dialogue with processes of abstract and universal reasoning. In a pluralist society, the particular narrative identity of Christian theology must be able to contribute to the public search for meaning, since the Christian narrative is a story of God's peace to all men and women of good will.[16]

A crucial aspect of the debate about the role of narrative in Christian theology and ethics is precisely the question of the relationship between identity and universality for Christian faith in a pluralist society. In particular, many exponents of an essentially narrative theology are strongly critical of any theology which gives a place to theological or philosophical

---

[16] The link between revelation, narrative and identity is developed at length in George W. Stroup's *The Promise of Narrative Theology: Recovering the Gospel in the Church* (Atlanta: John Knox Press, 1981). For Stroup, the crisis of contemporary Christianity is a crisis of identity, the loss of an identity that can enable Christians to live out a tradition with understanding and confidence. In secular and pluralist society 'the personal identity of many Christians is no longer shaped by Christian faith and the narrative that articulates that faith but by other communities and other narratives, narratives which have no necessary relation to the Christian community' (36). The theology of revelation is crucial to this question since 'Christian identity is something to do with the interrelation of knowledge of God and knowledge of self and revelation describes how that knowledge of God comes to bear on personal identity' (59). Since personal identity is based on narrative, on the dialectical relationship between the chronicle of the events of our life and our developing perception of them, then narrative is crucial to understanding Christian identity and revelation itself. The identity of the Christian community is similarly based on the narrative of the 'remembered past'. Revelation becomes an experienced reality 'at that juncture where the narrative identity of an individual collides with the narrative identity of the Christian community' (170). Stroup's interpretation rightly emphasizes the crucial intersection for personal faith between personal biography and community narrative, yet at the same time neglects the ways in which the identity of the community of faith itself is influenced by its reciprocal relationships to 'other communities and other narratives' in ways that can challenge and deepen its understanding of its own narrative.

anthropology, or which appeals to general human experience. In their rejection of philosophical and theological anthropology, they reject both the liberal Protestant tradition since Schleiermacher as well as all those strands of Catholic theology which include analysis of and reflection on human experience, transcendental theology in particular. This critique rejects the perspectives and methodology favoured by those theologians referred to in the description of the theology of mediation made above. The principal objection of the narrativist perspective to an appeal to anthropology or to 'human experience' is that it depends on epistemological foundationalism. This objection is both philosophical and theological.

Philosophically, it argues that any attempt to establish the truth of revelation by appealing to other 'grounds' of truth fails to recognize that there can be no final 'ground' or 'foundation' for truth, that there is no foundation in the Cartesian sense. The reason for this is that all epistemological foundations are recognized to be such only within a conceptual frame, and therefore assume the truth of this conceptual frame, which was itself to be supported by the purported foundation. The claim for foundations therefore results in vicious circularity. This argument contends that there can be no foundation for truth-claims which is independent of particular cognitive stances or commitments, and that therefore such particular stances cannot be justified by any foundation which might claim to be in some sense 'deeper' or more foundational than themselves. There is no 'bedrock' of knowledge which can be known as such by observers who have stripped themselves of all the accoutrements of particular stances.

The above argument relates to the most general epistemological claims. Allied to this, but somewhat more specific in its character, is the argument that a philosophical anthropology must be ruled out because it is intrinsically foundationalist in character. Any appeal to universal human experience in Christian theology or apologetics is a mistaken appeal to a purported foundation of truth, a foundation which – it is falsely claimed – can justify or clarify faith commitments in terms of anthropological themes which are less controversial because more foundational and therefore able to carry the *onus probandi* of Christian faith.

Philosophical or theological anthropology is further ruled out because it claims that there can be concrete experience prior to concrete language, that human experience can be conceived or spoken of in universal terms in some sense independently of specific narrative phenomena. The narrativist objection to this is that it is an impossibility, because of the strict union of experience and expression. There can be no universal themes in human experience because there is no universal narrative or language to express them.

Philosophically, then, the appeal to anthropological themes is ruled out in terms of the errors of both foundationalism and universalism. Theologically, the rejection of anthropology is fundamentally a rejection of any claims that would deny the utter priority of the Word of God: just as there can be no philosophical foundation which is prior to concrete language, so there can be no knowledge of God which is in any sense prior to God's own act of self-revelation, as expressed in concrete tradition. There can be no apologetics which moves from anthropological foundations to the truth of the Christian faith, since any such move reduces the Christian Gospel to the instantiation of a general truth, thereby depriving it of its uniqueness, its gratuity and its self-justifying priority.

These narrativist arguments draw attention to a question of fundamental importance for the self-understanding of Christian faith: what is the relationship between Christian revelation and the meanings and values which emerge from human experience, meanings and values which might become part of a philosophical or theological anthropology? This question is fundamental to the central concern of this book: the expression of Christian identity in ethical communication in the public forum of modern liberal societies. We will now consider this key question in the light of the development of Catholic teaching from Vatican I to Vatican II, and in the light of current theological debate, particularly in the work of Ronald Thiemann, George Lindbeck and David Tracy.

Vatican I ('Dei Filius') and Vatican II ('Dei Verbum')

In Catholic theology, a crucial change in the answer to this question can be seen in the development from Vatican I's *Dei Filius* (1870) to Vatican II's *Dei Verbum* (1965). In the document *Dei Filius*, the relationship between faith and reason, and the apologetic task in general, was conceived in a way which emphasized the possibility of a knowledge of God through the 'natural light of reason', which had the potential to know God through the 'things he has made'.[17] This natural knowledge of God provided a preamble to faith. Faith in divine revelation was only possible through a specific gift of faith as a supernatural virtue, yet this act of faith was rendered rationally responsible by the credibility given to the Gospel by the 'divine deeds' of miracle and prophecy. These 'divine deeds' were understood in apologetic terms, as attested historical facts of a supernatural character. Rather than being part of the *object* of faith, they were adduced as verified *grounds* for faith.

The strength of this approach lay in its affirmation of the possibility of knowledge of God outside the confines of the biblical communities of faith, its recognition that specifically Christian faith may develop, rather than contradict, knowledge of God derived from reflection on experience, and its emphasis that the act of faith could be a responsible act of a rational person. Its weakness lay in its concessions to rationalism and in its lack of historical sense. The 'natural knowledge' of God was not understood as being the product of the religious history of humanity, but rather as an abstract philosophical possibility. Revelation was conceived as super-added to this abstract philosophical knowledge of God. Finally, prophecies and miracles, rather than being seen as expressions of and responses to faith, were advanced as 'facts' which could in some sense be used as epistemological stepping-stones to affirm the credibility of the sacred texts which spoke of matters beyond the powers of natural reason to penetrate or verify.

The paradigm adopted at Vatican I was not foundationalist

---

[17] *Dei Filius*, ch. 2; DS 3004.

in a Cartesian sense, since it did not conceive of the natural knowledge of God as something which had to be *proven* in order to entertain the possibility of divine revelation. It affirms rather that God can be *known* – that the existence of a creator God is open to reason.[18] In its use of the 'divine deeds' of miracle and prophecy however, and in its overall conception of reason and revelation as two distinct realms of knowledge corresponding to 'nature' and 'supernature' it did lend support to an apologetic style which conceived of theology as grounded in a preamble of universal philosophical truths, whose certainty could only be doubted by those blinded by sin and error.

For Vatican II's *Dei Verbum*, in contrast, the mysteries of creation and revelation are fused: God both creates and reveals through the eternal Word. Revelation is not confined to the history of the Old and New Testaments, but is seen as coextensive with the history of the human race, reaching its culmination in Christ, whose coming was prepared for in the history of Israel. Since revelation is the invitation to friendship with God, it brings with it the gift of salvation and eternal life, a gift offered to all humanity, responded to through 'persevering in doing good'.[19] On this basis, there can be no dichotomy between the order of creation and the order of salvation. From the beginnings of the human race, God communicates Himself as saviour.

Just as the realms of creation and salvation are fused, so also are the realms of nature and grace. Revelation is not presented as an additional source of knowledge of divine mysteries, but as the divine source and foundation of human existence, enacted within human history and leading the human race towards its destiny of union with God.

[18] For Walter Kasper, in his *The God of Jesus Christ* (London: SCM, 1984), the affirmation of a natural knowledge of God in *Dei Filius* was not intended to assert that such a natural, 'unrevealed', knowledge of God actually exists, nor to define that the existence of God can be proven by the natural light of reason. The central issue in the affirmation of natural knowledge of God is 'simply the openness, in principle, of reason to God'. It is 'making a theological statement of a transcendental kind; that is, it is concerned with the condition for the possibility of faith which faith itself presupposes'. Vatican II 'integrated the abstract, transcendental theological approach of Vatican I into a concretely historical and salvation–historical perspective' (69).
[19] *Dei Verbum*, 3; Romans 2:7. Flannery, *Vatican Council II*, 98.

The fusion of the spheres of creation and revelation in *Dei Verbum* was the means of overcoming a conception of revelation as the communication of divine decrees inaccessible to reason. If God is conceived as knowable in a realm of nature without grace, then revelation is of necessity a supplement to the insights of reason rather than their foundation. For *Dei Verbum*, knowledge of God is given to human beings through their historical experience of God's self-communication, through personal and dialogic encounter. The truths of revelation are statements describing and interpreting this experience. The role of reason is to responsibly articulate this experience in relation to other dimensions of human knowledge and insight.

Both *Dei Filius* and *Dei Verbum* affirm the relationship between universality and particularity, but in crucially different ways. For Vatican I, universality was conceived of as prior in terms of the universality of natural reason. The light of natural reason was not 'revelation', but it did have the power to know God through reflection on human experience ('the things he has made'). Subsequent to and transcending this natural universality was the supernatural particularity of revelation. For Vatican II, in contrast, revelation began with the beginnings of the human race, has a universality coextensive with the universality of the human response to God in the religious quest, and achieved its definitive culmination in the particularity of Jesus of Nazareth. Reason reflects on this revelation, and shows that response to it is rationally responsible. In this way, *Dei Verbum* rejected epistemological foundationalism, in the sense of a rationalist and unhistorical system of knowledge on which revelation depends for its own veracity and credibility.

Thiemann, Lindbeck and Tracy

In contrast to 'foundationalist' theology, Ronald Thiemann proposes a 'descriptive' theology which 'seeks to illuminate the structures embedded in beliefs and practices'.[20] Narrative is crucial to this project of a 'descriptive theology'. For Thiemann,

[20] *Revelation and Theology: The Gospel as Narrated Promise* (University of Notre Dame Press, 1985), 72.

this appeal to narrative is emphatically not an appeal to a 'deep structure of expression of the temporal self', to a transcendental category of philosophical anthropology. If narrative were understood in this way, it would, he argues, become a new kind of foundationalism, a new grounding of theological claims on universal anthropological constants. Thiemann maintains, on the contrary, that 'descriptive theology opposes the systematic methodological affirmation of the primacy of anthropology in modern theology. The turn to narrative is one way of providing an alternative to that predominant modern tradition'.[21] Rather than being an anthropological 'deep structure', narrative is an interpretive approach to the biblical material which enables us to unfold the implications of the story which it tells.

On this basis, Thiemann argues that belief in God's prevenience, the basis of the theological doctrine of revelation, is 'a belief constitutive of Christian identity as formed by the Church's worshipping life'.[22] It is a legitimate and useful conceptual implication of the first-order narrative of Christian practice. This connection between revelation and Christian identity, as revealed in Christian practices, can be straightforwardly demonstrated. What is more difficult, as Thiemann acknowledges, is to show how God is both prior to and related to our own world of meaning, to show 'how the notion of "narrated promise" addresses the central problem of revelation, i.e. the difficulty of affirming both God's priority and his relation to our theological framework'.[23]

This is a point of crucial importance. The fatal flaw of foundationalism is that it cannot provide an ultimate foundation for a system or paradigm of knowledge, since that foundation can itself only be perceived from within the context of that system or paradigm. If knowing has an interpretive dimension, then there can be no ultimate knowing that is free of the interpretive elements that are justified within the context of a paradigm of interpretation, which is itself claimed to be based on a fulcrum of ultimate knowing. Philosophically, then, foundationalism fails. Theologically, its greatest fault is that it makes

[21] Ibid., 85. [22] Ibid., 101. [23] Ibid., 102.

God a dependent rather than a background belief. The authenticity of God's revelation is known by appeal to a foundation in self-authenticating human knowledge.

Yet if foundationalism is rejected, what relationship can be conceived between God and our system of understanding? If God is sheer prevenience, prior to all paradigms of understanding, how can the divine reality be conceived of in a way which is coherent with our understanding of reality as a whole? Any such system of general relationships threatens to result in foundationalism, since the divinity would be comprehended in terms of an interlocking set of interpretive categories. Thiemann proposes the category of 'narrated promise' to achieve the task of acknowledging the divine prevenience while at the same time bringing it into a relationship with our theological framework: 'the great advantage of the paradigm of narrated promise is that it conceives of God and humanity as essentially in relation and seeks to generate the distinctions between the two from within that relation'.[24] The act of promising is a category which allows a conception of God's priority to our framework of belief and at the same time his relationship to it. This is because a promise leaves the initiative with the promiser, but also requires someone accepting the promise.

The biblical narrative is a narrative of identity: it identifies the God of promise, the God who is prior to and yet related to human meaning. As the identity of the God of promise becomes clear through the narrative, the reader is invited to respond in faith and discipleship: 'If the reader does so respond, a context of interpretation is created in which the content and force of the text are logically prior to the correlative response. Thus the context for the illocutionary act can rightly be said to flow *from* the text *to* the reader. Promise and promiser must precede the faithful or doubting response of the recipient.'[25] While normally the context of interpretation functions to control the interpretation of the text, the text must be prior if it is the identity-narrative of the living God of the promise.

The text, then, becomes the narrative of the living God only

[24] Ibid., 109. [25] Ibid., 146.

when responded to in faith, but this faith grants the prevenience of God's word to its own response. Clearly, the doctrine of revelation implies that God's word and God's gift are prior to human response and enable that response. What is unclear in Thiemann's discussion is the motivation for the response of faith, the context of meaning which will lead anyone to relate to this text as the identity-narrative of the living God. The text creates a world of meaning for the believer, a world within which God has priority as its central character, but each reader comes to the text as a participant in a world of meaning which is not identical with that of the text itself. The text can only become the dominant context of meaning if it relates in some way to the context of meaning brought to it by the reader. This context of meaning may have been formed by other texts or other practices. The promises made in the text are responded to as true promises because they interrelate with the reader's own sense of reality.

The narrative identifies God as promiser, but Thiemann grants that the 'Gospel narrative can be God's promise if, and only if, he has raised Jesus from the dead. The Gospel's claim to truth thus demands acceptance of a deeply paradoxical claim which lies at the heart of the narrative's meaning.'[26] Yet, in critical response to Thiemann's account, crucial questions arise: what motivates the reader to accept this claim? What distinguishes it from any conceivable arbitrary claim made in any text? The acceptance of the claim that Jesus was raised from the dead is related to a sense of reality that the reader brings to the text. The reader responds to the promise of resurrection because it sheds light on his or her world of meaning. This does not mean that it is simply integrated into a pre-existent system. Belief in the resurrection may transform a world of meaning in fundamental ways, but initial response to it is made by someone inhabiting a world of meaning which is distinct from that of the text itself.

If response to the narrative of the living God can occur through the interaction of two worlds of meaning, then Thie-

[26] Ibid.

mann's strictures on philosophical anthropology as an *ancilla theologiae* are unjustified. The valid and fruitful function of anthropology is not to construct a narrative-free foundation for theological claims. This would indeed neglect the crucial role of concrete tradition in human knowledge. Rather, anthropology highlights those themes in human experience which are common, in significant ways, to different worlds of meaning. Anthropology draws attention to common experience in the concrete reality of different traditions. Such commonality makes possible communication and dialogue between traditions. It is also part of the process of appropriation of a faith tradition: a reader of the biblical text, who is not yet a believer in the God of Jesus, responds to the promise of resurrection from the perspective of a world of meaning within which this promise is the answer to a perceived need and the resolution of a tension between the experience of transcendence and the inevitability of death, a tension understood in different ways in different concrete traditions.

While epistemological foundationalism affirms the possibility of knowledge independent of any conceptual frame, the radical espousal of narrative theology affirms, in contrast, the generation of theological meaning and truth solely in and through a given, concrete text. Since this text is a particular narrative and a self-contained world of meaning, its truth-claims cannot be warranted by appeal to a world of experience external to the text. This would – it is argued – be an appeal to epistemological foundationalism, which derives from the illusion that there can be a world of experience independent of a text or of a particular interpretation of reality. Yet what this radically narrative conception fails to acknowledge is that the text itself is the product of a history, a witness to events which took place prior to the writing of the text. The biblical narrative of God as saviour is a product of a long history of human vicissitude, a dialectic of interpretation and experience, of ever-widening images of God. The God revealed in this history is the Lord of all nations and the creator of the universe, and it is to this God that the text refers.

Since the text itself was generated by dialectical relationships between given states of religious consciousness and new historical experiences of God, and reached its final form as the definitive testimony to a community's historical experience of God, the text has an inherent dynamism beyond itself: it refers to the reality of history, a history to which it witnesses. The history of revelation, which is part of the public world, has priority over the text, in the sense that the status and role of the text is as a witness to this history. This history is not simply the 'internal' history of a self-contained community, but a history open to a wide range of complex interactions with varied traditions and experiences.[27] Just as the text was developed in interaction with a multitude of concrete worlds of meaning in a historical context, so it invites response as the resolution to the hopes and questions experienced within the world of meaning of the contemporary reader. Part of the function of a philosophical or theological anthropology is to mediate in this relationship between the text and its hearers.

Thiemann argues that we should understand the doctrine of revelation not in terms of God's knowability, but as 'an account of God's identifiability'.[28] The identifiability of God as saviour is indeed a fruitful means of construing the biblical narrative, but it is the identifiability of God and his purposes in the events witnessed to in the Bible that highlights the interaction between worlds of meaning as the process of which the revelation of the God of Jesus was the culmination. A *leitmotiv* of the Old Testament is the challenge to identify God in new and unexpected ways, and to establish the living historical relationship between new revelations of God and the God of the Fathers. In these situations, human beings experience the revelation of God within the context of a given world of meaning, yet in ways which transform this world. The text that emerges is a text witnessing to a history of identifications of God in human

---

[27] The distinction between participant and spectator, internal and external history, is central to the interpretation of revelation developed in H. Richard Niebuhr's *The Meaning of Revelation* (London: Macmillan, 1941). For a critique of this distinction, see Pannenberg's 'Die Offenbarung Gottes in Jesus von Nazareth', in *Theologie als Geschichte*, 161, and E. Schillebeeckx, *Christ: The Christian Experience in the Modern World* (London: SCM, 1980), 50–63.

[28] *Revelation and Theology*, 153.

experience. Such a text invites contemporary response through its own power to evoke new and saving meaning in the realm of experience that the reader brings to it.

Thiemann interprets the meaning of revelation in terms of future promise. It is the concrete biblical word of promise which makes any experience of God possible, rather than human experience providing a realm of awareness within which the promise might be heard. This means, however, that the biblical promise can only come to us as an external word, a word which does not bear any relationship to the meanings we already experience. If the promise creates a world of meaning *ex nihilo*, then it threatens to become the authoritarian datum from the past that Kant rightly sensed to be a danger to human autonomy.[29]

In George Lindbeck's 'cultural–linguistic' model, religion, rather than being the outward expression of an inner experience of God, is an interrelated complex of externally observable phenomena – a language.[30] It is this external language which an individual is inculturated into, and which makes religious experience possible. A religion does not express individual experience, but enables it. It is the text of a religion which forms the world of the believer, rather than the experienced world of the believer forming the text of religious tradition. Because each religion is a given cultural fact, there can be no inner relationships between religions, any more than there can be inner relationships between different languages of different language groups. All that is in common between religions is that they relate in some ways to what human beings believe to be ultimate reality.

---

[29] For J. Moltmann, like Thiemann, faith cannot be grounded in our experience of the world, but rather in the word of promise: it is the word of promise, creating faith and hope in us, which makes experience of God possible; *Theology of Hope* (London: SCM, 1967), Part 2, ch. 4, 'Revelation and Knowledge of God'. Pannenberg argues in contrast that Kant's challenge to Christian theology of revelation retains its force. For Pannenberg, the notion of the 'Word of God' can be given its authentic role as a primary biblical symbol only in the light of an interpretation of revelation as history. Without a grounding in the interpretation of our common human history, 'the conception of the Word of God remains a mythological category and an instrument of unvalidated claims to authority', *Systematische Theologie*, vol. 1, 280.

[30] *The Nature of Doctrine*, 32–41.

From the perspective of this 'cultural–linguistic' understanding of religion, religious change must be understood not as resulting from new experiences, but rather as the outcome of the interaction of a given cultural–linguistic system with changing situations: 'Religious traditions are not transformed, abandoned, or replaced because of an upwelling of new or different ways of feeling about the self, world, or God, but because a religious interpretive scheme (embodied, as it always is, in religious practice and beliefs) develops anomalies in its application in new contexts.'[31] The role of prophets is not to proclaim new experiences, but to see how inherited religious beliefs can be reshaped.

Lindbeck's argument against the 'experiential–expressivist'[32] approach is essentially similar to Thiemann's critique of foundationalism. Both authors reject the notion of an insight, intuition or experience which is independent of a language or system of expression. Since experiences are known through language and insights are perceived in their relationship to a system of meanings, neither pre-linguistic experience nor primordial insight can ground concrete worlds of meaning. For Lindbeck, the 'experiential–expressivist' approach is characteristic of the liberal epoch in theology, of the attempt to proclaim the Gospel by relating it to focal themes in the experience of its audience. The error of this liberal project was to suppose that the concrete language of Christian faith was an expression of experiences that might find their counterpart in the experiences of contemporary human beings. Rather, the process of conversion must be understood in terms of an infant learning a new language, of someone who is unable to experience being given the skills and the words that make experience possible.

The choice that Lindbeck poses between the enigma of private and pre-linguistic experience and the reality of religion as a totally concrete linguistic world is as undialectical as Thiemann's contrast between narrative and foundationalism (whether anthropological or epistemological). What this contrast of opposites overlooks is the very process through which

---

[31] Ibid., 39.   [32] Ibid., 31.

the concrete text of Christian tradition was formed, a process characterized by the interaction of the developing biblical tradition with other religious and philosophical traditions and with a range of historical experiences. This interaction challenged the meanings present in the tradition, and resulted in the development of the tradition to ever-new and ever more saving images of God. Yet these challenges to the tradition could only be perceived and experienced as challenges because the bearers of tradition did not have their own possibilities of experiencing the world wholly formed by their own concrete tradition.

This dialectical relationship between tradition and experience in the development of biblical revelation is not adequately conceived in Lindbeck's appraisal of religious change as a matter of adjusting to anomalies in changing situations. The development of revelation from the patriarch's image of God as a tribal deity through the prophets' proclamation of Yahweh as the Lord of history to Jesus' experience of the loving and providential Father is not simply a matter of reconciling a concrete cultural organism to historical change. This development shows radical innovation, an innovation which cannot be satisfactorily conceived through the 'cultural–linguistic' model.[33] Such radical innovation is intelligible only in terms of a theology of revelation which recognizes the priority of a reality beyond the tradition itself, a reality which reveals itself in the public world, a reality which is the source of the tradition and the source of its transformation and development. This is particularly clear in the long history of the development of the tradition in the Old Testament. In the New Testament, in a much shorter time span, it is evident in the very different ways in which New Testament communities and writers experience

---

[33] The radical innovation characteristic of the biblical record is better understood with the aid of MacIntyre's notion of 'epistemological crisis' (*Whose Justice? Which Rationality?* (University of Notre Dame Press, 1988), 362), rather than as adjustment to anomalies – an epistemological crisis confronted, for example, by those prophets of Israel who had to understand the destruction of the Northern Kingdom, and eventually of Jerusalem itself, in the light of faith in Yahweh, and develop new conceptions of Yahweh's universal Lordship and relationship to 'the nations'.

the reality of Jesus as Lord and Saviour through the different cultural environments in which they live.[34]

The project of a narrative theology, in the radical form espoused by Thiemann and Lindbeck, involves a critique of the liberal theological enterprise. Theological liberalism, in this context, involves a conviction that the meaning or essence of human nature can be expressed in a philosophical anthropology, and that the truth of the Gospel can be shown by the way in which it complements, fulfils or develops this understanding of human nature provided by anthropology. Whether or not we give it the name 'liberal', this emphasis on anthropology need not involve epistemological foundationalism in the Cartesian sense. It does not require the Cartesian claim that knowledge of God can be based on epistemological premises derived from the certainties of introspective self-consciousness. What it does claim is that there are aspects of human experience which are characteristic of human beings irrespective of what concrete tradition they are a part of, that these experiences provide a means of understanding the nature of the human condition, and that they resonate with crucial themes of the Gospel.

Radical narrativism rejects these claims because of its insistence on the essentially narrative *locus* of all perspectives on the human condition and all evocations of human experience. This does provide an important corrective and warning for any use of philosophical and theological anthropology: the claim for the

---

[34] In 'Barth and Textuality', *Theology Today* 43 (October 1986: no. 3), Lindbeck argues that Christian theology must emulate Barth by proceeding on the basis of 'intratextuality', from within the world of meaning created by the text, into which other realities or experiences are inscribed or encoded. Opponents of Luther's and Barth's emphasis on 'intratextuality', whether conservative or progressive, made the error of thinking 'that the realities of which the Bible speaks are found in doctrinal, metaphysical, moral, experimental, or historical domains above, behind, beneath, or in front of the text' (365). In his 'Response to George Lindbeck' (*Theology Today* 43 (1983): no. 3), Thiemann notes that claims for the importance of 'intratextuality' in Barth's method must be justified in terms of his theology of revelation, since 'without that doctrine of revelation, or its functional equivalent, textuality, intratextuality and self-interpreting texts have no *theological* force.' (380) The prior question, however, is whether a one-sided emphasis on the text as formative of experience is adequate to the reality of biblical revelation itself, to the relationship between texts, tradition and experience in the development of the biblical narrative as a whole.

cross-cultural intelligibility of a particular theme in human experience must be made critically and tentatively. In particular, the emphasis on narrative reminds us that such evocations of human experience are not made through an appeal to human nature conceived of in abstraction from tradition, but rather in a context which is the complex resultant of a historical interaction of traditions.

What the use of anthropology rightly affirms, however, is that meanings and values emerging from a particular tradition do have an intelligibility beyond the bounds of that tradition. There are patterns of thought and responses to value which have achieved a *relative independence* from particular narrative traditions. They have done so through their inherent power to illuminate the human condition. The notion of 'transcendence', for example, points to a crucial dimension of human experience which can be evoked by and for a wide range of people, with varying affiliation to concrete traditions. This is not because it does not have its original context in religious tradition: the transcendent dimension of the human person is not known by pure and supra-historical insight, but through the interpretive horizon provided by the cumulative history of myth, religion and philosophy. Once it has developed through this process, however, it can be intelligible outside the confines of specific traditions. In experiences of joy and grief, freedom and responsibility, moral outrage and moral witness, human beings sense their spiritual connections to a greater reality, and can recognize what is intended by the concept of 'transcendence'.[35] Such concepts have achieved a relative independence of specific narrative: their ultimate coherence is within the interpretation of reality sustained by that narrative, but their intelligibility can be independent of the specific narrative context.[36] In this sense

---

[35] This is especially true, as Tracy emphasizes, when such experiences are 'united to the logos of appropriate expression', achieving successful artistic form. *The Analogical Imagination*, 134.

[36] In his *Metaphysical Horror* (Oxford: Blackwell, 1988), Leszek Kolakowski develops a critique of epistemological foundationalism while retaining the role of philosophy as a critical mediator between concrete traditions. For Kolakowski, our knowledge cannot reach an ultimate ground or foundation because the rules of logic themselves are based on such a ground and therefore cannot prove that it is the ultimate ground (31). The only ultimate ground is an infallible subject which must be everything it

they can function as 'mediating principles' which are crucial to a contemporary conception of natural law. The importance of such concepts for ethical communication will be emphasized in more detail in the next chapter.

This relative independence of focal anthropological themes and concepts is of great importance, since it enables a relationship between tradition and experience which is consonant with the process by which the biblical narrative was itself formed. The Gospel is proclaimed to human beings who can respond to it through the evidence of experience, who recognize its message as the intensification and confirmation of what they recognize in their experience. This recognition indeed involves the transformation and judgement of experience by the power of the Gospel, but this power is itself accepted as liberation rather than domination because it is recognized to be the answer to an experienced question. The relative independence of significant meanings and values from a particular narrative is crucial to the critical and autonomous role that experience plays in the response to the Gospel, to the fundamental relationship between a proclaimed Word and a free response in faith. The emphasis on narrative at the expense of anthropology fails to do justice to the dialectical relationship between tradition

knows since any distance between it and what it knows would abolish the certainty and wholeness of truth. For Kolakowski, the ground of knowledge is practical: through our moral actions we become aware of the difference between good and evil, 'in a movement, which, we feel, makes the Being grow or diminish as the result of the good or evil of our acts' (95). The self's sense of reality is linked to awareness of good and evil in a concrete community and in the history of this community. It is this practical knowledge which wards off 'metaphysical horror', the non-existence of both Ego and Absolute. Philosophy, in choosing a possible language or an epistemological standpoint, reflects the contingent choices of a civilization. Unless such a civilization is threatened by radical confrontation with another it remains in a physical and moral order sanctioned by myth and immune to scrutiny. It was philosophy's 'original sin' to challenge this order. Philosophy is a realm of 'the confusion of tongues', a confusion 'which is the revenge of mythology on the Enlightenment for the latter's arrogant attempt to demolish the former' (112). Yet, although philosophy cannot lay claim to an ultimate source of knowledge or values which is independent of that accessible to myth and revelation, it is a realm of cultural life which has its legitimacy through its power to 'absorb various mutually unintelligible idioms . . . idioms which occupy their respective niches in culture and prevent each other from becoming unrestrictedly dominant' (113). See also the concluding discussion of the relationships between religion and philosophy, sacred and secular, in Kolakowski's *Religion* (Glasgow: Fount, Collins, 1982), 223–7.

and experience. Because of this, it is not an adequate response to the contemporary challenge of proclaiming the Gospel in a pluralist society.

Through his *Constructing a Public Theology: The Church in a Pluralistic Culture*,[37] *Religion in Public Life: A Dilemma for Democracy*,[38] and his leading role in the Centre for the Study of Values in Public Life at Harvard Divinity School, Ronald Thiemann has made a distinguished contribution to the debate on the contribution of Christian tradition to the public ethical life of contemporary liberal and pluralist societies. In *Religion and Public Life* he has developed a nuanced and comprehensive advocacy for the value of religious contributions to public ethical debate, linking his argument to the role that 'revisionist liberalism' gives to the various beliefs and world-views in society in developing the 'overlapping consensus' which informs the value of democracy.[39]

Thiemann has a particular concern for Christian identity, in the context of the debilitating conflicts in American Christianity between conservatives and liberals and the urgency of the need to contribute to public ethical life.[40] Only a community which is confident of its own identity can have something valuable to say to democratic societies seeking to strengthen their core values in difficult times. This identity is based in the narratives and practices of Christian tradition, which give Christians a powerful message of hope to share with their fellow citizens. At the same time, the sources of this identity are public, in the sense that the narratives and practices of Christianity are publicly observable and accessible. As such, they satisfy 'the

[37] Louisville: Westminster/John Knox Press, 1991.
[38] Washington, D.C.: Georgetown University Press (Twentieth-Century Fund), 1996.
[39] For this argument, and its relation to Rawls' position, see especially chs. 5 and 6.
[40] See 'Toward an American Public Theology: Religion in a Pluralistic Democracy', in *Constructing a Public Theology* (Louisville: Westminster/John Knox Press, 1991), 40. Because of his commitment to liberal democracy as an ethical and political project, Thiemann has distanced himself from the term 'post-liberal' and from the views of Lindbeck and Hauerwas on contemporary culture and society, ibid., 23–5. Thiemann presents a critique of Hauerwas' views in his discussion of 'Sectarian Communitarians' in *Religion and Public Life* (Washington, D.C.: Georgetown University Press (Twentieth-Century Fund), 1996), 99–105. Hauerwas emphasizes the importance of Lindbeck's post-liberal theology for his own work in *Against the Nations: War and Survival in a Liberal Society*, Minneapolis: Winston Press, 1985, 1–9.

norm of public accessibility' which is desirable for any set of beliefs which is to become a basis for a contribution to public ethical debate.[41]

Although Christian beliefs are publicly accessible, in the sense that the content and phenomena of Christianity are openly available for public analysis, they do not – for Thiemann – claim 'publicity' in the sense of having significant relationships to general human experience. In his critique of David Tracy's arguments, Thiemann explicitly rejects this sense of 'publicness'. For Thiemann, Tracy's third criterion for 'publicness', that is, to 'provide philosophical warrants of sufficient generality to show that the theological position is grounded not in the particulars of faith or belief but in some possibility available to human existence generally', is unacceptable.[42] This is so not only in general theological terms but also because of its negative effects on the public communication of Christian beliefs, since 'by identifying genuine publicness with general philosophical argument, Tracy undercuts the ability of Christians to employ the specific resources of their traditions to engage in public conversation'.[43] Thiemann grants that Tracy's notion of the 'classic' is intended to give Christian systematic theology a character of public disclosure, but argues that this is vitiated by its dependence on a fundamental theology which appeals to universal human experience and a universal religious quest.[44]

Yet the notion of a 'classic' of meaning and value, which can have public resonance for members of different traditions, does of its nature depend on some form of common human experience. A classic cannot evoke new insights into the human condition, for human beings of different traditions, unless it is experienced as a response to questions, hopes and anticipations which arise in universal human experience. It may transform these hopes, and bring deeply felt but inchoate questions to articulate form, but its power to disclose is related to the experience, or pre-disposition, of the person or community who receives it. If it can be experienced as disclosive across different communities, then this power relates to experiences which are

[41] *Religion in Public Life*, 131–6.   [42] *Constructing a Public Theology*, 20.
[43] Ibid., 21.   [44] Ibid., 26.

characteristically human. In this sense, Tracy's criteria for publicness are intended precisely to enable the power of disclosure of the Christian 'classic' to have a public resonance.

In his discussion of the power of Christian narrative to contribute to public ethical debate, Thiemann argues that the parable of the Good Samaritan is a powerful evocation of love of neighbour as love of anyone in need. For Thiemann, this raises critical questions of public communicability in the contribution of Christian faith to social policy: 'Can this particular conviction be developed into a principle of justice with sufficient scope as to be persuasive to a broad and diverse populace? Does the Christian obligation to provide care for the neighbour in need resonate with a fundamental democratic value familiar to all citizens?'[45] Thiemann is right to argue that this principle of care for anyone in need can be communicated in the public forum, as well as in its 'home community' of Christian faith, as a powerful means of universalizing the scope of social care. Yet it is difficult to see how a principle which draws on the Christian value of love of neighbour, evoked by Christian narrative, can resonate with a value familiar to all citizens, unless some appeal can be made to general human experience. If the content of Christian faith is to be publicly communicated in ways which can contribute to the ethical life of a democratic community drawn from various religious traditions, then this implies that members of different traditions can recognize values and principles drawn from Christian tradition as answers to their own questions. In this sense, it is not clear how Thiemann's powerful contribution to the question of the role of religion in public life is fully consistent with his rejection of a role for general human experience in foundational theology.

REVELATION AND A THEOLOGY OF MEDIATION

An adequate theology of revelation seeks to do justice to both the radical uniqueness and gratuity of God's self-communication in Christ, and the universality which it has since 'God wills that

[45] *Religion in Public Life*, 158.

all human beings be saved' (1 Timothy 2:4). It has been argued above that a purely narrativist approach to revelation is not adequate to grasp revelation's universalist dynamic, since it conceives it as a given text rather than as a historical process.

Rather, the account of the theology of revelation developed here will give priority to the concepts of *mystery* and *historicity* in the interpretation of the meaning of revelation. For Christian theology, the concept of mystery has its *locus classicus* in Ephesians 1:9–10: 'God has given us the wisdom to understand fully the mystery, the plan he was pleased to decree in Christ, to be carried out in the fullness of time: namely, to bring all things in the heavens and on earth into one under Christ's headship.'[46]

What the biblical concept of mystery emphasizes is both the gratuity and uniqueness of revelation, and its inexhaustible richness. Revelation is the self-communication of God which makes it possible for God's human creatures to know and experience God and to participate in the divine life. It cannot be predicted, grounded, justified or superseded by any system of reasoning, since of its nature human reason is totally unable to establish a 'ground' which is more 'foundational' than the infinite ground of God's loving purpose. Similarly, Christian revelation cannot be reduced to a statement of what would otherwise be known, a quintessence of common human experience, an instantiation of a generally known truth. Of its nature, it exceeds all such experience and striving after truth, since it embodies the ultimacy of God's self-communication, an ultimacy which is unique and inexhaustible.

The mystery of the divine self-communication is historical, the concrete and particular incarnation of God become human. Through its historicity, its identification with the human condition in the life of Jesus of Nazareth, it achieves a radical completeness of the divine self-gift to humanity and to creation. Since this historicity is so crucial to its radical identification with humanity, then it cannot be replaced by general truths, and is expressed most fittingly in narrative, in language which expresses the texture of lived experience. Since it is mystery,

---

[46] Cf. Colossians 1:26–7.

embodying infinite richness of meaning, only narrative and symbol can adequately embody its meaning in ways which allow its plenitude of meaning and of meanings to be open to the reader and listener.

To emphasize the character of revelation as mystery and historicity is to interpret it as an event of inexhaustible meaning. Its character as historical event radicalizes its uniqueness and irreducibility. Its plenitude of meaning emphasizes its openness to all forms of meaning and truth, all of which are to 'be brought under Christ's headship'. The mystery of the divine plan is that all truth is to be understood in the perspective of Christ. The event which was the culmination of the history of Israel is also the event which will provide the key to the interpretation of all human history and the cosmos. The history of God's self-communication to humanity reached its climax in the resurrection of Jesus of Nazareth, which anticipated the fulfilment of human existence and of the cosmos in the *eschaton*.[47]

From this time on, the definitive character of a history, and of an interpretation of that history, is canonized: the resurrected Christ is the focal-point of cosmic and human history, and it is in and through him that all history, before and since, is ultimately to be interpreted. For this reason, although it does not occur at the end of human history, Christian revelation is not provisional, part of an endlessly self-improving and self-correcting process. It is an assurance of God's irrevocable self-gift to creation. As *historicity*, revelation is also the anticipated fulfilment of history.

At the same time, as *mystery*, the historical event of revelation remains open to the plenitude of meanings that it can evoke and inspire within the course of continuing human history. As

---

[47] The completeness of salvation in Christ, and at the same time its enactment through history, is held together in Ephesians 1:10 in a way described by Rudolf Schnackenburg in his *The Epistle to the Ephesians* (Edinburgh: T. and T. Clark, 1991): 'The universe has been unified in Christ and put under his rule finally and incontestably, and yet it will continue to be subjugated ever to a greater degree, in the earthly–historical space, to Christ's rule which is already established . . . What is already reality in God's world, which is beyond time, will be revealed and realised through the Church in the earthly–historical world which is bound by time' (61).

interpretations of human history, the biblical texts refer only to those historical communities which made up Israel and which figured in Israel's historical vicissitudes. It is, to some degree, also an interpretation of the significance of the Roman empire and of Greek philosophy. It is clearly not an interpretation of other ancient histories, such as the foundational histories of the Hindu and Buddhist traditions. The significance of *those* histories in relation to the incarnate Word awaited the discoveries, mutual contacts and reflective attempts of much later times. Even more evidently, and more importantly for our purposes, it is not an interpretation of human histories which come after the apostolic period. It offers the ultimate key to their interpretation, but awaits the coming of each historical age and the effort of believers to understand their times in the light of Christ. This effort of understanding, made in the light of the Spirit's guidance, is the development of tradition as an interpretive process. Just as revelation occurred as an interpretive process, achieving a definitive form canonized in the community-founding texts of Scripture, so the post-apostolic process of developing tradition occurs as a process of interpreting the meaning of the foundational revelation in the light of the Christian community's experience of history.

The process of tradition: interpretation and dialectic

This act of interpretation is a dialectical and reciprocal one. Not only does it explore the meaning of human history in the light of the realized promise of divine love, but at the same time it is able to develop the meaning of revelation – as inexhaustible mystery – itself. The Christian communities are involved in a historical process of interpretation of the mystery of revelation, a process which seeks to explore the meaning of the Christ-event in relation to all of history and creation. Because of this, it is inadequate to speak of Christian faith as a self-contained narrative, or as a language which defines a reality distinct from other realities: rather, Christian revelation is an event whose meaning develops in relation to all narratives and all languages. In this process of interaction, it is the mystery of God revealed

Theology of revelation and Christian identity 131

in Christ which has interpretive priority, but the meaning of this event is often only brought to light by interaction with human experiences and traditions which are other than those characteristic of the given state of Christian consciousness.

There are many historical examples of an interaction with the 'other' resulting in a developing understanding of Christian faith itself. Probably the most well known is the interaction with Greek philosophy which afforded Christian faith the tools for developing dogmatic definitions which were adequate to answering the questions posed by a philosophically sophisticated culture, and which achieved permanent historical importance. In more recent times, in Catholic history, the interaction with the liberal movements of the nineteenth and twentieth centuries resulted in a more profound and adequate understanding of freedom of conscience, in an estimation of the subjective rights of the person, which in earlier periods of Catholic history were dismissed in favour of the objective rights of institutionally established truths. In contemporary Christian theology, a major reappraisal of the relationship of humanity to nature is in process, a reappraisal which owes much to the religious experience of tribal cultures and to the recent experience of disillusionment with the abuse of human technological power.

One example that is germane to the ethical concerns of this thesis, and which demonstrates profound change in Catholic thought, is the development of Vatican teaching on the social question. While there is no doubt that much of this development expressed the spontaneous commitment of Catholic leaders and thinkers to the lot of the working class, it is equally clear that this development was radically affected by the need to respond to the challenge and critique posed by other world-views – in this case, by socialist ideologies and by Marxism in particular.

Although it concerns the question of political freedom more specifically than the social question, it is useful to consider the reaction of Gregory XVI to Lamennais' *Paroles d'un Croyant* (1834) in the encyclical *Singulari Nos* of the same year.[48] For

[48] On Lamennais, see, for example, B. Reardon, *Liberalism and Tradition: Aspects of Catholic Thought in Nineteenth-Century France* (Cambridge University Press, 1975), chs. 4

Gregory, any movement which threatened the established order of authority was to be condemned. Lamennais' book 'corrupts the people by a wicked abuse of the word of God, to dissolve the bonds of all public order and to weaken all authority. It arouses, fosters, and strengthens seditions, riots and rebellions in the empires.'[49] Earlier, in the encyclical *Mirari Vos* (1832), he had declared that 'divine and human laws cry out against those who strive by treason and sedition to drive the people from confidence in their princes and force them from their government'.[50] This rejection of liberalism, and of any movements of political and social change in the nineteenth century, had its well-known apogee in Pius IX's encyclical *Quanta Cura* and the accompanying *Syllabus of Errors* (1864).

A comparison of these declarations with the documents of the Second Vatican Council is an instructive example of change in the internal structure of a tradition. The document *Gaudium et Spes*, Vatican II's *Pastoral Constitution on the Church in the Modern World*, promulgated in 1965, emphasizes the importance of dialogue with all people of good will. This dialogue is to be based on the common human imperatives of developing a just and humane society. While the Council bases its own understanding of the meaning and purpose of human life on the biblical teaching of the creation of the human person in the image of God and finally on the incarnation itself, it emphasizes that this understanding of humanity is open to dialogue and co-operation with other understandings that share common values. Section 21 of the document recommends 'sincere and prudent dialogue' with atheism on the basis of a common commitment to the 'rightful betterment of this world'.

Together with this recognition of the importance of dialogue, the document emphasizes that the church 'altogether rejects

and 5. A critical modern edition of *Paroles d'un croyant* is edited by L. de Guillou (Paris: Flammarion, 1973). In June 1832, Gregory XVI had sent a papal brief to the Polish bishops, condemning the Polish rebellion against the 'legitimate rule' of the Russian Czar. This had made a deep impression on Lamennais, and prompted the writing of the *Paroles*. See *History of the Church*, ed. H. Jedin (New York: Crossroad, 1981), vol. VII: *The Church between Revolution and Restoration*, 289.

[49] *Singulari Nos, On the Errors of Lamennais*, 6, in *The Papal Encyclicals 1740–1878*, ed. Claudia Carlen (Raleigh: McGrath, Consortium, 1981), 250.
[50] *Mirari Vos, On Liberalism and Religious Indifferentism*, 17; ibid., 239.

atheism' together with the notion that commitment to otherworldly hopes lessens Christians' commitment to the need to develop this world.[51] The document does note that the spread of atheism can be blamed partly on believers themselves, to the extent that 'they fail in their religious, moral or social life',[52] although it does not explicitly admit that the history of Catholicism does include many episodes when emphasis on hope for the next world lessened a practical commitment to social change. Simply through its denial of the inevitability of such religious alienation, however, the document shows the impact of Marxist ideas on the church itself. The document insists that 'hope in a life to come does not take away from the importance of the duties of this life on earth but rather adds to it by giving new motives for fulfilling those duties'.[53] The document's concern to emphasize the importance of building up earthly society through social change, and its firm rejection of any image of religion as offering purely other-worldly hopes, shows a clear and significant change of emphasis from earlier teaching. The rejection of the Marxist theory of religious alienation is accompanied by a greater concentration on the importance of Christian faith as a commitment directed to the amelioration of this-worldly conditions.

For Catholicism in the 1960s, then, the effects of encounter with an ideological opponent and – at times – dialogue partner were to draw attention to a problematic aspect of Catholic tradition: whereas Gregory XVI was content simply to

---

[51] Article 21 (Flannery, ed., *Vatican Council II* (Dublin: Dominican Publications, 1996), 184, 183).

[52] Article 19 (ibid., 182).

[53] Article 21 (ibid., 183). In his commentary on the relevant section of *Gaudium et Spes*, in the *Commentary on the Documents of Vatican II*, edited by H. Vorgrimler, vol. v (London and New York: Burns and Oates, Herder and Herder, 1969), J. Ratzinger notes that the Council's discussion of these questions had its context in a concern to answer atheism by emphasizing the meaning of a Christian humanism and by addressing the question of theodicy, rather than simply condemning Marxism. In this sense, the Council accepted 'the comprehensive question represented by Marxism as also concerning the Church itself' (150). Ratzinger goes on to comment that Christian 'contempt for the world' has in fact weakened commitment to worldly tasks, and that the Council's insistence to the contrary was to some extent an unfounded assertion: 'Here . . . a deeper examination of conscience was needed and it should have been admitted that at bottom, after all, we owe it to the atheists' attack that we have become properly aware once more of our own duties' (156).

condemn Lamennais' hopes for Catholic commitment to social and political liberation with a reminder of the Pauline teaching on respect for worldly authority, the Second Vatican Council emphasized the role of faith as an inspiration to such social reform.

What this indicates is that the encounter with different forms of socialism between the 1830s and the 1960s had brought home to Catholicism the insufficiency of a teaching that emphasized the acceptance of the poor man's lot in life and the assured hope of heavenly bliss.[54] The eventual effect of this encounter had been to put the most basic belief, the mystery of God's revelation in Jesus Christ, into a new relationship with social reality. Formerly, this basic belief had been linked to social reality through the intermediary belief in the divine warrant for existing worldly authority. This intermediary belief had been accepted as part of natural law, supported by divine revelation, although it had never been given dogmatic status.

By the 1960s, however, this belief had been rejected and replaced by a commitment to support for social and political change that embodied fundamental ethical values: the divine warrant for any actually existing worldly authority had been reinterpreted in terms of an emphasis on the authentic authority of any secular power that genuinely embodied those ethical values that expressed the creator's purposes for humanity. Confrontation and dialogue with an ideological opponent, which had interpreted the social facts of nineteenth- and twentieth-century life in a radically different way, had played a role in provoking Catholicism's re-assessment of the structure of its own teaching: beliefs that had earlier been taken for granted had been dispensed with, and had given way to a new focus on the ethical implications of basic beliefs. In this case, then, the

---

[54] Paul Misner, in his *Social Catholicism in Europe: From the Onset of Industrialization to the First World War* (New York: Crossroad, 1991) notes a strong awareness of this insufficiency in the work of Bishop Wilhelm Emmanuel von Ketteler. Von Ketteler's writings show an awareness that 'pastorally, it was of the greatest momentum for the church to bestir itself. Inaction was tantamount to abandoning vast numbers of the working masses to a "proximate occasion of sin". To preach other-worldly rewards while not lifting a finger to help the working masses would lead predictably to mass alienation from Christianity. Already they were turning to other sources of support that were "indifferent to Christianity or downright hostile to it"' (144).

effect of dialogue over ethical matters, such as the conditions of industrial society, had been to impel a clarification of what were basic and essential beliefs that could be given a new social significance, and what were inessential beliefs that could be left in the past.

The interaction of Catholic teaching with socialism and the social question is a good example of some general characteristics of the interpretive process of the development of tradition – the process that attempts to understand the world in the light of Christ, and to understand the meaning of Christ through experience of the breadth and depth of history and the cosmos. These general characteristics of the interpretive process stem from its dialectical relationship with historical experience. In this dialectical process, the historical reality of the Christ-event retains priority and controls the development of meaning, but the character of this event as mystery means, in principle, that its content is always open to new and unpredictable development.

This interpretive process is a critical one, in so far as the interaction between Christian tradition and the 'other' must involve critical discernment to judge whether or not new and other perspectives offer a potential enrichment of tradition or, rather, something essentially inimical to its character. It is a distorted one, because at any given stage of the development of tradition, its shape bears the scars of the struggle to maintain personal and institutional power in the all-too-human dimensions of the church's life, a struggle for power that often blinds the church both to the needs of contemporary humanity and to the harmful effects of its own processes of action. It is characterized by conflict: a conflict of world-views; a conflict of social interests; a conflict of claims to power. At times, this conflict can lead to a hard-won development of insight. It is dialogic at those times when the conflictual element of dialectic can be overcome in a recognition of the goodwill and authenticity of the other, and in a preparedness to affirm the commonality of the search for truth.

To speak of Christian tradition as characterized by a dialectical process is not to subscribe to historical determinism of a

Hegelian or Marxist kind, a necessary process of evolution of divine life or the historical development of material forces driven by an inevitably conflictual dynamism. It is rather to acknowledge that Christian tradition has developed through interaction with the 'other', an interaction characterized so often by conflict, but sometimes by friendship and harmony. The concrete results of this interaction are always unpredictable, and bear witness to the role of the Spirit in the church's life, bringing new forms of life out of the pains of growth and struggle.

In the history of the interaction between the Catholic Church and Socialism we see these dialectical characteristics of an interpretive process at play. From the beginnings of the socialist movement in Europe in the early nineteenth century, the teaching authority of the Catholic Church attempted to exercise critical discernment in relation to these new and radical forms of social thought. In general, this resulted in a forthright rejection and denunciation of socialism. This attempt at critical discernment was a partially distorted one, in which the deeply rooted relationships of the Catholic Church with the property-owning classes played a key role. It was also a notoriously conflictual one, involving severe conflict between the Catholic Church and the socialist and anarchist parties, which had the most tragic consequences in such events as the Spanish Civil War. This dialectic was not simply a matter of conflict, but rather of conflict leading to a higher truth, to insights that were achieved only through the pain of confronting an opponent and acknowledging the spur to growth that that opponent sometimes was. Such insights and acknowledgement were present in the teaching of the Second Vatican Council, a teaching which emphasized the value of dialogue. On the socialist side, they were present in the reformed Marxism of the thinkers of the Prague Spring and the Marxist–Christian dialogue of the 1960s.

A THEOLOGY OF MEDIATION AND CHRISTIAN IDENTITY

The understanding of revelation in terms of mystery and historicity, and of tradition as an interpretive and dialectical process, give us good reason for preferring the 'theology of mediation' as the most adequate conception of the relationship between Christian identity and the other meanings and values that the Christian community encounters.

In the discussion of models of Christian identity earlier in this chapter, it was noted that two of these models place great emphasis on the concrete and self-contained character of Christian narrative tradition. What these models rightly affirm is that, since Christian faith is a response to divine revelation, which is itself gratuitous and ineffable, then Christianity's own identity is based on a reality which cannot be explained or justified in any system of meaning which claims to be larger or more comprehensive than revelation itself. We cannot demonstrate the reality of revelation by standing outside the circle of faith and showing its necessity.

A theology of mediation shares this insistence that revelation is self-*grounding*: what it does not accept is that this means that Christian tradition or Christian narrative are self-*contained* in any sense that obscures or denies the relationship between the Christ-event and the presence of the Spirit in human history as a whole. A tradition which accepts that the Spirit is present in creation and in human history must seek to speak of God in ways which take account of the fruits of the Spirit wherever and whenever they are to be found. The Christian tradition, founded as it is both on the affirmation of God's intimate relationship with all history and all creation, and on the witness to God incarnate in Jesus of Nazareth, is intrinsically oriented to a mediation between universality and particularity. The task of a theology of mediation is to preserve the identity of Christian faith in a way which is at the same time an affirmation of its openness to the work of the Spirit in the world.[55]

Because of this, a theology of mediation is predicated on the possibility of mutual comprehension and dialogue between Christian faith and other worlds of meaning. This dialogue is possible on the basis of the analogies between the experiences contained in different faith traditions. Traditions can grow and

---

[55] Such an interpretation of Christian identity has affinities with Paul Lakeland's conception of an 'apologetics in face of postmodernity' in his *Postmodernity*, 91.

interact with each other through the recognition of common features of the human condition. This interaction is sometimes a matter of relatively peaceful dialogue – more often, perhaps, it begins in the pain of conflict and finds resolution in insight and mutual recognition only after a long and turbulent history of engagement. An understanding of Christian tradition or Christian narrative as a self-contained world of meaning fails to do justice to the ways in which a tradition can grow through the interaction between its own witness and the challenges it encounters in the course of history.

Yet, if a theology of mediation places such emphasis on interaction with other worlds of meaning, what can assure it of Christian identity? If it does not find its identity in a self-contained narrative or tradition, what defines it in relation to what is other than itself? In its ethical communication – a fundamental concern of this study – how does it affirm an identity that has something distinctive to communicate? Most importantly, how does it remain faithful to its identity as a witness to the reality of God's self-communication in Christ?

The Christian community founds its identity in its witness to the risen Christ. This witness affirms, in faith, that the mystery of God has been revealed in the life, death and resurrection of Jesus of Nazareth. The faith of the earliest Christian communities was expressed in texts that combined narrative and interpretation. Through a process of discernment within later Christian communities, these texts were recognized as canonical and inspired, as texts which are inextricably and constitutively linked to Christian identity, both in their recounting of the narrative of the history of revelation and in their interpretation of this narrative. Because of this, any Christian theology must be subject to the true meaning of these texts. Yet their true meaning is in the witness they give to the Christ-event. The biblical texts point beyond themselves to the events of revelation, events which are incarnated in human history. The uniquely revelatory significance of these events makes them different from all others, yet their reality as events in human history, as the incarnation of God in a human being, gives them – at the same time – a continuity with all human history.

This simultaneous difference and continuity indicates a particular kind of relationship between Scripture and history in the interpretation of the Christ-event: while the text of Scripture has a normative and constitutive role, it is to be interpreted in the light of the community's experience of its own history and the history of humanity in general. Because Scripture's role is to witness to the Christ-event, whose meaning can be known more fully through human history, it is possible for the community to recognize – in the light of historical experience – that certain biblical texts are deficient as testimonies to divine revelation, reflecting the beliefs of particular ancient cultures rather than articulating truths constitutive of Christian identity.

If Christian tradition develops as an interpretive and dialectical process, devoted to the articulation of the meaning of the mystery of Christ, what defines the identity of this process? How does it distinguish between what is compatible and what is incompatible with the meaning of Christian revelation? What is essential is that this process is engaged in by a witnessing community, whose own identity is based in Christian tradition, and whose life is guided, in the Spirit, by the ideal of Christian discipleship. The discernment of Christian tradition can only be lived out by those who have staked their own identity on the truth of God's revelation in Christ, and who are committed to Christ's vision of the Kingdom.

It is an essential characteristic of a witnessing community to be committed to preserving the authenticity of its tradition. In developing meanings through the interpretive process of tradition, the community constantly judges these new meanings in the light of an already agreed tradition. The shape of this tradition is marked – in its specifically theological aspect – by the history of dogma, of community judgements which give definitive shape to the meaning of Christian mystery – not to limit its scope and richness, but to define parameters of meaning within which authentic tradition can develop. This process is engaged in by the church as a whole, since it is the church as a whole which witnesses to faith, and which encounters the historical challenges which motivate the process of interpretation. At the same time, a necessary dimension of the witnessing community — and of this interpretive process — is a teaching authority, which can articulate the normative shape of tradition arrived at through the discernment of the whole witnessing community. In this way, a theology of mediation preserves an authentically Christian identity, firmly based in the normative tradition of a witnessing community. At the same time, this tradition, as a devoted interpretive response to the mystery of Christ, is constantly open to the human, historical world which gives challenge and stimulus for the interpretive process.[56]

If a theology of mediation can convincingly answer the charge that its conception of tradition lacks a clear Christian identity, how does it respond to the criticism that it is driven essentially by a desire to identify and legitimize Christianity by a comprehension of universal reality, rather than by an identification with concrete praxis, and especially with the suffering and marginalized? The fundamental response to this criticism is that the impetus for a theology of mediation is given precisely through Christians' encounter with human need and human suffering in all the concrete situations of history. The universality of a theology of mediation is not an avoidance of the pain of particularity, but springs from the desire to relate all encounters and engagements with the 'other' to the mystery of Christ.

Because it does develop through engagements with what is 'other', a theology of mediation is necessarily involved with human conflict, estrangement, incomprehension and alienation. The discussion of some aspects of the development of

[56] From this perspective, I can agree with Charles Davis that 'what the Christian tradition embodies is the narrative of an argument. It has constantly been threatened with dissolution and saved by the reconstruction of its narrative — a retelling that incorporates new insights or even revolutionary changes of interpretation', *Religion and the Making of Society: Essays in Social Theology* (Cambridge University Press, 1994), 110. Within contemporary social conditions, which encourage the development of a personal identity based in cultural universalism, Davis argues that our reasons for belonging to a tradition are essentially 'for personal growth and for the rich individuality of concrete religious faith' but not because it is in some sense ultimate truth or because 'to be a member of it should constitute the basic social identity of a religious person' (149). Yet a conception of Christian revelation — and of Christian identity — based in both universality and particularity can affirm cultural universalism in a way that is grounded in the particularity of a relationship with Jesus of Nazareth, a relationship fundamental to an individual's social identity.

Catholic social teaching, earlier in this chapter, attempts to demonstrate the extent of this conflict and tension in just one aspect of the development of tradition. In this case, it was a response to the sheer physical want of the new working classes, together with the challenge posed by the church's opponents and critics, that motivated the development of church teaching. In other cases, a theology of mediation helps to develop tradition by encountering other forms of conflict and estrangement. In relatively recent history, these have included: the fraught relationships between Christianity and other world religions, especially during the imperialist and colonial periods, yet still of very great urgency; the bitter conflicts between the church and scientific endeavours, so fateful for the faith and Christian identity of countless members of the educated classes; the recent conflicts between traditional conceptions of gender roles in the church and the feminist movements. In all of these cases, what motivates a theology of mediation is not primarily a desire to achieve theoretical understanding, but rather the experience of pain and conflict – whether physical, communal, intellectual or psychological – in the life of the Christian in the world. In responding to this experience, a theology of mediation seeks to overcome the pain of conflict in a genuinely dialectical way. In this sense, it offers a conception of Christian identity as a form of Christian discipleship which is open to and engaged in the conflicts of human history, and which seeks to bring peace and mutual respect through new insight into the meaning of the mystery of Christ for the world.[57]

If a theology of mediation is the most adequate basis for Christian identity in a self-consciously plural world, how does this relate to the central concern of this study, that is, the

---

[57] In his plea for a 'recovery of mystery', in *The Making of Moral Theology: A Study of the Roman Catholic Tradition* (Oxford: Clarendon Press, 1987), John Mahoney makes a strong link between a theology of mystery and *koinonia*, understanding the church's identity as an agent for universal *koinonia* as an expression of the mystery of Christ: 'in so perceiving itself as the place and the agent of moral theology, the Church at the same time receives as its charge the gift and task of deepening not only its own, but also all men's fellowship with each other and with God, in whose own nature all are called to be sharers, or *koinonoi* (2 Peter 1:4). And such call to further the *koinonia* of all humanity constitutes also the first and overriding, or architectonic, task of moral theology' (345).

relationship between Christian identity and Christian ethical communication in the public forum? As we have seen, this relationship is particularly concerned with the connections – in the context of modern liberal societies – between a theology of revelation and conceptions of the worth of persons in community. It is important, at this point in the argument, to consider the positions of two works which are specifically concerned with these issues, and which present points of view which are different both from each other and from my own. John Milbank's *Theology and Social Theory*[58] argues for an understanding of Christian identity as a self-contained narrative of peace which is intrinsically opposed to the secular 'ontology of violence'. Andrew Shanks' *Civil Society, Civil Religion*[59], in contrast, advocates a non-confessional civil religion based on the revelatory power of twentieth-century history, at the service of a discursive society of justice and solidarity. An examination and critique of the arguments of these two works will serve to delineate further the distinct position presented in this study, that is, a conception of Christian identity and Christian ethical communication which is based on the essential link between particularity and universality, historicity and mystery. My own argument has, in common with Milbank's and Shanks' arguments, an emphasis on Hegel's seminal importance for the debate, and a critique of their interpretation of Hegel is therefore a key aspect of any attempt to differentiate their positions from my own.

The basic thesis of Milbank's *Theology and Social Theory* is that there is no such thing as social theory conceived of as a theory of society that is independent of, and more fundamental than, theological commitments. All conceptions of society express a theological vision, or lack of one: secular reason, then, which claims to be the source of a science of society which can subject theology to criticism, turns out to be a theological (or antitheological) vision, which competes with the Christian vision. In this light, the relationship between religion and society is not a matter of competing 'religious' and 'social' factors, but rather of

[58] Oxford: Blackwell, 1990.   [59] Oxford: Blackwell, 1995.

conflicting religious visions which have their social counterparts. Christianity offers an alternative religious vision to other religious and secular visions, together with an alternative social reality based on peace, charity and justice. The method of *Theology and Social Theory* is systematically to criticize the key traditions in social theory, revealing their theological assumptions, and then to advance the Christian 'metanarrative' of peace as an alternative social theory.

Milbank notes that the tasks of his own work can be understood in Hegelian terms, and he recommends the resumption of four 'Hegelian tasks': 'first, a theological critique of Enlightenment; second, a historical narration of the interconnection between politics and religion; third, a self-critique of Christian historical practice; fourth, and most importantly, the transformation of the Greek philosophical logos through encounter with the theological logos, so that thought itself becomes inescapably Christian, and one is "beyond secular reason"'.[60] Yet, although Hegel's questions are the right ones, 'he fails decisively just at the points where he promises most'.

For Milbank, the strength of Hegel's vision is in his understanding of the historical effect of Christianity on the development of conceptions of freedom and the ethical life of communities – unlike other social theorists, Hegel does not reduce Christianity to social phenomena, but gives it a causative status. For Milbank, 'the relationship of Christianity both to the morality of subjective freedom and to *die Sittlichkeit* is the key crux of Hegel's ethical and political theory and the one most relevant to this book. Here, especially, I am both for and against Hegel'.[61] Milbank argues that Hegel failed in his attempt to link Christian faith with an ethical life of peace and justice because he relied on philosophical dialectics to 'prove' the absolute character of the content of Christian faith, rather than allowing the narrative to speak for itself. Both the character of the ethical life he speaks of, and the way it is justified, are vitiated by his reliance on sources outside the Christian tradition. For Milbank, the true way of developing a Christian social and

[60] *Theology and Social Theory*, 147.   [61] Ibid., 162–3.

ethical vision is to draw from the Christian narrative itself, as 'something only to be believed in by faith and searched for through practices', rather than to seek a rationally demonstrable link between the absolute and socio-political life.[62]

Milbank's critique of Hegel, then, is that the Christian narrative itself could achieve Hegel's goals much more effectively than Hegel's metaphysical system. He sees a related error in social theologies which draw on Rahner's transcendental theology. Milbank makes a critique of a number of Catholic theologians, who, he argues, have rightly espoused the cause of radical social justice, but who base this on an erroneous reading of the relationship of Christianity and reason, of 'narrative' and 'dialectics'. This critique stems from his argument that the 'integralist revolution' in Catholic thought, the theological affirmation of the union of grace and nature, had two sources: one French – Blondel and *la nouvelle théologie*, the other German – principally Rahner. Von Balthasar, although writing in German, is strongly identified with the former approach. These two theological schools had in common an emphasis on the integration of grace and nature, but they sought to achieve this in ways which had very significant and contrasting implications. The Blondel–De Lubac–Von Balthasar school emphasized the fundamental character of the Christian narrative itself, and sought to achieve a union of nature and grace by catching up all of human existence into the world of the Christian narrative – this had, for Milbank, the positive effect of giving foundational status to the Christian narrative itself, as a self-grounded world of meaning. The Rahnerian school, in contrast, affirmed the autonomy of the world, and the validity of social theory as an understanding of this world. The result is that Christianity becomes merely an overlay, an understanding of a specifically 'religious' sphere of life.

For Milbank, Rahner's mistake was to begin from universal human experience, and to seek to add a Christian dimension to this. Milbank argues that this implies that we have access to such experience in a way that is independent of narrative.

---

[62] Ibid., 173.

Further, it implies an acceptance of the validity of 'secular reason' in interpreting this experience, and of the validity of a dialogue between Christian faith and 'secular reason' in achieving a full understanding of the relationship between sacred and secular. None of this is compatible with Milbank's own view that Christianity and 'secular reason' are competing 'total interpretations' of reality.

Milbank sees the source of Rahner's error in his doctrine of the relationship of nature and grace. Ironically, although Rahner 'sincerely wishes to guard against what he perceives as the dangers of "naturalism" . . . by upholding the otherness, the unprecedented character of grace', he cannot give this 'otherness' any content, because he claims 'that this otherness is present in the *a priori* structure of every created human spirit'. For Milbank, this results in a 'thoroughly naturalized' understanding of human ethical norms, since Christian revelation is understood as simply making explicit the universal availability of grace. If it is a universal a priori, then the concrete contents of Christian narrative add nothing to it: 'The historical events, the human acts and images which can alone be the site of supernatural difference, are here reduced to mere signs of a perfect inward self-transcendence, always humanly available.'[63]

The result of this is that political and liberation theologians 'embrace secular social science with enthusiasm because they refuse the truly non-extrinsicist historicism of Blondel, de Lubac and von Balthasar, and embrace Karl Rahner's ahistorical metaphysics of human subjectivity'.[64] So, for Milbank, contemporary German and Latin American political and liberation theologians either see the dimension of 'transcendence' simply as the motivation for social and political action whose content is understood in secular terms, or else the process of liberation is itself understood as the site of 'transcendence'. The social ethics which follows from the Rahnerian approach does not recognize a specific Christian content, but acknowledges only a Christian 'motivation'. Thus, by trying to recognize the autonomy of the secular and the gratuity of grace, Christian

---

[63] Ibid., 223.   [64] Ibid.

ethics is deprived of the content and distinctiveness of the Christian narrative, and is filled with the bogus insights of 'secular reason'.[65]

For Milbank, this approach must be rejected in favour of one which puts the community of the church, the true site of Christian praxis, at the centre. A Christian social ethics must be one with a distinctively Christian content, based in the Christian community – this can only be based in a theology which understands society on the basis of the Christian narrative, and which engages in 'directly theological discourse about the sociohistorical: without this, theology occupies the pre-theologically determined site of transcendentalist metaphysics'.[66]

Milbank's rejection of any approach based on the universal characteristics of human transcendence goes together with an emphasis on narrative and history: theology is not in combat with a universal 'secular reason' – rather, Christian theology is one narrative competing with others. He rejects MacIntyre's arguments for the possibility of mutual understanding in the rationality of traditions, maintaining that 'secular reason' cannot be countered by a dialectic of traditions, but only by the assertion of a different narrative: 'My case is rather that it is only a mythos, and therefore cannot be refuted, but only out-narrated, if we can persuade people – for reasons of "literary taste" – that Christianity offers a much better story.'[67] Milbank defends this approach as the affirmation of rhetoric over dialectic, the 'persuasion' of faith, rather than the groundless claim that dialectics can demonstrate that any one narrative is superior to all the others.

Milbank's critique fully endorses post-modernism's rejection of all forms of universal rationality. Yet he recognizes that the negative potential of post-modernism is that it is an absolute historicism, based on an ontology of 'difference' which accepts the sheer givenness of power, resulting in an ethical nihilism. This post-modern ontology of violence and difference is the most honest and clear-sighted understanding of secularity, and

---

[65] Ibid., 240.   [66] Ibid., 249.
[67] Ibid., 330. See Markham, *Plurality and Christian Ethics* (Cambridge University Press, 1994), ch. 8, for a detailed discussion of Milbank's critique of MacIntyre.

can only be countered by an alternative ontology of peace, based in the Christian narrative, the distinctive source of 'theology as a social science'. The task of this 'theology as social science' is to give an account of a distinct kind of society, the church, which contrasts with the ontology of violence. In an important sense, this theology takes up Hegelian tasks, since it is a theology of history which sees theological ideas at the source of social ethics, but it rejects Hegel's fundamental errors: abandoning any attempt to graft faith onto reason, it seeks to develop a specifically Christian *logos* and *praxis*.

Milbank takes Augustine's *City of God* as his key source for a conception of a Christian narrative and Christian community that is a radical alternative to the secular world of violence. The path of peace over violence cannot be based in universal and self-evident objective reason, but only in the persuasive force of a narrative. Christianity 'from the first took the side of rhetoric against philosophy and contended that the Good and the True are those things of which we "have a persuasion", pistis, or faith'.[68] An ontology of peace, which can embrace difference in a relationship with the infinite, is the meaning of Christian narrative and of the Christian community as *altera civitas*. Since the disillusionment of the Enlightenment, since the manifestation of the logic of secularity in the post-modern ontology of violence, there is no other alternative to this choice between the Christian community, truly living out the story of peace, and a world of violence.

Theology and Social Theory is a powerful statement of an understanding of Christianity as a self-contained narrative which is in opposition to the character of the secular world, and which rejects any attempt to mediate between the Gospel and the secular world through universalist reason or an appeal to transcendence. Milbank is right to identify the main positive content of Hegel's social theology in the links between Christian theology and political and subjective freedom and, at the same time, to reject Hegel's attempt to 'sublate' Christian narrative in a metaphysical system. Yet Milbank's general critique of

[68] Ibid., 398.

secularity fails to recognize the great positive value in Hegel's theory of the relationship between Christianity and society, which affirmed both the mutual autonomy of church and state, and the importance of the Christian faith for a state based on human dignity.

For Hegel, human dignity, formed in the crucible of a liturgical relationship to the infinite God, could also have a profound influence in the secular world. Although church and state were separate and distinct, the spiritual and moral sense of value received in a religious context could be maintained in all walks of life. In this sense, religion provided a 'horizon' of human value that could not be ignored and which could inform the character of secularity as well. This emphasis is quite distinct from Milbank's 'two cities' theology of history, which does not recognize the autonomous value of secularity. Hegel's metaphysics and political philosophy did not do justice to the narrative character of Christianity, nor to its irreducibly eschatological character, but this should not blind us to the positive value of his understanding of the relationship between the Christian experience of human value and the affirmation of human rights in the secular sphere.

Milbank's critique of Rahner's theology fails to recognize the links between historicity and transcendence in Rahner's thought. It is a misjudgement of Rahner to say that he asserts that Christian teaching merely 'makes explicit' the universal availability of grace. Rahner's theology is fundamentally concerned to hold together both the reality of God's universal salvific will and the historical and particular character of God's self-communication in Jesus of Nazareth. For Rahner, the universality of revelation flows from an earnest and consistent appreciation of the doctrines of the universal salvific will of God, of sanctifying grace and of the necessity of grace for faith.[69] Since God's salvific will is universal, and since faith is necessary for salvation, then the grace of saving faith is offered by God to all humanity. Yet this saving faith is only possible as a

---

[69] See, for example, Rahner's presentation of this in Rahner, K. and Ratzinger, J. *Offenbarung und Überlieferung*, Quaestiones Disputatae (Freiburg im Breisgau: Herder, 1965), 14.

response to God's own self, to the grace of the divine revelation as self-communication. The universality of God's salvific will implies the universality of revelation: God communicates his own self to all of humanity as the saving mystery, giving the gift of faith and inviting the response of human freedom.

Rahner's theology combines this affirmation of the universality of revelation with an emphasis on its historical and Christological character. This question was of particular concern to him, since he believed that it is the notion of historical revelation, rather than the possibility of a transcendental relationship to God, which is the greatest obstacle to contemporary acceptance of the Christian Gospel.[70] Rahner put the question of the relationship between transcendence and historicity to himself in terms similar to Milbank's critique: if God is already present as the absolute ground of every creature's life and maintains creation in existence, then how can God become any more present to his creation through historical revelation? If the divine Spirit already dwells in the heart of every human being, elevating the human person to the plane of the 'supernatural existential', then what is the meaning and purpose of history and of a relationship to God mediated by history? Rahner's answer to this question is that the transcendence of the human person does not exist in a historical vacuum but is rather developed through concrete interaction with the historical world. The relationship between the self-communication of God and the believing response of men and women is a relationship of freedom and therefore a historical relationship. Since we are historical beings, and since the personal self-communication of God can only take place in the concreteness of human history, then the history of God's own revealing and saving action is known through our history. The historicity of transcendence is not merely a human historicity, but also 'a history which really is the one true history of God himself, and a history in which the unchanging and untouchable God manifests his power to enter into the time and the history which he as the Eternal One has created'.[71]

[70] Ibid., 12. [71] Rahner, *Grundkurs des Glaubens*, 146–7.

The reconciliation of the transcendental and the historical is finally that 'history is ultimately precisely the history of transcendence itself'.[72] Transcendence must be understood as something which is realized and developed within history, but at the same time the human person as a historical being must remain aware of her own transcendental freedom as the 'condition which makes genuine history possible'.[73] Since the subject's involvement with the concrete historical world is precisely the mode in which the subject finds and posits itself in a definitive way, then salvation itself is an event which happens within history.[74] It is in the concrete acts of personal history that the human person affirms her response to the self-communication of God. The self-communication of God has an historical 'event character', since the response to it which allows it to become effective in the life of the person is a response made through concrete historical choices.

For Rahner, transcendence and historicity are not opposed but, rather, complementary: the human person develops and expresses transcendent freedom through involvement in historical situations. The event of the divine self-communication is transcendental, but precisely as such has a real history. It is coextensive with all human history, since all human history is an expression of human freedom. Transcendental revelation does not occur as non-historical introspection. Rather 'concrete history is individually and collectively the history of the transcendental revelation of God'.[75] In this sense, Rahner's theology of revelation affirms both the universality and the historicity of the graced relationship between the 'holy mystery' of God and the human creature.

In the light of this theology of the historicity of transcendence, Rahner's theology is in no sense an attempt to show that we can achieve a sense of the meaning and intentionality of human transcendence in complete abstraction from the content of Christian faith. It is rather an attempt to understand the transcendence of the human person *in the light of* Christian faith,

---

[72] 'die Geschichte gerade im letzten die Geschichte der Transzendentalität selbst ist', ibid., 145.
[73] Ibid.   [74] Ibid., 50.   [75] *Offenbarung und Überlieferung*, 18.

in a way which allows contemporary human beings to explore the relationships and analogies between their own experience and the Christian tradition.[76] The concept of transcendence used by Rahner, inspired by the experience of freedom and love, is informed by the content of Christian tradition, but at the same time provides a key to reflection on human experience which can enable and encourage reflection on the tensions and affinities between a narrated tradition and the meanings and values which emerge in contemporary culture. Because of its relative independence from the content of tradition, it can provide a bridge between that tradition and other conceptions of the human condition, a bridge which is of crucial importance both for the individual's appropriation of tradition and for the tradition's capacity to engage in dialogue.

Rahner's theology of human transcendence and the universality of revelation was developed in tension with restrictive and extrinsicist theologies of revelation and grace in the ecclesial context, and, in a secular context, with existentialist and transcendentalist philosophies of atheistic humanism. David Tracy's theology puts a similar emphasis on the relationship between particularity and universality in a context where the historical character of traditions and the reality of contemporary cultural pluralism have come into more explicit focus. Tracy's argument is that different traditions can recognize the power of disclosure inherent in the 'classics' of disclosure originating in the 'intensification of particularity'. Tracy's arguments for conversation between traditions, based on the mutual intelligibility of particular 'classics' of disclosure, are in harmony with MacIntyre's

---

[76] In his *Immortal Longings: Versions of Transcending Humanity* (University of Notre Dame Press, 1997), Fergus Kerr points out that Rahner's concern was essentially apologetic: seeking to overcome 'the impotence of the neo-Scholastic theology which he had inherited to bring people to God . . . He sought to show how Christian claims, however bizarre and disorientating they may seem, actually fit with ordinary everyday human experience. This is, of course, something to be seen only in retrospect. The absolute mystery to which all knowledge and loving are related, as transcendental analysis of human subjectivity discloses, has in fact been revealed by the dispensation of grace in the history recorded in the Bible. Given that this self-revelation of God has occurred, Rahner wants to discover what must be true about the structure of human knowledge and loving for such a revelation to be recognized and received' (178).

arguments for the possibility of critical argument between traditions, including the recognition by a particular tradition that a competing tradition may be able to answer its own questions better than itself. It is insufficient for Milbank to argue that MacIntyre's case for a dialectic of traditions is irrelevant, since what is at stake is a clash of 'myths' that can only be decided by reasons of 'literary taste'. This would be true only if no mutual understanding or intelligibility were possible between the Christian myth and other myths in our common human world. Yet this is simply not the case: the classics of particularity can speak to those outside the confines of particular traditions. This fact is of central importance to an understanding of our contemporary human situation, and to a theology of the work of the Spirit in the world.

Milbank's contrast between a church community informed by a narrative of peace and a secular world fuelled by an ontology of violence is a seriously inadequate interpretation of the relationships between the church and the secular world – quite apart from the fact that it neglects the meaning, role and influence of the other world religions. While the church finds its identity in the concrete narrative of the Gospel, it recognizes that this narrative has a meaning which can find expression, in particular ways, within the secular world as well. Because the church, and the Gospel which it proclaims, witness to the God who created the world, both church and Gospel are, of their nature, oriented to the world, a world which bears the marks of human sin but also manifests the signs of the work of the Spirit. Part of the church's relationship to the world is to discern and support those movements and ideas within secular culture which do reflect the work of the Spirit, bearing witness to the values of creation. To a considerable extent, certain values – such as the dignity of the person – are influential in secular culture because of the historical influence of Christian traditions themselves, and Hegel's philosophy is a seminal interpretation of why this is so. This demonstrates that the power of Christian narrative can influence those who do not identify with the concrete Christian community, because it remains a fundamental source of meaning within their lives. Christian narrative has a universal ethical meaning, a meaning in ethical and social practice which finds its ultimate cognitive 'home' in Christian faith, but yet has its own practical self-evidence in its power to liberate and do justice. In terms of ethical communication, Christian identity can be understood as the relationship between the particularity of narrative and the universality and intelligibility of its implications for human existence. This will be a particular concern of the next chapter.

Milbank's critique of the Enlightenment fails to recognize the value of the discursive ethical practices which are a fundamentally important part of the Enlightenment's contemporary heritage. It has been part of the argument of this book that these discursive practices, in order to achieve their potential of universal solidarity, do find their context and fulfilment in an ontology of communion, an ontology which the Christian theology of revelation can inform and inspire. The fundamental weakness of the Enlightenment tradition was to seek universal ethical solidarity through the universalization of subjective will – a weakness which had its source in the rejection of any religious or metaphysical ground for the 'givenness' of human solidarity, an objective foundation of human moral unity. At the same time, it must be recognized that the open, discursive practices that were given such impetus by the Enlightenment have been of immeasurable value in the development of democratic societies and have often been a source of instruction and example for the internal affairs of church communities. For these reasons, a contemporary theology of Christian identity and ethical communication must affirm the value of such discursive practices, while seeking to support and inspire them with the narrated traditions of Christian faith.

Andrew Shanks' *Civil Society, Civil Religion* offers a very different conception of Christian identity and the social meaning of Christianity. For Shanks, our contemporary need is for religion to act as the Spiritual dimension of civil society. In contrast to other versions of civil religion as a spiritual source and legitimation of various forms of social order, Shanks argues for civil religion as a source of healing and reconciliation inspired by the revelatory power of the twentieth-century experience of totalitarianism, war and genocide. The concept of revelation should not be restricted to the foundational event of Jesus Christ, but should rather be expanded to include all those events which disclose to us the meaning of the human condition, and which can inspire the virtues of solidarity. For Shanks, it is clear that traditional Christian confessional loyalties had very varied moral implications for the reaction to Nazi genocide and Soviet totalitarianism: a 'civil theology' would relativize such loyalties in favour of a religious spirit explicitly dedicated to citizenship in solidarity, drawing on the revelatory potential of these twentieth-century upheavals.[77] In this sense, the whole point of a 'civil theology' is to 'expand the range of historical experience which is brought to bear upon our understanding of salvation'[78] and our 'interpretation of religious symbolism',[79] in order to maximize the 'critical–communitarian expressiveness' of Christian faith and Christian liturgy.

Shanks considers the contemporary concern of Christian communities to maintain a distinctive identity to be a defensive response originally formed in the age of the martyrs, in opposition to Roman civil religion. This defensive response, which sometimes acquired a neurotic character, needs to be overcome so that the churches can be open to the 'revelatory shock-stimulus to theological reflection inherent in the global twentieth-century phenomenon of totalitarianism'.[80] For Shanks, an open church is one that reproduces the full range of moral conflict, excluding only intolerance, and differing from the world only in the exemplary manner in which it handles conflicts. Such an environment would be hospitable to the practice of critical civil religion. In contrast to this, he argues, contemporary churches are characterized by 'a pastoral

---

[77] *Civil Society, Civil Religion* (Oxford: Blackwell, 1995), 212. Shanks' conception of revelation has affinities with that developed by Gabriel Moran, in his *The Present Revelation* (New York: Herder and Herder, 1972). Rejecting the 'revelation as history' paradigm, Moran looks for different sources for a revelation based at the grass-roots of present universal human experience, since revelation should 'refer primarily to the worldwide religious experience of living people' (227). He suggests examples of such foci of experience in humanistic and existential psychology, the worldwide struggle for human rights, and the ecological movement.
[78] Shanks, *Civil Society, Civil Religion*, 72.   [79] Ibid., 77.   [80] Ibid., 22.

monoculture',[81] emphasizing communal unity rather than provoking political discussion. Because of this they lack sensitivity to the sin implicit in social and political structures.

For Shanks, 'civil theology' is 'civil' because it is transconfessional, and oriented to freedom and solidarity, but at the same time it retains its theological character through its 'counterbalancing orientation towards the absolute'.[82] Civil theology is 'exploration, from a theistic perspective, of the requirements of moral solidarity in the face of oppression in so far as the need is for a spirit of moral solidarity transcending all confessional boundaries'.[83] Drawing on the work of the Czech philosopher and signatory of Charter 77, Jan Patočka, Shanks uses the term 'solidarity of the shaken' to refer to the fundamental solidarity of human beings who are united in their 'shakenness', in their resistance to the threat of utter inhumanity and nihilism.[84] A 'civil theology' would go beyond particular loyalties in order to help achieve this solidarity, and would be inspired by this solidarity, in turn, in the task of discerning the meaning and challenge of the present moment, as a *kairos* of potential revelation.[85]

In contrast with confessional Christian theology, which constantly correlates the present age with specifically Christian tradition, 'civil theology' finds its methodological independence in the analysis of the 'virtues of discernment' crucial to detecting the signs of hope in the 'signs of the times'. These virtues of discernment are 'free spiritedness', a 'flair for tradition' and 'generosity', and Shanks devotes considerable space to illustrating the meaning of these virtues through, in particular, Nietzsche, Hegel and Levinas respectively. The 'virtues of discernment' are linked not to the apologetic requirements of any particular tradition, but rather to the needs of a society striving for justice and solidarity. Such discernment is particularly necessary since, for civil theology, revelation always

---

[81] Ibid., 91. [82] Ibid., 67. [83] Ibid., 115.
[84] Charter 77 was a document issued in 1977 by a group of Czech dissidents, including Václav Havel and Patočka, challenging the Czechoslovak communist govenment to abide by the terms of the 1975 Helsinki Declaration, to which it was a signatory.
[85] Shanks, *Civil Society, Civil Religion*, 138.

needs to be identified afresh, because it is not intrinsically linked to any foundational event but rather found in the events of contemporary life. Through the cultivation of the virtues of discernment we are enabled to sense the potential in the present moment for inspiring and supporting a society based on discursive practices devoted to preserving justice and human rights. Shanks sees the concrete meaning of a 'solidarity of the shaken' in, for example, Václav Havel's 'anti-politics', subverting the power of political parties in order to allow critical ethical lobbies to play their full role in public debate. One consequence of such a model, he suggests, would be state funding for non-party critical lobbies. The role of the churches is to leave behind confessional boundaries in dedication to the common task of energizing a society which is free from propaganda and inspired by the 'solidarity of the shaken'.

Hegel plays a key role in Shanks' account of the origins and meaning of 'civil theology'. For Shanks, Hegel begins from a purely civil–theological problematic, seeking to rescue the whole theological tradition of the church from the church as a defensive and confessional institution so that it could become a 'civil–theological' tradition and a vital contribution to the civilizing of politics.[86] In this sense, Shanks argues, Hegel combines two of the key virtues of discernment: he reconciles 'free spiritedness' with a 'flair for tradition', showing – despite Nietzsche – that Christianity does have affinity to the free spirit. Hegel's 'civil theological' rendering of Christianity seeks the widest possible basis of rational solidarity 'in defence of a civilization rendered dangerously fragile by "the death of God".'[87]

Despite this great potential as a 'civil' theologian, Shanks argues that Hegel is still a spokesperson for 'Christendom', and the civil–theological potential of his work has to be distinguished from his Christian apologetics. Hegel's definitive link between the incarnation and the development of human freedom is an aspect of his Christian apologetics that need not be carried over into a civil theology that can have more pluralist

[86] Ibid., 114.   [87] Ibid., 168.

sources.[88] For Shanks, 'the metaphysical pretensions of Hegel's thought are very much bound up with his own distinctive strategy of confessional apologetics'.[89] Yet, even though this Christian and metaphysical metanarrative has collapsed, this does not necessarily entail the abandonment of Hegel's 'macro-solidarity reinforcing theory' of civil theology.[90] In one sense, as Shanks notes, the whole of Hegel's mature theology could be seen as a response to the French Revolution's Terror, devoted to the question of how a form of Christian faith could be developed which would help to bolster civil society against such catastrophes.[91]

Shanks' interpretation of Hegel has much in common with my own, especially in the role that he gives to Hegel as the exponent of a freedom, rooted in religious tradition, that could bear fruit in the ethical and political life of civil society. Yet, in my view, Shanks' interpretation of Hegel fails to do justice to the substantive and instrinsic links between Hegel's Christian theology and his theory of *Sittlichkeit*. For Hegel, the definitive character of the incarnation, and its universalization in the course of human history through the work of the Spirit, were at the root of the modern ethical and political conception of human dignity. This link was made real in contemporary life through the union of human and divine in the life of the religious community and the experience of liturgy. Because of this, Hegel as 'civil' theologian cannot be contrasted with Hegel as 'Christian apologist': it was precisely the content of Christian revelation, for Hegel, that could bear fruit in modern freedom. Contrary to Shanks, I would argue that Hegel's metaphysical *Aufhebung* of religious *Vorstellung* was not part of a strategy of reinforcing Christianity's confessional character – on the contrary, it weakened it, by claiming that a set of metaphysical truths, an 'absolute knowledge', could be distilled from Christianity and that – at least for philosophers – this 'absolute knowledge' might make religious *Vorstellung* redundant.

Shanks' general thesis is a powerful and stimulating defence of 'civil theology', which makes a very good case for the need

[88] Ibid., 145. [89] Ibid., 166. [90] Ibid., 176. [91] Ibid., 186.

for theology and the churches to commit themselves to the discernment of the potential for justice and freedom in the disclosures of human experience in contemporary life. His thesis has much in common with my own argument concerning the links between disclosure and discourse, revelation and ethical dialogue. Yet there is a crucial difference between Shanks' theology of revelation and that advocated in this study, a difference that has fundamental consequences for Christian identity in ethical communication. Shanks makes it clear that 'civil theology' does not give a normative and foundational revelatory status to the Christ-event. Rather, it seeks to discern the revelatory potential in contemporary events of human suffering and upheaval, drawing attention to the solidarity and goodness that such 'negative revelations' can throw in stark relief. Civil theology consciously relativizes the revelatory claims or traditions of any particular confession, seeking to draw together various groups for the sake of a common moral challenge. To do otherwise, he implies, would be to run the risk of repeating what happened in the churches' responses to twentieth-century totalitarianism, when confessional loyalties often stifled and muted moral responses, or – at the least – were not predictive of the kinds of responses Christians would make.

For Shanks, the criterion for 'civil theology' is the contribution that it can make to a society of justice and solidarity, a contribution made through the discernment of the revelatory meaning of contemporary events. Yet what criteria are to discern which contemporary events are revelatory, and how they are to be interpreted? What criteria should be used to interpret the political disasters and incalculable human tragedies of twentieth-century history? These questions highlight the fundamental importance of religious traditions for human existence in the face of radically threatening historical change. The nature of a religious tradition is to provide a fundamental and definitive criterion for the interpretation of experience, based in a founding event of the revelation of God. This tradition provides a means of interpreting experience for all ages to come. It has been emphasized in an earlier part of this chapter that this interpretation should be understood as a dialectical process, so that the infinite meaning of the founding event becomes more and manifest in the course of history. Yet, without the light thrown on human existence by this founding event, there is no fundamental criterion for interpreting human history. In the face of the Holocaust, for example, if there is no normative tradition of the ultimately redemptive power of the love of God, what kind of interpretation is possible? For those caught up in such events, it was precisely the definitive character of religious revelation that gave them the resources to survive in hope. If the contribution of theology to political and ethical life is to speak of the absolute – an absolute that can be the source of the dignity of even the most degraded and the guarantee of hope for even the most abandoned – then it can only speak effectively if it speaks with a confidence and identity based in definitive revelation, that manifests the absolute in a way that has permanent and universal meaning. Nothing less than this can give theology the power to be truly prophetic in the face of the propaganda of money and power and the horrors of totalitarian violence.

Because of this, the valuable aims of a 'civil theology' cannot be achieved by relativizing the status and meaning of religious revelation. The resources for social justice and solidarity must be drawn from religious traditions which retain their identity and their source in definitive revelation. How then can religions be 'civil-ized'? How can religious believers be led to put the most urgent moral concerns of the age ahead of confessional differences? Shanks' argument does indeed point to a weakness in any conception of religious identity which is indifferent to the moral and religious meaning of the secular world, and to the potential that secular history has to make the meaning of the mystery of Christ real and present to us. Yet it does not refute the need for identity based in definitive revelation. Religious traditions with this sense of identity have shown strong commitment to interfaith dialogue and to support for social justice and human rights. A strong sense of identity is no intrinsic obstacle to respect for other traditions, and to a commitment to contribute to a common sense of universal ethical norms. For the Christian tradition, what is crucial is that this commitment to the cause of goodness in secular history, to the strengthening of solidarity in civil society, is understood to be a necessary and constitutive dimension of a response to God's revelation in Christ.

Christian identity implies that Christians must ultimately look to the sources of their own faith for the criteria of belief and action. However much they affirm the wide range of contemporary movements of emancipation and conscientization, the self-consciousness of Christians will involve critical reflection on the present meaning of evangelical criteria, a reflection which tries to distance itself from identification with the spirit of the age, in order the better to witness to the Gospel and to minister to the needs of our age. Such distancing, of course, may result in a re-doubled affirmation of leading features of the spirit of the age – such as the concern for human rights. Yet a consideration, for example, of the responses of nationalistic Christians to World War I, or of many Catholics' uncritical and enthusiastic embrace of conservative romanticism as an antidote to the Enlightenment and the French Revolution, is an historical reminder of the need to maintain such critical independence.

The discipline of distancing oneself from the spirit of the age is quite different from ignoring the 'signs of the times'.[92] Christians must ask themselves whether what they are doing ultimately flows from Christian criteria of action, but they are often inspired to look at the sources of their own faith afresh by the Spirit-filled events and movements that are part of human history. The theology of mediation is grounded in the conviction that Christian revelation is the ultimate and definitive form of the universal self-offering of God: the momentum of Christian faith to mediate with contemporary culture does not spring from an appeal to a rationality which transcends revelation but rather to the universality inherent in revelation itself. In responding to the signs of the times, Christians attempt – often in a painfully dialectical process – to achieve a fuller understanding of the meaning of their own faith, to do justice to the

---

[92] *Gaudium et Spes*, 4.

universal scope of its symbols. Since such 'signs of the times' are a crucial source of theology's vitality, then Christian identity cannot be adequately based on an existing tradition which is conceived to be self-sufficient. Christian identity is formed and re-formed in the process of understanding the relationship between the Gospel and all those movements of thought and action which call for reaction and response. This is the way the tradition itself was formed, and the way in which it remains alive.

We began this chapter with the affirmation that the project of universal ethical dialogue and ethical community, as expressed in the Kantian notion of the 'kingdom of ends', receives its ontological grounding in the theology of revelation, in which the mutual respect of human persons is grounded in their communion with the three-personed God and with each other. The orientation of human autonomy to truth finds its fulfilment in participation in the truth of infinite being. In terms of the question of the communication of the Christian theological vision in the ethical projects of liberal societies, this led to an inquiry into the relationship between Christian theology of revelation and the other meanings and values of a pluralist world. In particular, it occasioned the question of the identity of Christianity in a post-modern context.

Three conceptions of Christian identity were proposed. Two of them place particular emphasis on the self-contained character of Christian narrative and tradition. The third emphasizes that Christian faith must see itself as in a process of mediation of meaning with a universal dynamism. The understanding of Christian faith as essentially a self-contained narrative, and the accompanying critique of any use of philosophical and theological anthropology, were subjected to criticism, with the argument that this did not take sufficient account of the interactive process by which Christian revelation itself developed. Further, a positive proposal was made in terms of a theology of revelation focussing on the themes of mystery and historicity. This theology of revelation results in a theology of tradition as a dialectical process of interpretation. In this process, the *identity* of Christian revelation is preserved through the essential historicity of the Christ-event, a historicity which is uniquely and irreducibly communicative of infinite mystery. At the same time, the *communicative* character of Christianity is motivated by the Christian calling to 'bring all under Christ's headship', in so far as the fullness of the mystery of Christ is known through coming to know the world that was created in and through Christ and which finds in Christ the anticipation of its reconciled and fulfilled future.

CHAPTER 4

The communication of Christian ethics in the public forum

The previous chapter has developed a conception of Christian identity based in a theology of mediation of universality and particularity. It is now time to consider how this conception of Christian identity is expressed in ethical communication in the public forum, for the sake of maintaining and strengthening the sense of the worth of persons in community. Any conception of Christian identity must have communication at its core, in so far as all Christian identity is rooted in evangelization. For a theology of mediation, evangelization as communication has a particular concern for the potential for self-understanding and reciprocal learning inherent in the communicative process.

The specific emphasis of this study is on the nature of Christian ethical communication in the public forum of liberal and pluralist societies. In chapter 1, some of the fundamental features of such societies were highlighted, in particular liberalism's own problems of legitimation and the tensions between liberalism and particular revealed traditions. Chapter 2 addressed the various ways in which philosophy since Kant has attempted to ground the ethical concept of the worth of persons. Firstly, it offered an interpretation of the different ways in which the relationships between revelation, reason and ethics have been understood since Kant. Secondly, it presented a critical analysis of the ways in which Kant himself and neo-Kantian thought attempt to ground autonomy and ethical universality (a 'kingdom of ends') in various forms of rationality. Finally, it argued that the relationship between the autonomy of the individual and ethical universality can only be fully sustained in an ontological relationship with the infinite, a relationship which is summed up in the the concept of revelation, as the self-communication of the divine *communio*.

This relationship is ultimately based in theological discourse, rather than in philosophical concepts, since a public metaphysics is dependent on theological commitments. As we have seen in the discussion of theological discourse and religious narrative in the last chapter, however, certain concepts – or 'mediating principles' – drawn from a philosophical and theological anthropology can achieve a relative independence of a specific narrative tradition and have considerable communicative power. The purpose of the present chapter is to consider the implications of this theology of revelation for the communication of Christian ethics in the public forum.

Christians who have sought to participate in ethical debate on the basis of generally shared methods of argument have made very extensive use of two great traditions of ethical reasoning which did not recognize any constitutive relationships between ethical values and particular religious traditions. The theory of natural law, first developed in classical culture and subsequently integrated into Catholic thought, argued that ethics could be based on 'right reason's' perception of the order inherent in things. 'Right reason' itself was conceived of as a human faculty possessed universally and independently of particular historical traditions. The Catholic theory of natural law presupposed, of course, a creator God who was the source of the order and objective teleology of nature, as expressed in natural law, but recognition of the creator and his will for humanity could – in abstract terms – be achieved independently of particular religious traditions, even though in the usual concrete case it was the assistance of revelation that enabled human beings to overcome the distortions of sin and error and to know the true deliverances of 'right reason'. The Kantian theory of the autonomy of ethics, by contrast, placed the objective character of ethical truth in the universality of reason and freedom, rejecting the notion of 'natural law' as heteronomous. It was at one with the natural law tradition, however, in affirming that insight into ethical truth was independent of particular religious traditions. While the natural law theory, particularly as expressed in the First Vatican Council, spoke of particular revelation as clarifying and intensifying our perception of natural law, Kantianism rejected such revelation as at best superfluous and at worst a powerful source of heteronomy. Contemporary awareness of the crucial role of historical tradition in making possible certain perceptions of and responses to reality has encouraged a different interpretation of the relationship between religion and ethics. While it is clear that there are many ethical constants in human culture, based on the fundamental similarity of basic human needs, we can also discern different ethical emphases that are related to different interpretations of the meaning and purpose of human existence. These interpretations are themselves linked to religious visions or world-views. Max Weber's studies of the different forms of 'secular ethic' generated by different religions are a classic example of research into such links. The strength of the theory of 'natural law' is that it identifies common, trans-historical human goods and needs and the ways in which ethical action might fulfil them. The power of Kant's categorical imperative is to identify the fundamental characteristics of a society made up of free and rational human beings. Yet the actual goals that human beings set themselves, and the value that they place on each other, can be fundamentally affected by visions of life that are grounded in historical religious traditions.

These questions make up an important part of the debate about the relationship between 'modern' and 'post-modern' understandings of culture. Contemporary discussions of the possibility and meaning of a public culture emphasize that the public character of ideas and insights can no longer be defined purely in terms of a universal rationality, in terms of a 'modern' paradigm. There has been increasing awareness of the contribution of specific and particular traditions to public culture, and of the dangers of eliminating such traditions in favour of a reductionist conception of agreed public truths. This discussion has particular relevance for theology. If the public forum can no longer be exclusively defined as a place cleared of all particular traditions of belief and value, but rather as the place where such traditions meet in dialogue, then theology, the articulation of a specific faith tradition, can make its own contribution to this dialogue. If the public forum is a matter not of public reason versus particular and private faiths, but rather of maintaining, developing and affirming faith in those values essential to our common life, then the insights of Christian faith can contribute to it.

For these reasons, contemporary Christians, of many different communities, have increasingly drawn on the symbolic and narrative resources of their own tradition to develop contributions to public ethical debate. In so doing, they are able to make a distinctive and powerful source of insight available to the public realm. Christians seek to affirm the central value of liberal societies, the worth of the human person, by setting personal life in the context of a Christian vision of the meaning of human existence. They seek to affirm their society's public values from the resources of their own particular tradition.

This is a task of great urgency and importance, and at the same time a delicate and complex one. It is in the realm of ethics that the contribution of Christian faith is both particularly relevant and particularly controversial. It is particularly relevant, since Christian faith bears its most evident fruits in the ways it can be of service to our common humanity, as an integral aspect of the call to evangelize. It is particularly controversial, since members of liberal and pluralist societies are particularly sensitive to Christians asserting how others should live. The contribution of the Christian vision to public perception of and respect for the worth of persons has inestimable value, yet it rests on the presupposition that this vision can be communicated in the public realm in ways that are intelligible to those who are not members of the Christian communities. A Christian ethics, which self-consciously draws on its own traditions in public debate, can show a clear awareness of its own historical and traditional character. Yet it thereby renders problematic its relationship to the public forum.

If the premises of Christians' ethical arguments are in the revealed sources of their own tradition, how can these arguments have any force for those who do not share these premises? If the premises of Christian arguments in Scripture and tradition are unimportant, then there is no reason to refer to them in developing a Christian ethical stance on public issues. But, if they are important, their intelligibility becomes a critical issue. Their content must be developed and communicated in ways which can enrich the public forum. The alternative is for Christians to retreat from publicness, to see the ethical implications of their tradition as relevant only for those who fully share its premises. Yet this would be to imply that the Christian Gospel can bear ethical fruit only for the church, and not for the world. It may benefit the world through the ethical life and witness of those who belong to both a Christian community and a wider, public community, but it cannot be part of a common and public search for ethical truth. A Christian ethics which draws on the resources of Christian tradition for the sake of the public realm must be both particular and universal, communal and public: it must affirm the foundations of its own traditions in the historicity of revelation, and yet demonstrate the relevance of the values implicit in these traditions for our common humanity.

THE COMMUNICATION OF ETHICS AND THE THEOLOGY OF REVELATION

The ethical situation in liberal societies can be characterized as a tension between pluralism and consensus. Such societies exhibit crucially important areas of consensus, centred on the rights of the individual and the primary values of freedom and tolerance. Many social and communal rights, as well, are the object of considerable consensus. At the same time, ethical pluralism has had profound and far-reaching effects in shaping the character of liberal societies. Our understandings of the meaning of human existence, of the goals of personal life, and of the relationship between individual and communal existence, are all strongly pluralist.

This tension between pluralism and consensus is the context in which the identity of Christian ethical communication is shaped. Different forms of Christian identity interpret this tension differently, assessing the potential for ethical communication – and the mode of that communication – accordingly. Christians face the task of discerning the possibilities for communication marked out by this tension: informed by fundamental theological perspectives on the nature of Christian identity, they must choose how to respond to a situation where possible options include a commitment to the broadening of consensus, the intensification and affirmation of particular stances and forms of communal life within the plurality of voices, as well as complex and particular negotiations between their own received traditions and new ethical perspectives emerging in the historical development of the societies of which they are a part.

Christians are called to communicate a fundamental ethical vision of the worth of persons in community, a vision based in the revelation of divine love. Yet, as we have seen in the previous chapter, the mode of communication of this vision is fundamentally affected by different understandings of Christian identity, conceived theologically in terms of different conceptions of revelation. These different conceptions are marked by contested interpretations of the relationships between the particularity of Christian narrative and general human experience, between the integrity of self-contained tradition and openness to historical change and innovation, between church and world. The previous chapter sought to develop a theology of revelation, informed by the focal concepts of mystery and historicity, which affirmed both the narrative character and the character of disclosure of Christian revelation, and the development of its meaning through a dialectical process of tradition in a pluralist historical context. The purpose of the present chapter is to explore the implications of this theology of revelation for the task of Christian ethical communication in the public forum, employing it both as a critical criterion for assessing different approaches and as the basis for the recommendation of a particular conception of this task.

How, then, should we conceive of a Christian ethical contribution to contemporary pluralist societies? One set of responses to this situation is based on the premise that a public ethics must be based on ethical insights drawn from rational reflection on human nature and human experience, without appealing to the content of particular traditions. This general approach has two major forms: one more closely associated with the natural law tradition, the other emphasizing the autonomy of ethics and more influenced by Kantianism. Characteristic of the 'natural law' version of this approach is an emphasis on the permanent importance and value of certain philosophical insights into the nature and purpose of human existence. For this approach, these insights should be the basis for common and public judgement on ethical matters. They are both communicable to anyone open to critical rationality, and sufficiently substantive to give society a sound ethical basis. From this perspective, Christian moral teaching should emphasize this shared body of insights, and not attempt to introduce uniquely or distinctively Christian claims, since they cannot be shared by others and do not belong in the public forum. For this conception, based in a substantive understanding of philosophical universalism, Christian faith can add distinctive motivation to our commitment to a common ethical enterprise, but it has nothing distinctive to offer to the content of this enterprise, since this content can be derived from public rationality.

This approach to natural law has a powerful commitment to universality and intelligibility, but it can pose a number of problems for Christian identity when this universality is conceived of in ways which lack a sense of historical development or the role of traditions. If there are substantive ethical stances which can be justified by a public metaphysics or a philosophy universally accessible to reason, then it becomes difficult to explain differences in ethical perspectives without being tempted to resort to a claim of the moral blindness of those who do not share belief in what is claimed to be universally evident. We need only recall how obsolete some purported contents of natural law have become to be reminded how dangerous and misguided such a claim can be. Further, a rationalist and ahistorical conception of natural law runs the risk of cutting the church off from the historical process through which the meaning of fundamental ethical values is found – a process grounded in the lived experience of those who seek to give expression to ethical traditions in concrete forms of life. A purportedly universalist ethics which is cut off from this historical process can become little more than assertion, acquiring a dogmatism and authoritarianism which is in direct proportion to its claimed universalism.

The other form of this conception, which emphasizes the autonomy of ethical reasoning in a broadly Kantian tradition, does not encounter these problems, since it is based not on a body of ethical knowledge claiming permanent validity, but rather on a process of ethical reasoning emphasizing the worth of the human person in a historical process of development.[1] This approach emphasizes the autonomy of the ethical – of practical reasoning in its own right – from religious traditions, while at the same time setting ethics within a Christian context through its distinctive motivation and intentionality. This

[1] In general terms, this conception is characteristic of the 'autonomy school' in Catholic moral theology, particularly as represented by J. Fuchs, A. Auer and B. Schüller. Fuchs' 'Gibt es eine spezifisch christliche Moral?', *Stimmen der Zeit* 185 (1970): 99–112, and Auer's *Autonome Moral und christlicher Glaube* (Düsseldorf: Patmos, 1971, second edition 1984) were two of the most influential expressions of this approach. During the 1970s, this school of thought was challenged by those arguing for a morality based specifically on Christian faith, notably B. Stoeckle, *Grenzen der autonomen Moral* (Munich: Kösel, 1974), and J. Ratzinger, *Prinzipien christlicher Moral* (Einsiedeln: Johannes Verlag, 1975). A somewhat different version of the 'autonomous morality' approach, giving more emphasis to the role of revelation, was expressed by W. Korff, in his *Norm und Sittlichkeit* (Mainz: Matthias Grünewald, 1973), and K. Demmer, in, e.g., *Deuten und Handeln* (Freiburg im Breisgau: Herder, 1985). In his *Faith and Ethics – Recent Roman Catholicism* (Dublin: Gill and Macmillan, Washington: Georgetown University Press, 1985) Vincent MacNamara noted that 'a great lack in the debate has been some discussion of the key term, i.e. revelation' (89). MacNamara went on to argue that both parties seem to be using the Vatican I notion of revelation: the *Glaubensethik* school refers to the moral truths found in Scripture, while the autonomy school 'regards a revealed morality as carrying the implication of being unintelligible'. Thus 'what divides the parties is also what unites them'. MacNamara noted the need for a contemporary theology of revelation to be applied to these problems. The critical lacuna that MacNamara identified was further reflected in an undeveloped sense of the role of concrete traditions in their relationship to public communicative reasoning, an obstacle which, in Catholic theology, was principally overcome by David Tracy in his *The Analogical Imagination* (New York: Crossroads, 1981). For presentations and discussions of this debate as a whole, see C. Curran and R. McCormick, *The Distinctiveness of Christian Ethics*, Readings in Moral Theology 2 (New York/Ramsey: Paulist Press, 1980), N. Rigali, 'The Uniqueness and Distinctiveness of Christian Ethics', in *Moral Theology: Challenges for the Future. Essays in Honour of R.A. McCormick*, ed. C. Curran (Mahwah: Paulist, 1990).

approach has the great strength of emphasizing that ethics – as the recognition of the human good – must have a commonly intelligible and communicative character. Practical reasoning, if it does concern our common human welfare, must involve insights and processes of argument that are publicly communicable. Yet the weakness of this emphasis on the autonomy of ethics is its failure to attribute sufficient importance to the role of traditions in the development of a vision of the human good. The insights into the meaning of human existence that are at the foundation of practical reasoning are formed in traditions: in this crucial sense, ethical reasoning is not 'autonomous' from Christian tradition, but rather formed by it.

In his influential work *Autonome Moral und christlicher Glaube* (*Autonomous Morality and Christian Faith*), the German Catholic theologian Alfons Auer speaks of ethical value as grounded in the human experience of transcendence, as an assent to the claim that reality makes on us.[2] It is this experience, independent of any religious interpretation, which is the source of our awareness of ethical obligation. The distinctive contribution of Christian faith to ethics is in terms of its integrating, stimulating and critical functions, rather than as a tradition which embodies and enables this experience of transcendence in its own distinctive terms.[3]

Auer is right to emphasize that the response to ethical value springs from an experience of the transcendent character of the human which need not be explicitly linked with religious values. The key to his conception of the autonomy of the ethical is that the ethical response to the claim of reality is not linked to any assent to religious world-views: 'the real meaning and the immediate usefulness of the concept of the autonomy of morality is in its affirmation that the (ontological) foundations of practical ideals can be found in varying interpretations of the depth dimension of reality, some of which do not include radical metaphysical or religious commitments'.[4] Yet the interpretation of this 'depth dimension' as indeed communicating an ethical claim is linked with our interpretations of reality as a

[2] *Autonome Moral und christlicher Glaube* (Düsseldorf: Patmos, 1984 edition), 16–21.
[3] Ibid., 188–95.   [4] Ibid., 30.

whole: it is such traditions of interpretation that give the ethical claim a particular scope and force. An individual may not have made a personal decision in favour of a religious world-view, but may still be the heir of religious interpretations of human reality which give human persons a particular value. It is concrete religious traditions which have, historically speaking, made such interpretations of human existence possible, and which remain as the only contexts within which understandings of human transcendence are truly 'at home'.[5]

To speak of human beings as characterized by transcendence, or of a 'depth dimension of reality', is already to use categories of language and interpretation which are not shared by secular moral philosophy, precisely because the language of human transcendence is not 'at home' in philosophies which have renounced any ontology of the human. Chapter 2 of this study sought to demonstrate that contemporary neo-Kantianism grounds ethics not in human transcendence, in a substantive ethical sense of the word, but rather in various understandings of rational universalizability. The ethical project of this form of moral philosophy is the project of developing ethical paradigms which do not require appeal to the category of transcendence, with its metaphysical and religious associations. While (as argued in the previous chapter) concepts such as 'transcendence' can have a relative independence from particular traditions, in so far as they can become intelligible outside tradition-

---

[5] Auer notes that 'from the perspective of Christian revelation, in any case, human nature cannot be defined without this reference to transcendence' (ibid., 21). Yet this reference to revelation as the context within which the human person is known as transcendent runs counter to his attempt to show the essential independence of ethics from religious contexts of meaning. My own view is that the autonomy of morality does not consist in its independence from religious or metaphysical world views, but rather in the freedom of practical reason to make normative judgements within the horizon of meaning drawn by the meanings and values characteristic of a tradition. The great value of Auer's work is in its contribution to affirming this latter meaning of the autonomy of ethics. I would agree with K. Hilpert, in his *Ethik und Rationalität: Untersuchungen zum Autonomieproblem und zu seiner Bedeutung für die theologische Ethik* (Düsseldorf: Patmos Verlag, 1980), that Auer's reference to transcendence is problematic in a context intended to be independent of religious world-views (ibid., 562), but not with his contention that the notion of autonomy is essentially the product of atheistic humanism, and therefore of dubious usefulness in moral theology.

bearing communities, they do depend on such traditions for their coherence and sustaining background of meaning.

In general terms, Auer's approach expresses the paradigm of the relationship between reason and revelation characteristic of Vatican I's *Dei Filius*. For this paradigm, natural reason provides a universal capacity for insight into meaning and value which is subsequently supplemented and refined by the historical revealed traditions. Yet the experience of contemporary secular philosophy is that these meanings and values are not evident to a rationality shorn of all associations with historical traditions rooted in concrete disclosure.[6]

A second kind of response takes a very different stance on the question of the commonality of public ethical insight. For this conception, there is no substantive body of shared insight which can be sustained by a public metaphysics or by any substantive public consensus. The different conceptions of human nature and purpose that exist in contemporary pluralist societies provide no basis for agreement about moral claims that go beyond a bare minimum of respect for individual freedom and security and basic contractual obligations. Any public ethics can be based only on this minimum. Any more substantive ethics must be inextricably linked to the narratives of particular moral communities, narratives which are so closely fused with the communities that identify with them that they are unintelligible to others. The truth-claims of these particular narratives cannot become the basis of a public ethics.

This conception has at least two variants. One is a secular ethics which accepts radical ethical pluralism and argues that any public ethics, and the political and legal institutions associated with it, must be based on a minimalist contractarianism, which can tolerate diverse private ethical communities in its

[6] The critique of Auer's work by B. Stoeckle in his *Grenzen der autonomen Moral* was also characterized by a clear dependence on Vatican I's conception of revelation, criticizing what Stoeckle saw as the assumption that human beings can achieve a sufficient and reliable knowledge of their own nature without the help of any 'ausser- oder übermenschliche Auskunft' ('information from a source external to or beyond the human'), 86. The use of concepts of this kind supports MacNamara's judgement that a Vatican I conception of revelation both 'divided and united' the participants in the controversy between the proponents of an 'autonomous ethics' and an 'ethics of faith'.

midst, so long as they respect the radical difference between public and private worlds.[7] Another is a Christian ethics – and an understanding of Christian identity – which affirms the highly specific character of Christian life and Christian ethics and the radical distinctiveness of its concerns and priorities from those of the state and the public forum.[8] Both understand pluralist societies in terms of radical dissonance, and can agree on the necessity of a radical distinction between public and private ethical worlds, because the truth-claims of private worlds cannot be persuasively communicated in the public forum.

The conceptions of ethics as contractual rationality and as the particular ethos of the Christian community have in common a denial of the public relevance of Christian revelation. This is because both see this revelation as essentially particular, as the internal history of a confessing community. The meanings and values associated with this internal history cannot have relevance to the internal histories of other commu-

---

[7] A conception developed, for example, by H. Tristram Engelhardt in his *The Foundations of Bioethics* (New York: Oxford University Press, 1986). Engelhardt's dichotomy between an objective secular morality and the 'voluntary' morality of various cultural communities expresses a similar perspective to Peter Strawson's 'Social Morality and Individual Ideal', in *Christian Ethics and Contemporary Philosophy*, ed. I. Ramsey (London: SCM, 1965). For Strawson, too, there must be a distinction between certain fundamental social obligations and those life styles which express individual ideals. Strawson's discussion raises two crucial questions: whether the basic social obligations that he speaks of can in fact be adequately interpreted without any recourse to historical traditions of meaning and value which incapsulate religious or metaphysical concepts and insights, and whether these basic social obligations themselves, conceived in essentially contractual terms, do justice to the inalienable worth of the individual to which, as B. Mitchell notes, the 'traditional conscience', whether Christian or secular, owes allegiance (cf. Mitchell's discussion of Strawson's position in his *Morality: Religious and Secular* (Oxford: Clarendon Press, 1980), ch. 4).

[8] A position advocated by Stanley Hauerwas in his *A Community of Character: Towards a Constructive Christian Social Ethic* (University of Notre Dame Press, 1981) and many other works. In his *The Gospel in a Pluralist Society* (Grand Rapids: Eerdmans, 1989), Lesslie Newbigin argues that, although the church will promote programmes for social change, it is primarily the life of the local congregation 'as itself the foretaste of a different social order' (231) which will have something to offer to what is by now an essentially pagan society (218–19). Newbigin argues, however, that it is part of the role of the church 'to provide the public truth by which society can be given coherence and direction' (223), while Hauerwas's writings argue that the Christian narrative is so intimately connected with the life of Christian communities that Christian truth-claims cannot be communicated within the public forum.

nities, nor, *a fortiori*, to the public forum, which, through its pluralist character, is essentially a space devoid of meaning and value, a space which can be filled only by agreements between strangers.

What is crucial to this conception is the belief that a revealed tradition only has meaning and force for the particular community whose life, practices and world-view are comprehensively shaped by it. Stanley Hauerwas' most fundamental objection to conceptions of Christian ethics as informing or inspiring a public commitment to democracy and human rights is that such conceptions reduce Christian revelation to a species of 'knowledge' which can be dissociated from the believing community which is shaped and sustained by it. Both his moral philosophical perspectives, based in a conception of virtuous practices founded in narrative,[9] and his theological understanding of the church as a redeemed community in radical distinction from the secular world of violence,[10] motivate a rejection of any notion of the 'generalizability' of Christian ethical perspectives for the sake of a public ethics: 'to be saved is to be engrafted into a body that reconstitutes us by making us a part of a history not universally available. It is a history of real people whom God has made part of the Kingdom through forgiveness and reconciliation. Only a people so bodily formed can survive the temptation to become a "knowledge" in the name of democracy. Only such a people deserves to survive.'[11]

For Hauerwas, the danger of emphasizing the revealed character of the Bible is that it can 'give the impression that Scripture can be known and used apart from a community that

---

[9] See, for example, Hauerwas' critique of the 'standard account' of moral rationality in favour of an ethics of narrative, virtue and character in S. Hauerwas and D. Burrell, 'From System to Story: An Alternative Pattern for Rationality in Ethics', in *Why Narrative? Readings in Narrative Theology*, eds. S. Hauerwas and L. Gregory Jones (Grand Rapids: Eerdmans, 1989).

[10] A position developed at length in *The Peaceable Kingdom* (University of Notre Dame Press, 1981). Hauerwas firmly aligns himself with Milbank's account of 'the secular' in *Theology and Social Theory* (Oxford: Blackwell, 1990) in his 'Positioning: In the Church and University but not of Either', in *Dispatches from the Front: Theological Engagements with the Secular* (Durham and London: Duke University Press, 1994), 198.

[11] 'The Democratic Policing of Christianity', in *Dispatches from the Front*, 106.

has been formed and sustained by it'.[12] From the perspective of Hauerwas' narrative and communitarian ecclesiology, the concept of revelation can imply that Christian faith is a truth that can somehow be dissociated from the ethical praxis that makes it visible and active. To speak of Christianity as a resource for a public ethics is to imply that Christian revelation can have significance for the unconverted, that the 'world' can learn from Christian 'knowledge' without the transformation of life that must occur if this 'knowledge' is to have any intelligibility. The Christian church, for Hauerwas, does not serve the world by attempting to communicate Christian ethical perspectives to it, but rather by demonstrating the distinctiveness of the Christian form of communal life, a distinctiveness that is marked by the radicality of the difference between Christian and secular existence.[13]

The two kinds of response exemplified in the thought of Alfons Auer and Stanley Hauerwas demonstrate fundamental differences in their implicit theology of revelation. In Auer's approach, ethics can be said to be 'autonomous' in the sense that the affirmation of human transcendence need not involve a link to its source and context in historical religious traditions. In Hauerwas' perspective, by contrast, Christian revelation – understood especially as the narrative character of Scripture – becomes intelligible only to those who are a part of a highly distinctive faith community, living a life transformed by this narrative. While the first approach, in Rahner's terms, dissociates 'transcendental' from 'categorial' revelation, the experience of human value from the historical traditions which mediate it, the second is informed by a theology of revelation which rejects both the point and possibility of communicating Christian revelation to the 'world': the point – because of the radical ethical difference between Christian existence and modern secularity; the possibility – because of the incoherence of a notion of revelation as 'knowledge' which can be abstracted from the life of a faithful community.

---

[12] *A Community of Character*, 57.
[13] See, for example, Hauerwas' argument in 'The Church and Liberal Democracy', in *A Community of Character*, Part 1.

Commensurate with their radically different theologies of revelation, these two kinds of response are strongly at variance in their judgement of the character of pluralist societies. The first argues for the possibility of substantive common insights based on a common philosophical culture, the other for a minimalist public ethics and a rich but incommunicable private ethics. In terms of the tension between ethical consensus and ethical pluralism, while the first response projects a consensus based on autonomous ethical principles, underestimating the influence of concrete traditions, the second exaggerates the extent of pluralism and neglects the potential for mutual understanding between traditions. Both of these options are inadequate because they misread the character of pluralist societies and the associated relationship between shared rationality and particular traditions.

The first conception – especially in its 'natural law' variant – conceives public ethical rationality as a substantive body of truths which can be agreed on independently of the insights evoked by particular narrative traditions. This fails to recognize that the coherence and meaning of substantive ethical insights is associated with visions of human nature and purpose which derive from such traditions. This conception conceives of philosophical reflection as an independent source of substantive ethical insights, rather than as a discipline of critical reflection on the ethical significance of the concrete traditions of meaning and value given in culture. For this conception, it is difficult to explain, for example, why there is such massive disagreement about the question of abortion, since the rights and wrongs of the matter should be open to the philosophic and scientific consensus of a common ethical culture.

The second option, by contrast, misinterprets our situation by denying the real elements of common culture which are present in pluralist societies and the public influence of particular narrative traditions. It does not do justice to the significant areas of consensus between different religious and ethical traditions over substantive questions of human rights, which play an important role in pluralist societies. It fails to acknowledge that ethical movements inspired by particular religious discourses have made crucial contributions to a public ethics of human dignity. In terms of Christian identity, it implies a theology of revelation which gives inadequate attention to the relationship between the particularity and universality of the divine self-communication, the incarnation in Christ and the work of the Spirit in the world.

It is necessary, then, to argue for a third conception which can do justice to the reality of cultural pluralism, to the significant elements of ethical consensus, and to the public contribution that particular traditions can make to this common culture. This third conception does not deny the existence of elements of a common ethical culture, but shows an awareness that such a common culture can only be sustained and enriched by drawing on the communicative potential of particular traditions. It interprets the traditional notion of natural law not as a body of philosophical insights that are independent of tradition, but rather as an affirmation of the possibility of genuine and substantive communication between traditions. Such communication gives an important role to mediating principles, which – as argued in the previous chapter – can achieve a relative independence from specific traditional contexts and a degree of public intelligibility. This conception rejects the radical bifurcation of public forum and private communitarian tradition by arguing for the possibility of particular traditions achieving significant mutual intelligibility and contributing sustaining insights to the life of the public forum. Such a conception, I would argue, is most appropriate to conceiving the task of Christian ethical communication today.

The first two conceptions tend to conceive of Christian ethics and public ethics in 'two-tiered' terms. For the first conception, invoking a public metaphysics or the autonomy of ethics, the Christian community itself responds to the distinctive appeal and challenge of the Gospel, while, outside this community, the God-given power of 'right reason' enables all people of good will to recognize and respond to the fundamental goods of human existence. For the second option, based on a strictly narrative approach, encounters and relationships outside particular communities are governed by essentially contractual or prudential considerations. Within particular communities, a strong and substantive mutuality is possible, but necessarily without significant influence on practice and legislation in the public forum. What is intended by this third conception is a challenge to the 'two-tiered' character of the other conceptions – in particular, a challenge to any insistence on the 'impermeability' of the division between the two 'tiers'.

It is evident that this third conception is closer to the first than the second. While the first conception saw 'natural law' or autonomous morality as informed by the content of a commonly held philosophy, the third conception argues that the concept of 'natural law' refers to what can be assented to by a communicative process of public rationality, drawing on the traditions which share public space in a pluralist culture. The third conception differs from the first in so far as it does not posit a world known by 'reason' distinct from a world known by 'faith tradition', or a 'transcendence' independent of traditions of disclosure, but rather recognizes that all perspectives on the world are influenced by concrete tradition – in this sense, it attempts to reflect more adequately the difference between the theologies of revelation of Vatican I's *Dei Filius* and Vatican II's *Dei Verbum*, and to express what I have called a theology of mediation. What the first and third conceptions have in common, however, in marked and significant difference from the second, is the emphasis on the substantial character of a public ethics, on the possibility of achieving a public ethical consciousness that goes beyond the limits of a minimalist contractarian ethic. In this sense, the third conception is an attempt to preserve the best features of the first in the light of a post-modern cultural consciousness.[14]

[14] The commonalities and differences between these two conceptions are discernible in the two key statements of the American Catholic Bishops' Conference on public ethical matters. It is the express intention of *The Challenge of Peace* (Washington, D.C.: National Conference of Catholic Bishops, 1983) to address two distinct but overlapping audiences that require two complementary but distinct styles of teaching. In essential continuity with more traditional conceptions of natural law, this pastoral letter employs the distinction between 'the premises of the Gospel' and 'a conscience based on reason' as the principal means of identifying the two different (albeit 'overlapping') audiences of Catholics and 'the wider civil community, a more pluralistic audience' (11). The subsequent pastoral, *Economic Justice For All* (1986),

What are the implications of this third conception? As we have seen, it is based on the premises that a substantive common ethical culture is not simply given, that it must draw on particular traditions, and that these particular traditions are communicable or intelligible in the public forum. These premises, however, are disputed, since it could be argued that if such particular traditions are intelligible in the public forum, then their intelligibility is explained by the fact that they appeal to commonly shared insights. But, if these insights are indeed commonly shared, then the contribution made by these particular traditions is not in fact distinctive, but is rather an affirmation of what is already publically known, a philosophical commonplace.

This conception, then, faces the challenge of showing that it is not in fact alternating between the two other conceptions: that it is either simply reaffirming truths that are philosophical commonplaces, in which case there is no need for them to be sustained by the vision of particular traditions, or else introducing points of view which are not communicable or intelligible in the public forum, and thereby perpetuating the dichotomy between public and private ethical worlds. The attempt to show the public relevance of Christian narrative might, in fact, be no more than the affirmation of ethical insights which are both logically and culturally quite independent of any and all tradition, in which case the reference to Christian narrative is superfluous, or the assertion of a distinctively Christian ethical position, based on Christian narrative, which is incommunicable to other groups in the public forum. What is at stake is the possibility of achieving common insight in a cultural situation where it is recognized that such commonality must be based on

> displays a greater emphasis on the role of tradition as the formative source of ethical insights, as well as a more historical sense of the relationships between faith and reason and of the influence of traditions beyond their 'home' community. This document has its basis in a conviction of the worth of persons, which has biblical roots but 'is also supported by a long tradition of theological and philosophical reflection and through the reasoned analysis of human experience' (15), a convergence of traditions which is reflected in the fact that the 'overall Christian perspective on economic ethics' is 'subscribed to by many who do not share Christian religious convictions' (32).

an acceptance that meaning and value have their source in particular experiences mediated by tradition.

This approach also faces very real challenges in terms of Christian identity, since it must embrace the task of expressing this identity through engagement with the plurality of voices and traditions which claim a hearing in our contemporary world. Christian identity is rooted in the historical particularity of revelation in Christ, and Christian ethical communication must always seek to express the distinctive meaning of the Christian Gospel. At the same time – as was argued in the previous chapter – a full response to the mystery of Christ implies an openness to truth, the gift of the Spirit, wherever it is found. Informed by such a conception of Christian identity, the Christian community must commit itself to developing ethical consensus and a sense of global ethical community through the difficult process of dialogue between world religious and philosophical traditions. Further, it must acknowledge that any process of dialogue is marked by reciprocity, and that the path of coming to know the other is also the way to a new self-knowledge – for Christians, a new knowledge of Christ.

Such a conception of Christian communication is based in Christian identity while at the same time being open to the public community. As we have seen, it is grounded in a particular theology of revelation, one that affirms both its particularity and historicity and its universal scope and relevance. This theology of revelation, advocated in the previous chapter, differentiates itself from a strictly narrative, post-liberal or cultural–linguistic theology of revelation by its emphasis on this bond between particularity and universality, on the potential communicability of the meanings of Christian revelation, a communicability based in their resonance with the 'internal word' of the Spirit in the hearts of women and men. In my own account, this theology drew heavily on theologies of mystery, transcendence and universal history. It is now time to consider a different attempt to link the particularity of Christian ethics with public communicability, on the basis of a Barthian theology of the word.

In his *Community, Liberalism and Christian Ethics*,[15] David Fergusson shows strong sympathy for communal understandings of Christian ethics, and at the same time argues for the need for a Christian understanding of 'moral perception outwith the Christian community'.[16] He seeks 'to defend many of the criticisms and insights of theological communitarianism, while yet maintaining a commitment to a residual liberalism'.[17] This theological stance attempts likewise to do justice to the church's position in liberal societies, a situation 'which is neither establishment nor marginalization', in which the church must both differentiate itself from secular society and at the same time contribute to the common good.

To understand and maintain this commitment to public moral dialogue and the common good, what is needed 'is a theological explanation of why there might be common ground in the absence of common theory', a theological expression of a 'simultaneous commitment to ontological realism and epistemological contextualism'.[18] For Fergusson, this can be achieved on the basis of Barthian theological principles, since 'The character of the world as created and redeemed by God in Jesus Christ as the arena for the action of the Holy Spirit, and as moving towards an eschatological identity already revealed, provides a basis for explaining moral activity everywhere.'[19]

This search for 'common ground without common theory' on Barthian principles informs Fergusson's critique of aspects of Lindbeck's and Hauerwas' communal interpretations of the theology of revelation and of Christian ethics. In Fergusson's view, Lindbeck's theology of revelation leaves unresolved the question of the knowability of God. A rule theory of doctrine and an interpretation of religious tradition in cultural–linguistic terms cannot, for Fergusson, give sufficient account of the connection between the mode of signification and the thing signified. This gap in Lindbeck's theory calls for 'a doctrine of revelation which defends the notion that, in some sense, God is, within God's own self, who God is for us in the stories of Israel

---

[15] Cambridge University Press, 1998. New Studies in Christian Ethics.
[16] Ibid., 7.   [17] Ibid., 172.   [18] Ibid., 166, 167.   [19] Ibid., 166.

and Jesus'.[20] This problem of the link between Christian narrative and the reality of divine revelation also has a bearing on the universality and communicability of that revelation. Although Fergusson defends Lindbeck from a general charge of isolationism,[21] he does note that Lindbeck, in contrast to MacIntyre, does not have 'any notion of translatability in the presentation of the cultural–linguistic model of religion. This absence prevents due attention being devoted to the possibility of cross-fertilization between traditions and to the influencing of a tradition by external forces.'[22]

Fergusson's critique of Hauerwas is informed by a strong sense of the need to distinguish between revelation as the informing principle of a community's life and revelation as an event to which the church bears witness. Hauerwas' constant emphasis on the communal character and context of Christian faith means that the principal weakness in his theology is 'its overdetermination of the distinctiveness of the church. This is reflected both in an attenuated reading of the person and work of Christ, and in a reluctance to describe the possibility of ethical perception and action outwith the Christian community.'[23] Hauerwas emphasizes community in ways which threaten the pre-eminence of Christology, since 'the church is not the extension of the incarnation, but exists to bear witness and to live faithfully in light of this unrepeatable and unsubstitutable event'.[24] This tension in Hauerwas' theology between the church as 'extension of the incarnation' and as witness to it is linked, for Fergusson, with the problems in Lindbeck's approach, since there is a danger that a cultural–linguistic model of religion 'reduces theological truth to performance according to the form of life created by the narratives of Scripture'. While this account does 'capture the self-involving nature of religious language', it can jeopardise 'the realist claim that the truth is not of our own making', but rather 'constituted by the way things are independently of and prior to correct performance'.[25]

The answer to this danger of linking the truth of revelation to

[20] Ibid., 38. [21] Ibid., 41. [22] Ibid., 132.
[23] Ibid., 67. [24] Ibid., 69. [25] Ibid., 70.

performance can be found, for Fergusson, in a distinction between 'the linguistic practices of the community, the words of Scripture and that to which these ultimately refer'.[26] In a Barthian perspective, this requires a threefold understanding and stratification of the Word of God as including the witness of the church, the words of Scripture and Jesus Christ, the Word of God revealed: 'The confession of the church depends upon the normative witness to Scripture. Yet Scripture itself only bears witness through the activity of the Spirit to its central theme and object, Jesus Christ.'[27] An emphasis on the distinction between Christ and the church is also a means of emphasizing Christ's relationship to the world, since 'a theology which distinguishes more clearly between the Word of God *extra nos* and the church's testimony to it, has the resource to account for the possibility of secular witness'.[28]

The recognition of the work of the Spirit outside the church, then, is based on a theology of revelation which emphasizes that the church always remains a witness to a divine truth which can, in some sense, be known and responded to outside its confines. What does this mean for an ecclesially conceived ethics? Is it 'capable of accommodating and reinterpreting older claims about natural law, the orders of creation and natural rights'?[29] If the church can communicate on ethical matters with society as a whole, this can contribute to a common 'vision of the common good', since 'a religion which presents human life as a gift held in trust, as having a purpose conferred upon it, and as capable by grace of achieving a measure of goodness is likely to have an important social role to exercise'.[30] The church's contribution to the common good must have some means of common moral appeal, and the language of human rights is the only plausible candidate for any global moral language.[31]

While founded in the distinctiveness of the divine incarnation in Christ, the Christian church can communicate with other perspectives and traditions in a pluralist society in order to affirm and uphold the common good, to recognize 'common

[26] Ibid.   [27] Ibid., 71.   [28] Ibid., 74.   [29] Ibid., 78.
[30] Ibid., 154–5.   [31] Ibid., 168–9.

ground without common theory'. What is called for is a 'differentiated yet positive relationship between the common good that is sought by the Christian community and those principles on which civil organization is founded', a relationship correlating with a proper distinction between church and state.[32] The church needs some doctrine of the state since it 'seeks something like a social consensus concerning religious toleration and freedom . . . a polity which will respect the conditions under which it can worship and witness'.[33] Christian theology can affirm secular claims about the dignity of the person and the rights of the individual on the basis of the affirmation of that religious freedom which is essential to the life of the church itself.

The key to Fergusson's account of an ecclesial ethics which is engaged with public questions of the common good lies in a theology of revelation which sees the church as witness to a divine revelation of universal scope and significance. This accords with my own emphasis, in the previous chapter, on the distinction between the narrative of Christian tradition and the history of revelation to which it bears witness. This distinction was emphasized as crucial to a recognition of the work of the Spirit in the world, and of the possibility of the church's understanding of the mystery of Christ being challenged and deepened through its encounter with the world. To this extent, a theology of revelation which draws on Barth's theology of the word and a theology of revelation which owes much to Karl Rahner can be in accord on the key principles which undergird a publicly communicable Christian ethics.

At the same time, the differences between these approaches are informed by differences in the theology of revelation, principally in terms of the meaning of Spirit in the world. By seeing the church essentially as witness, a theology of the word lessens the ethical contrast between church and world and recognizes that divine revelation is oriented to all humanity: the church is epistemologically privileged, as the witness to divine revelation, but an ontologically realist stance affirms the objec-

[32] Ibid., 156. [33] Ibid., 159.

tivity of divine revelation's universal scope and the work of the Spirit in the world. Yet, for reasons based in classical positions in Reformed theology, this recognition of the work of the Spirit in the world is not complemented by a theology of human transcendence. My own presentation of a communicable Christian ethics – reflecting in a similar way a debt to Catholic classics – emphasizes such a theology of human transcendence as the anthropological counterpart of an emphasis on the Spirit's work in the world. As has been argued, a theology of transcendence is grounded in and energized by particular revealed tradition, yet at the same time is authorized by revelation itself to recognize human transcendence as universal. From the perspective of a theology of the word, an anthropology of human transcendence threatens the gratuity and uniquely saving power of the Word of God by overstating the revealing presence of the Spirit, the *verbum internum*, in the heart of the human person as the 'image of God'. Yet from the perspective of a theology of human transcendence, the affirmation of the Spirit's work in the world can only be meaningful if it resonates with the *verbum internum*, that prior gift of the Spirit which enables us to hear the Spirit's promptings in the concrete circumstances of life.

What difference does this make in specific terms for the relationship between church and world? As we have seen, there are fundamental commonalities between Fergusson's approach and my own. Yet the difference in terms of a theology of human transcendence has significant effects for the interpretation of the meaning of human rights and the relations between church and state. Fergusson notes that 'it is not clear that the concept of human rights is necessarily tethered to the assumptions of liberal individualism'.[34] Despite the criticisms levelled against it, he argues that the language of human rights can articulate the 'minimum conditions necessary for membership of a moral community' on 'the basis of a substantive notion of the common good'. This implies the recognition of a 'thin' uni-

---

[34] Ibid., 168.

versal morality distinct from the 'thick' moralities of particular communities of meaning.

These arguments can support the church's commitment to human rights in the public forum, but they lack specifically theological justification, a justification important for giving commitment to human rights a role in the church's own self-understanding. If human rights – as the expression of human dignity in community – are based in a theology of human transcendence, for which the 'image of God' concept is a *locus classicus*, then they can become a constitutive part of the church's self-consciousness as a witness to God's work in the world. Further, if – as the previous chapter sought to demonstrate – the church's understanding of the mystery of Christ is deepened by its engagement with the world, especially with human suffering, then its commitment to human dignity and human rights must be integral to its theological self-understanding.

Fergusson's justification for the role of the neutral, liberal state is conceived in explicitly theological terms, since only such a state can give believers religious freedom and the church the 'social space' it needs as a worshipping community. In this sense, liberal freedoms can be given an explicitly theological grounding, a grounding of key importance to the historical origins of the liberal state as a means of protecting religious freedom. Further, since both church and state are penultimate to the Kingdom itself, the state can have an 'ameliorative role of protecting citizens from abuses'.[35] These theological considerations drawn from the nature of religious freedom and from eschatology are powerful arguments for a state which does not intrude on the individual's spiritual freedom and which is modest in its claims to power and efficacy. They are less effective in justifying the role of the state as an active agent for the common good, as an expression of the communal character of human existence which can play an effective role in limiting the power of private economic interest and providing some of the conditions for human flourishing in the context of equality of opportunity. Such a justification for the state's positive role –

[35] Ibid., 158.

which must always be tempered by the theologically grounded limitations on the state that Fergusson draws attention to – can be offered by a theology of human dignity in community grounded in a transcendent relationship to God, which can act as a powerful source of the affirmation of democratic institutions. The major concern of the second chapter of this book was to argue that such a theology can affirm the ethical and political universality of neo-Kantianism, while giving a theological ground to human dignity about which neo-Kantianism must remain agnostic.

ETHICAL INSIGHT AND RELIGIOUS DISCOURSE

I have argued that conceptions of the communication of Christian ethics in the public forum are formed by notions of Christian identity based in a theology of revelation. This led to an advocacy of an approach based on a theology of revelation that seeks to unify particularity and universality, and that, unlike the two other conceptions described and criticized in this discussion, affirms both the rootedness of a sense of human dignity and human transcendence in particular tradition and the recognition and affirmation of their universality as an integral part of the church's own self-understanding and mission.

What role, then, should specifically religious discourse play in Christian ethical communication in the public forum? If the conception I am advocating is to be coherent, religious discourse should be seen *neither* as superfluous to ethical insight *nor* so essential to it that ethical insights cannot be shared without fully sharing in the faith described by religious discourse. This means that the role of religious discourse in ethical communication should be conceived as evoking and enriching possibilities of ethical insight, which are intelligible in their own terms. Substantive ethical insights have their source and coherence in the vision of human existence characteristic of religious discourse, but, if this ethical insight is indeed an insight into truth, a truth about our common human life, then its truth can be evident in ethical terms, in the heightened possibilities of common human life that it can enable. Since ethics is practical, the spirit of human *praxis*, then the truth of ethical insight becomes evident in the *praxis* that it informs.

This conception, then, makes a distinction between the coherence of the vision of life associated with a particular form of ethical practice, and the intelligibility and meaningfulness of such practice in experiential terms. It argues that religious visions of life are linked, in fundamental ways, with the vision of human existence and destiny associated with forms of ethical practice, especially all those forms which go beyond a minimalist contractarian ethics between independent agents. At the same time, it recognizes that ethical practice, because it enhances the goods of our common human existence, can be intelligible in its own terms, without explicit reference to the broader visions of life and foundational beliefs which give it coherence. This means that, to a certain extent, it is possible to communicate the meaning of an ethical vision in practical ethical terms, without presupposing that its background beliefs must also be accepted.[36]

It can be argued, for example, that the virtue of altruism has ultimate coherence only within a theological conception of human existence, since, for any individual, devotion to the path of altruism must be made on the basis of an assurance that it will be a path leading to self-fulfilment through love of others, rather than merely to destruction at the hands of exploiters – an

---

[36] In his *Deuten und Handeln*, K. Demmer stresses the complex and dialectical character of the process by which religious traditions influence ethical insight and practice. For Demmer, there is no direct connection between religious world-views and ethical norms, but such world-views do provide a new context within which ethical insight and judgement take place: 'Correspondences are perceived between faith and ethical insight, mediated through faith's anthropological implications' (94). The revelation of God in Jesus Christ changed the fundamental presuppositions of ethical insight and practice, giving rise to a significant historical influence of Christian faith on the content of ethics (110). Because of this significant but indirect relationship between faith and ethics, Demmer speaks of the 'relational autonomy' of ethical reason. It is autonomous within its own sphere, but cannot be grounded purely formally, without some reference to its content, and this content relates to a historical field of conditions (79–81). The stress in chapter 3 and the present chapter on the 'relative independence' from concrete tradition of such concepts as transcendence is also intended to affirm both the context of such concepts in traditions of narrative and disclosure, and their power to illuminate human experience beyond the confines of the communities which bear such traditions.

assurance based on faith in the meaningfulness and benevolence of providence, or, in Kant's terms, on the existence of a 'highest good' which reconciles virtue and happiness. At the same time, once certain conceptions of altruism become influential in a culture, their inherent ethical value becomes evident through the sheer appeal of the praxis they make possible, and they can be adopted by many who have no belief in the theological horizons which originally formed their ultimate context.

Since Christian discourse, which derives from revelation, is a discourse about God's purposes for human life, then its ethical implications must have a concrete and intelligible meaning in terms of that human life, a meaning which has a practical and self-evidential quality. Any other understanding of Christian ethics breaks the fundamental unity of God as creator and God as revealer, God as the source of the goodness of human life and relationships and God-in-Christ as the revelation of the eschatological destiny of human persons. This is not to deny that we receive a particular vision of creation through revelation, nor to assert that an ethics which purports to be based on creation can in any sense bypass the specific content of Christian revelation. What it does affirm is that the self-revealing God is the God of creation, and that the possibilities for human existence evoked in Christian discourse are possibilities that develop and enrich the meanings inherent in the goods of creation.

The role of religious discourse, then, is both to evoke and to give coherence to new possibilities of ethical meaning, which can be communicated and understood in ethical terms. Yet this does not mean that religious discourse is a ladder which can be thrown aside once the heights of ethical perspective have been reached. While ethical insights have a real practical intelligibility apart from the discourse that evokes them, they do depend for their continued vigour and coherence on the enrichment they derive from such discourse. Ethics has a truth evident in practice, but this truth of practice seeks a world of meaning within which it makes sense to be committed to that kind of practice. Consider the traditional principle of the universal destination of created goods.[37] Religious discourse is the source of this principle, since it invokes creation by a benevolent God as the origin both of the goods of the earth and of the equal dignity of human beings. The role of these religious convictions is to provide a transcendent ground for a principle of fundamental equality in the distribution of goods. Although the principle has its source in religious discourse, since it invokes the concept of creation and a purposeful creator, based in the stories of creation, it is intelligible in practical ethical terms to those who do not share religious faith in a benevolent creator. A principle of fundamental equality in the distribution of goods, which limits the right to private property in reasonably concrete ways, is a principle which is highly controversial in the political forum but quite intelligible in practical terms. The social solidarity that it calls for is a form of life whose value for human beings has an evident practical appeal.

Belief in the created or gifted character of this world, then, is not essential to the public forum's openness to this principle. It can be stated as an ethical principle of equality of access to the fundamental necessities of life, without recourse to religious language. As such, it can act as a key source of particular social policies and objectives. Yet religious discourse remains a crucial source of the coherence and force of this principle, a principle subjected to critique by various ideologies of individualism. Practical ethical commitment to this principle is sustained by an understanding of human existence within which it is a clear imperative. Without such a background understanding, a principle may have practical intelligibility, but lose its persuasive force as an ethical principle which expresses the true character of human communal existence. An understanding of radical human equality as grounded in creation can affirm the principle

[37] As stated, for example, in *Gaudium et Spes*, 69: 'God destined the earth and all it contains for all people and nations so that all created things would be shared fairly by all humankind under the guidance of justice tempered by charity. No matter how property is structured in different countries, adapted to their lawful institutions according to various and changing circumstances, we must never lose sight of this universal destination of earthly goods. In their use of things people should regard the external goods they lawfully possess as not just their own but common to others as well, in the sense that they can benefit others as well as themselves' (Flannery, *Vatican II*, 248–9).

of the universal destination of the goods of the earth against understandings of human existence that make exclusive and absolute connections between human desert and human achievement. In contrast, an argument for an unlimited right of private property derived from individual freedom, opportunity and effort may express a philosophy of individualism based ultimately on a vision of the world as an intrinsically meaningless terrain awaiting the stamp of human self-assertion. The role of religious discourse is to affirm a coherent vision of human existence within which human freedom and human equality can be understood in relation to a God of freedom who has created human beings with a fundamentally equal dignity. Such a vision can provide the sustaining context of meaning which can affirm the principle of equality of access to fundamental necessities in a context of ideological tension.

Similarly, the ethical concept that every human being has equal worth in the most fundamental sense must be generally intelligible and must bear fruit in recognizable human goods. Hence the argument that democracy is the polity most likely to bring peace, security and wealth to its citizens. Yet this does not mean that religious conceptions have no sustaining relationship to the conception of human nature at its root. Most democracies ensure, to a varying extent, the welfare of those who have nothing to contribute to the general community in terms of generally recognized 'goods'. As J. L. Mackie notes, reasoning from a strictly secular and empiricist viewpoint, such welfare is a 'gratuitous extension of morality'.[38] It is in accord with the fundamental dispositions of some moral traditions, but religious doctrines of human worth are integral parts of those traditions. It was part of the argument of chapter 2 that an infinite foundation for human worth in *communio* with God gives the human community of discourse a unique scope and depth, so that the inclusion of all, however marginalized, is not 'a gratuitous extension of morality' but rather the achievement of its true meaning.

In summary, then, I have argued that the Christian tradition

---

[38] *Ethics: Inventing Right and Wrong* (Harmondsworth: Penguin, 1977), 194.

does inform general ethical principles that can be enunciated independently of a specifically religious background and that have a practical evidential quality. These principles, however, are sustained by their relationship to a set of background beliefs embedded in religious discourse. These background beliefs provide a context of meaning that supports the coherence of ethical principles, as well as maintaining their strength and plausibility in the context of ideological conflict. The role of this sustaining religious discourse is particularly important in the dialectic, characteristic of a pluralist culture, between practical understandings of the human good and various visions of human nature.[39] Practical principles receive assent through the human fulfilment they enable, but this assent is limited and insecure if such principles appeal to goods which have no place within larger visions of life. The principle of the universal destination of goods, for example, is insecure in relation to an understanding of life which is fundamentally in terms of individual achievement. This reciprocal relationship between practical principles and larger visions of meaning and value is a crucial aspect of Christian ethical communication in the public forum.

The role of religious background beliefs for ethics can also be expressed in terms of the importance for ethical action of reflective self-understanding. If self-understanding is an important accompaniment and illumination of motivation and action, then the interpretation of the foundations of the moral life will affect the extent to which we seek to alter or strengthen our dispositions, to intensify or ignore them. An interpretation of

[39] In his *Religion in Public Life* (Washington, D.C.: Georgetown University Press, 1996), Ronald Thiemann notes that John Rawls allows for an appeal to 'comprehensive doctrines', including religious beliefs, in situations when society is not well-ordered, so long as the purpose of this appeal is to restore the ideal of public reason itself (*Political Liberalism* New York: Columbia University Press, 1993), Lecture VI, part 8, 'The Limits of Public Reason'). Thiemann interprets this as a 'small, but welcomed opportunity for religious convictions to enter public debate; however, the opening created by this argument may be far wider than Rawls supposes' (86), since liberal societies are not so well ordered that they have a stable and continuing 'overlapping consensus'. The meaning and application of democratic values are, to the contrary, continually contested and negotiated and 'comprehensive doctrines', including religious beliefs, play a key role in this process (87–8).

the world which judges objective and universal moral claims to be unintelligible and illusory may modify moral dispositions to the extent that, for example, the moral claim is felt to be no longer a transcendent and universal human bond, but rather a type of prudential reciprocity necessary to the stability or survival of particular, local human societies. Similarly, an interpretation of the moral life which integrates it into a religious vision may reinforce and develop specifically moral dispositions, giving self-understanding to an individual's experience of value in human relationships by offering an interpretation of human existence in terms of God's creative love.

This relationship between the practical intelligibility of ethical principles and their dependence on a context of religious belief relates to the notion of mediating principles, often expressed in terms of a philosophical or theological anthropology, which was discussed in chapters 2 and 3. Such mediating principles as – for example – the universal destination of goods, the sanctity of life and the dignity of the human person are both context-dependent in a logical or theoretical sense and intelligible in their own terms in ethical practice. They do not derive from a tradition-independent metaphysics, since they all spring ultimately from religious visions of existence. Yet they can be invoked without specific appeal to such religious background beliefs. Their intelligibility and plausibility, however, is critically subject to particular states of cultural and ethical consensus or conflict. All of this has crucial implications for the understanding of 'natural law', not as a statement of tradition-independent metaphysical principles, but rather as an expression of such mediating principles, which derive from the contexts of meaning formed by religious traditions, yet have a relative independence from them. In this sense, 'natural law' is a crucially important recognition of human commonalities, and at the same time limited in its influence and persuasiveness by the degree of consensus between the traditions of meaning and value that are influential in a particular cultural context.

This understanding of the role of religious discourse in relation to ethical communication is informed by the theology of revelation and tradition developed in the previous chapter, which understood the union of universality and particularity to be based in the historicity of the revelation of the infinite mystery of God. Because revelation is the revelation of the mystery of the God who is creator and saviour, it evokes ethical insight into the universal meaning of creation: as mystery, its development in tradition is open to the unpredictable growth that interaction with human history will bring. Further, because revelation is founded in historical epiphany, the true meaning and coherence of creation, and of the ethical insights which seek to respond to the goods of creation, are grounded in the power of Christian narrative, concretely, in the person of the risen Christ.

WITNESS, VISION AND NORM

What does all this mean for the ways in which Christians should seek to communicate their ethical beliefs as a contribution to the public forum? Given that not everyone shares a commitment of faith to Christian narrative, but that Christian ethical beliefs can have a practical public intelligibility, dependent on particular situations of cultural consensus or conflict, what kinds of communication of these beliefs can occur? How is Christian identity expressed in this communication? In the first place, it is crucial to focus on the church as the subject of communication, a church whose own sense of identity will shape the ways in which it communicates with society as a whole. A reflection on Christian ethical communication must first consider the church itself as communicator.

The Christian church is a community founded in the historical particularity of the revelation of God in Jesus of Nazareth. Its life focusses on the retelling and celebration of this event, the irrevocable and definitive self-communication of God to humanity. The church witnesses to Christ through discipleship, through the attempt to follow his path in word and deed, and imitate his complete and self-emptying devotion to the coming of the Kingdom of God, the Kingdom that will usher in a realm of love, justice and freedom for all creation. Through this life of discipleship, inspired by word and sacrament, the church becomes a community of ethical life, a community which seeks to develop its members in a life of virtue, especially those virtues most characteristic of Jesus of Nazareth – compassion, forgiveness, justice, reconciliation. The church seeks to be a community where all members know themselves to be equal as disciples of Jesus, one body in a community of love which respects and recognizes the gifts of all its members. Through this common life of love and discipleship, the church can communicate an extraordinarily powerful ethical witness to society as a whole, a lived example of the meaning of a 'kingdom of ends', in which the unity of a common life is based in the worth of all its members. Through participation in this community, individual Christians are formed in the life of Christian virtue and are given the sense of identity and purpose which are such powerful sources of ethical commitment to the needs of their fellow human beings in society as a whole.

The primary form of Christian ethical communication, then, is practical witness to a form of life by the Christian community itself. Clearly, such communication can be distorted and even nullified in particular contexts by the failure of Christians, whether individually or institutionally, to live the life of discipleship – a failure often intensified by its juxtaposition with lofty claims. Apart from this obvious point, there are a number of other considerations which should qualify an emphasis on Christian communication as essentially a matter of practical witness by the church as a self-contained ethical community. Identification with the church community can be a means of nourishing and intensifying ethical commitment for the sake of the world, but can also become an identification with the needs and interests of a particular human group, to the ethical detriment of society as a whole. This is especially true in times of crisis, when the church can be tempted to preserve its own institutional interests to the detriment of its commitment to human rights.[40] Further, although Christian ethical life is founded in discipleship to the person of Christ, and formed primordially by the Gospel narrative, it is also – as was argued

---

[40] A point made very clearly in Shanks' discussion, noted in the previous chapter.

in chapter 3 – developed by its historical interactions with the 'other', through and in whom Christ may be encountered in unpredictable and challenging ways. Because of this, all Christian communication – including communication through practical witness – has a reciprocal character: it seeks to give a witness in the world to the Kingdom of God, while recognizing that its encounters with the world may deepen its own sense of the Kingdom. In this light, the sense of Christian identity expressed in the church as ethical communicator must be one which retains the tension between particularity and universality, its discipleship to the historical and risen Jesus and its openness to the mystery of God experienced in and through the world.

In the first place, then, the Christian community communicates its ethical vision through practical witness, through the attempt to live out the values of the Kingdom within a community of faith. The power of communication through practical witness, however, must be complemented by communication through word and image, through the attempt to evangelize by offering others resources for new hope stemming from a new vision and understanding of the world. It is crucial, however, that these forms of communication are themselves distinguished into what could be called the *visionary* and the *normative* dimensions of ethics. This distinction corresponds to different contexts within the public forum and to different kinds of ethical language.

The visionary dimension of ethics is the communication of those larger pictures of human origin, nature and destiny which are most closely associated with religious narrative and religious discourse in general. Although this dimension is crucial in terms of its role as the ontological background of ethical principles, it is not immediately concerned with normative implications. This dimension of ethical communication appeals to the more specifically cultural contexts of the public forum: intellectual debate, the arts, the media, education and so on.[41]

---

[41] As David Hollenbach notes in his 'Politically Active Churches: Some Empirical Prolegomena to a Normative Approach', in *Religion and Contemporary Liberalism*, ed. P. J. Weithman (University of Notre Dame Press, 1997), 'religious traditions and communities are among the principal bearers of the cultural sources for our

In the language appropriate to this dimension of ethics, Christians can seek to show that their faith proposes a vision of humanity that gives invaluable resources to our common life. They will present the content of Christian narrative as a vision of human fulfilment, a vision that makes public truth claims, that it is right and proper to articulate within the public forum.

At the visionary level, the crucial form of public communication is the richness of Christian religious discourse itself. Those who do not found their faith identity on this narrative may yet respond to it as a source of meaning and an illumination of the human condition. We cannot say that Christian narrative means everything to the believing Christian and nothing to the non-Christian. On the contrary, the stances of professing Christians towards Christian narrative vary markedly, just as the attitudes of those who do not identify themselves as Christians can range from complete indifference or hostility to profound respect and sympathy for the meaning of Christian narrative. Within the public forum, there are many non-Christians whose fundamental attitudes are receptive to the values expressed in Christian narrative, just as many Christians are receptive to the insights embodied in the narratives of other religions. It was noted above that part of the nature of this third conception of ethical communication, associated with a theology of mediation, is to challenge the 'two-tiered' character of the other two conceptions, and to argue for an important degree of 'permeability' between these 'two tiers'. This 'permeability' stems from the fact that Christian ethical communication cannot assume that its audience falls reasonably neatly into two groups that might be called 'church' and 'world'. Rather, contemporary social and religious conditions are characterised by a plurality of audiences for Christian communication, with greatly varying degrees of affiliation or indifference to the church – including a variety of forms of membership of the church by baptised Christians

understanding of the human good. They can evoke not only private self-understanding but public vision as well . . . Religious communities make perhaps their most important contribution to political life through this contribution to the formation of culture' (305).

themselves, and a variety of stances towards the Christian faith by members of other communities of belief.[42]

The normative dimension of ethical communication, on the other hand, is concerned with the whole range of social, legal and political norms, that is, with those areas that exert most direct and keenly felt pressure on people's lives. It is in this context that the public evidential quality of ethical principles is most stringently demanded, and where the debate between different understandings of the meaning and purpose of human life is most hard fought. In this context, reference to the religious premises of ethical principles is usually inappropriate, since it is an appeal to premises not shared by many participants in the debate. In the context of normative argument, a focus on the practical meaning of ethical principles, on the manifest human good that they can enable, is what is called for.

Bearing in mind this distinction between the visionary and normative dimensions of ethical communication, in what sorts of ways can Christian ethical beliefs be communicated in the public forum?

The communication of Christian ethics as vision has both an interpretive and an artistic character. In art, it communicates through the plenitude of meaning characteristic of the successful creation of an artistic image. As interpretation, it com-

[42] The variations in styles of membership and degrees of inculturation in church communities is a consideration given too little consideration by Hauerwas in his frequent contrasts between church and world. Hauerwas does confront himself squarely with the charge that he is fantasizing about a church that does not exist, and that he does not serve, nor is subject to the discipline of, any particular church (*Dispatches from the Front*, 20). He grants that he can 'in no way in principle defeat such a response' to his arguments, and answers this charge through the category of friendship. Acknowledging that 'friends are not a church' (20), he nevertheless seeks to convey an understanding of his service to the church in terms of friendship: 'By trying to submit my life and work to the imaginative demands of the practices and discourse of the church through time, I hope to serve my friends and even more hopefully make some new friends' (25). In his 'Moral Communities and Christian Ethics', in *Moral Leadership in a Postmodern Age* (Edinburgh: T. and T. Clark, 1997), Robin Gill, while supporting the general approach of communitarian Christian ethics, influenced by MacIntyre and Lindbeck, notes that 'it tends to produce a picture of churches as moral communities which fits ill their social reality'. For Gill, 'the challenge . . . is to find ways of expressing Christian distinctiveness which do not exaggerate the theological and sociological distinctiveness of churches as moral communities. As yet this is a challenge which has occupied the attention of too few Christian ethicists' (50).

municates through the success of the attempt to coherently understand our common life in the light of Christian faith. An important part of this effort of understanding is the development of philosophical interpretations of the human condition informed by the Christian vision of life. Both artistic creation and intellectual interpretation are forms of language that can be devoted to a hermeneutic of human experience motivated by Christian faith. Indeed, a crucial aspect of the relation of religious faith to ethics is the confidence and energy that faith can give to this task of interpreting the human condition, a confidence based in the faith that the world and our own existence are meaningful, and that the chiaroscuro of experience will repay the patient and demanding task of discerning hope and promise.[43]

There are a number of roles which such a communication of vision can play. Firstly, the communication of the Christian vision can offer a context of reinforcement and enrichment of the concept of human worth and dignity, setting individual autonomy in the context of communal life. In particular, as was argued in chapter 2, the Christian vision of the union of human persons with each other in the divine *communio* can give depth and universality to a commitment to a community of discourse. The Christian narrative has the power to disclose the value of persons in relation to God, the source of all value, breaking down all limitations imposed by power and prejudice. This is not to claim that it is the churches who have always recognized and condemned such limitations, nor to deny that secular liberal and socialist thinkers have often been at the forefront of expanding the range of application of the principle of the worth of persons, but rather to contend that the Christian narrative offers powerful spiritual resources for the continuing affirmation of what is most valuable in liberal societies.

Secondly, the Christian narrative of disclosure can offer a portrait of the human condition which is of crucial relevance to political life. Christian teaching offers an understanding of human existence as created for goodness, marred by sin,

[43] cf. D. Tracy's discussion of religion from this perspective in ch. 5 of his *Plurality and Ambiguity: Hermeneutics, Religion, Hope* (San Francisco: Harper and Row, 1987).

redeemed by self-sacrificial love, destined for freedom in community and sharing in the common goods of creation. Such theological emphases can give a creative service to politics by offering a concrete portrait of the human condition which is both realistic and optimistic, and which can provide a means of integrating a range of values.[44] The attempt by contemporary Catholic social teaching, for example, to develop an understanding of human community as characterized by freedom and solidarity, setting the right to private property within the context of the universal destination of created goods, makes a contribution to the debate over the social nature of property which is distinct from both economic liberalism and Marxism. In the Protestant tradition, Reinhold Niebuhr's prophetic deployment of the resources of the Christian tradition in engaged commentary on the politics of his day provides a rich and nuanced example of the ways in which the Christian portrait of the human condition can assist the search for truth in public life.

The above two categories refer, broadly speaking, to the relevance of Christian traditions to the ethical life of a liberal community – to its core value of the worth of persons and to the portrait of the human condition that informs its decisions and

[44] In his *Christian Perspectives on Politics* (London: SCM, 1988), J. Philip Wogaman speaks of 'theological entry points' into politics, arguing that 'it may be better to treat Christian doctrines as presumptive rather than definitive in the guidance of specific human action. By that I mean that a theological view with clear political ramifications should lead us to adopt those ramifications provisionally but with openness to the possibility that they should be set aside for sufficient reason. Theological entry points can help us to define initial presumptions in the political realm' (123). Wogaman suggests ten such 'theological entry points': the sovereignty of God, the transcendence of God, human finitude, covenant, the theology of the cross, justification and grace, the doctrine of creation, original sin, eschatology, and ecclesiology (113–22). For W. Korff, in his *Norm und Sittlichkeit*, while revelation gives human dignity a final ground, it does not imply any difference of content: theological ethics, that is, ethics informed by revelation, does not bring new anthropological structures to the foundations of ethical rationality, but rather gives these structures 'their final *arche*, which as *arche* simply is and as such does not allow of any further differentiation; it is an *arche* which is concerned not with varying goods, but with the good as such' (112). Yet a Christian vision of life, while not conveying new anthropological information in empirical terms, does offer a multifaceted interpretation of the meaning of human existence. As such, the theological character of ethics is not limited to providing an ultimate ground, but can also include the kinds of interpretive keys that Wogaman identifies as 'entry points'.

commitments. Yet the specifically religious practices and rituals of the Christian churches can also be of great public significance to liberal, pluralist societies. This third category would emphasize that human communities are projects sustained by faith and hope, and that the worship which is offered to God in their midst is crucial to the continuing vivification of that faith and hope. This has become particularly clear in the contemporary 'disenchantment with disenchantment',[45] in the search for spiritual meaning in societies which until recently were judged to be subject to an irreversible process of secularization. This search for spiritual meaning can take many forms, not all of them oriented towards a vision of hope for historical human communities. If the Christian liturgy can bear witness to the God of hope as a God who calls men and women together in community, then it offers a crucial service to humanity in liberal societies.

The work of the Christian artist can develop a realized portrait of the Christian vision of the union of suffering and hope in human experience, interpreted in the light of the paschal mystery. Such a portrait can influence many members of society who do not share the faith of Christians in Jesus Christ, but who respond to the power of disclosure of this portrait of their own humanity. Although formed by the distinctive contours of the Christian story, it achieves intelligibility through analogy with the experiences of others and can offer resources for a common attempt to inspire hope in the midst of failure. Christian intellectuals can contribute to public debate in ways which draw attention to the resources their tradition has to offer to the common task. All of these forms of communication can emphasize the distinctiveness of the Christian tradition, while respecting the impartiality of the public realm and the plural character of society.

The extent to which the committed proclamation of the Christian vision has a prophetic – in the sense of 'counter cultural' – character can only be judged in specific contexts and circumstances. There are situations in which the church will be

---

[45] cf. David Tracy, *Blessed Rage for Order* (New York: Seabury Press, 1975), Part 1, ch. 1.

essentially affirming developments which have been pioneered by secular movements, as well as those, by contrast, in which it must denounce much of the spirit of the age. The comments of Adrian Hastings, in a British context, illustrate the importance of such specific judgements by drawing attention to the church's relationship both to the reality of ethical progress in post-war liberal societies, and to its temptations and fragility:

> There are periods in human history when the organised city of man has appeared to be endeavouring to seek very much what the City of God is seeking. There develops a sort of alliance – sometimes a dangerous and deceptive alliance – between them. In our own century that was, I believe, the case from the 1940s to the 1970s. The age of the United Nations, of the winding-up of empire, of the blossoming of the Commonwealth, of the welfare state and the National Health Service, the ending of capital punishment, was, at least for this country, an age in which the church could have little of a prophetic voice because it could only confirm what society and state were endeavouring to do. Within that wide context, however, there could still be a need for outspokenness and contestation over specific issues, as Archbishop Ramsey showed on several matters. Perhaps there is a self-complacent quality in such periods; anyway, they do not last. Today we are certainly in a different situation.[46]

At the *normative* level, Christians can communicate their ethical beliefs by affirming fundamental ethical principles which are implied by their own narrative and which are also publicly intelligible in practical ethical terms. In doing so, they may demonstrate the ways in which such principles flow from their own religious beliefs, but should also make clear that the truth of these principles has its own intelligibility in ethical practice, and is therefore open to everyone of good will. Certain mediating principles – such as the sanctity of life, or various formulations of human rights – which may enjoy considerable consensus in the community, play a particularly important role here.

It is at the level of social practices, and the norms that govern such practices, that the reality of reciprocity between the Christian vision, Christian normative ethics and historical

[46] 'Theology and Contemporary Reality' in *The Shaping of Prophecy* (London: Geoffrey Chapman, 1995), 27.

experience is most powerfully evident. The previous chapter developed an understanding of Christian identity in terms of a theology of mediation that has its practical meaning in the encounter with the pain of suffering and conflict in historical change. A part of this work of mediation is the attempt to understand the relationships between the Christian vision itself and new forms of life and understandings of the world which embody new ethical perspectives. It is evident from the historical record that Christian narrative gives no unambiguous or self-evident answer to the ethical challenges of slavery, democracy, socio-economic justice, the rights of women or the imperatives of ecological consciousness. Rather, Christians were challenged in each of these cases to develop their understanding of this narrative, and the vision that it informs, by integrating new forms of ethical consciousness and sensitivity with it as a development of the Christian ethical tradition. In this sense, participation in public normative debate is both a means of communicating the principled wisdom of Christian tradition, and an opportunity to learn from the experience of all those whose needs, interests and aspirations motivate them to engage in such debate.

Ethical communication at the normative level is, in pluralist societies, a process usually characterized by elements of controversy and conflict – sometimes to an intense degree. This reflects both the different ethical visions involved, as well as the distorting effects of the assertion of power and particular interest. In such circumstances, mediating principles receive only limited assent, become controversial in their scope and application, or clash with other ethical principles which are deemed to be of equal or greater importance. Because of this, appeals to 'natural law', as a consensus of ethical wisdom, become less plausible.

In liberal societies, the question of abortion is probably the most significant example of this. This question can be understood as a clash between different hierarchies of good. One conceives it as legitimate for the good of human autonomy – in the case of an adult parent or parents – to override the life of the foetus; the other argues that the right of an innocent human individual to life cannot be overriden by any other good. These hierarchies of the good are linked to broader visions of human nature and purpose, which themselves may be linked to religious premises that play a role in giving the associated ethical stances force and coherence. The possibilities of reciprocal communication are also imperilled by complex histories of power, conflict and mutual distrust, which include the suppression of women in society and church, and the attempted marginalization of religion and religious communities by social and political groups asserting the autonomy of the individual.

Ethical controversy in the public forum, since it is often not conducted on shared premises in such broader visions, must focus on the specifically ethical goods involved. References to the purposes of the creator are references to premises which are not shared, and whose relationship to the ethical question at stake is unclear for many participants in the debate. Communication of normative principles demands particularly stringent relevance and intelligibility. At the same time, Christians can communicate the meaning of those ethical goods in ways which are formed by their own religious vision – a vision which enables them to see the goods of human life in a particular light and in particular mutual relationships. Christian critique of abortion can develop and affirm understandings of human existence which imaginatively link the desire for autonomy and self-expression with respect for the beginnings of human life. Motivated by their own narrative, but oriented towards the public forum, Christians can unfold the inherent ethical logic of a stance oriented towards the protection of innocent human life. This must be accompanied by words and actions which seek to overcome the bitter history of conflict referred to above through an affirmation of the rights of women, especially through a commitment to forms of service which welcome and support the bearing of children.

With the question of abortion, the distinction between visionary and normative communication is most difficult to sustain, since, in the present ethical and cultural climate, the normative principle of the foetus' right to life is generally perceived to be inextricably associated with a religious vision of life. In this case, rather than being seen as interdependent but significantly distinguishable modes of communication, the 'visionary' and the 'normative' are perceived to be one and the same by those who argue that the principle of the foetus' right to life is publicly unintelligible and expressive of a strictly private vision. This distinction between visionary and normative ethical communication also runs counter to any theology of Christian life, grounded in an explicit or implicit theology of revelation, which would deny that any 'vision' can be abstracted from the concrete life of the Christian community and communicated to the world, and also – for related reasons – reject the notion that Christians can and should engage in public normative debate on the basis of general principles without particular narrative content.

For Hauerwas, this is especially true in the realm of marriage and procreation, where a Christian ethic can be based not on any considerations of nature or natural law but rather on a reflection of the 'political' role of the church, that is, of its role as an alternative polity to the world. A Christian ethic of sex must be specifically Christian and not an ethic for all people. To understand why marriage is exclusive for the Christian, Hauerwas argues, we need a recovery of the political function of marriage in the Christian community: marriage and procreation are signs of hope in God. As such they play a crucial political role in marking out the distinction between the church and the world. Christian marriage is a covenant which bears witness to God's covenant with his people, Israel and the church.[47] It is this political function of Christian marriage that should be the perspective from which we judge the issue of abortion.

For Hauerwas, pro-choice activists have been right to argue that opposition to abortion depends on religious premises.[48] The question of abortion should not be argued in terms of the relationship between rights: 'the question is not "Is the fetus a human being with a right to life?", but "How should a Christian regard and care for the fetus as a child?"' What is required is

[47] *A Community of Character*, 176–91.   [48] Ibid., 196.

not abstract arguments about conflicting rights, but rather 'a normative account of parenthood correlative to the ends of a community'. Since we live 'in a culture where there is no such normative account', only the church can fulfil its political function of providing it as an alternative to the world. The point and purpose of marriage in such a community is to 'serve a symbolic function denoting God's loyalty to his people and as such as the appropriate context for reception of new life'.[49] Because of this function, the married couple must always be ready to 'welcome the stranger', to welcome new children into the world. It is this specific Christian narrative context that makes abortion wrong and marriage exclusive. The specificity of his grounding of marriage in Christian narrative leads Hauerwas to go so far as to say 'I do not know why people who are not Christians have children.'[50] Christian opposition to abortion in the public sphere has failed because 'by attempting to meet the moral challenge within the limits of public polity, we have failed to exhibit our deepest convictions that make our rejection of abortion intelligible'.[51]

Since a liberal pluralist society has no agreed method for solving such moral conflicts, it becomes 'a political necessity, anchored in our society's profoundest moral convictions, that an issue such as abortion be considered on grounds independent of the kind of persons we would like to encourage in our society', independently that is, of virtues and character.[52] It is Hauerwas' contention that Christians should not consider the issue on such grounds, since their ethical outlook is inextricably entwined with a particular narrative and the virtues that develop in symbiosis with it. The decision against abortion is not made on the abstract grounds that the foetus is a 'human being', but on the character of the Christian community which 'sees in the fetus nothing less than God's continuing creation that is destined in hope to be another citizen of his Kingdom. The question of when human life begins is of little interest to such a people, since their hope is that life will and does continue to begin time after time.'[53]

[49] Ibid., 210.   [50] Ibid.   [51] Ibid., 212.   [52] Ibid., 217.
[53] Ibid., 227.

Hauerwas is right to emphasize the prophetic and, in that sense, political, character of a Christian ethos of marriage and parenthood. A realized Christian commitment to faithful marriage and committed parenthood can be a sustained witness to hope in God's future and gratitude for God's gift of life. Further, a Christian community which supports this form of life can be inspired by such hope and gratitude to live as an alternative to the sense of disintegration and loss of meaning which constantly threatens any society giving pre-eminence to individual autonomy. In situations of extreme conflict between the life of the church and the 'world', the possibilities for Christian ethical communication may be restricted to the most fundamental one: the witness of living a form of life, best understood – philosophically – in Aristotelian terms. In recent history, this was most obviously the case in totalitarian societies of right and left, where Christians were denied any form of public communication and thus forced to confine their work of evangelization to private witness – a witness which, nevertheless, could and did have a gradual public effect in varying ways.

Yet liberal societies, whose difficulties of ethical communication stem not from totalitarian control but from cultural conflict, exacerbated by various forms of economic power and interest, present a different kind of challenge: the achievement of fundamental ethical consensus through both private and public witness as well as through the public communication of vision and argument. While the witness of a form of life remains the source and ground of other forms of communication, their necessity and importance should not be denied, even in the hardest cases of entrenched ethical and political polemic.[54] To do so is to deny the relevance of Christian revelation as a truth

[54] In his 'Catholic Classics in American Liberal Culture', in *Catholicism and Liberalism: Contributions to American Public Philosophy*, ed. D. Hollenbach and R. B. Douglass, David Tracy notes the possible negative consequences of restricting Christian contributions to public life to a narrative-based witness, or to coalitions between like-minded groups. The departure of shared norms of public rationality can precipitate a slide from coalitions of witnessing communities to the clash of interest groups in an impoverished public realm (202). For this reason, Tracy argues for a recognition both of the narrative roots of ethical stances, and of their public and shareable effects, providing transformative possibilities and possibilities of disclosure for all reflective persons.

for all, and to restrict it to the narrative of a particular community. If – as in the case of abortion – this revelation can sustain fundamental ethical principles, such as the sanctity of life, then it has a public ethical relevance. Further, its communicability can be enhanced by expressing these principles in the language of rights, since such language expresses fundamental ethical imperatives in ways which have contributed towards the development of a global ethical consensus at crucial times, notably the enunciation of the Universal Declaration of Human Rights in 1948.

Clearly, the use of the language of rights can only be effective when related to a coherent hierarchy of goods, and it is this which is so deeply contested in the case of abortion. At the same time, there are means of communicating a hierarchy of goods – in this case, the subordination of individual autonomy to sanctity of life – to those outside a particular community and its form of life. The connection between a narrative, with its form of life, and a specific ethical stance is not so immediate as necessarily to exclude those who do not participate in this form of life from understanding such a stance – nor to imply that all of those who participate (to some degree) in this form of life *ipso facto* accept this stance.[55] As has been argued, a historical process of experience, dialectic and integration, which includes the testing-ground of normative argument, is the means by which the specific ethical implications of Christian narrative have been developed.

This becomes more evident when we call to mind that not all members of the Christian churches accept that the Christian form of life necessarily entails a complete prohibition of abor-

[55] In her *Moral Action and Christian Ethics* (New Studies in Christian Ethics, Cambridge University Press, 1995), Jean Porter notes MacIntyre's and Hauerwas' claims about the causes of modern moral confusion in the breakdown of a moral tradition, and responds 'that it is not obvious that our widespread moral disagreements can be explained exclusively in terms of a pluralism of moral traditions,' since this presupposes 'that the Hebrew–Christian moral tradition, unlike the dominant ethos in modern liberal democracies, is a unified tradition, in which moral arguments can be settled by an appeal to its definite boundaries. It is far from clear that this is the case, however ... the Christian churches today are not generally models of unanimity and concord on the difficult issues of the day, and it does not seem that this is a new situation' (16–17).

tion. Many of them seek to be persuaded by specific normative arguments that the life of the foetus must not be subordinated to any other goods, and to be informed of the empirical evidence relevant to the attribution of moral status to the foetus. Their experience of Christian narrative and community will, it is to be hoped, predispose them to accept such arguments, but these arguments must still be made in order to convince them that this specific ethical stance has its own force and intelligibility in a range of circumstances. For many, it is not an immediate and self-evident implication of Christian narrative, but one which must be mediated by concrete ethical argument. Conversely, those who (to greatly varying degrees) do not share Christian or religious faith, can nevertheless be open to the specifically ethical force of a stance which respects the sanctity of life in ways informed by reasoned argument and empirical evidence, especially when their personal sense of life's meaning responds to a hopeful vision of the gifted character of new life, and when their experience of Christian communities has shown them that a prophetic resistance to abortion need have nothing to do with the degradation of women. In the case both of many members of Christian communities, and of many who understand their lives in secular terms, the connection between a religious form of life and a strong stance against abortion is not so exclusive as to nullify the point and purpose of specifically ethical argument, despite its inherent difficulties in the contemporary public forum.

One way to sum up the task of Christian ethical communication in a pluralist society is as the imperative to speak of God neither too early nor too late. If God is spoken of too early, if reference to religious discourse is made when what is required is a demonstration of the ethical coherence and effectiveness of a certain stance, then violence is done to the character of ethical debate. If specific principles have their own value in ethical terms, then reference to God's will or purposes can appear to be little more than an appeal to authority, which has no intrinsic bearing on the character of the ethical goods in question. Similarly, references to the life of Jesus may not of themselves offer specific guidance in developing the implications of an ethical principle for contemporary life. They, too, may be perceived simply as references to the authoritative founder of a particular group's identity, rather than as points of view which can give new insight to all participants in a debate. In many contexts, such premature and inappropriate religious references function to close debate by the assertion of particular and incommunicable identity, rather than leading it forward by offering a distinctive and illuminating perspective.

Yet a Christian contribution to the public forum in pluralist societies would not be fulfilled if God was spoken of too late or not at all. When societies step back from their immediate ethical disputes, with their normative and legal consequences, and consider the visions of human existence which inform and inspire their attempts to develop a coherent hierarchy of the good, then talk of God has a crucial role to play in developing an understanding of human existence. In this case, God-talk is not the insertion of an authoritarian premise in an ethical argument, but rather the development of a vision of human existence and its meaning in relation to an infinite mystery who creates, loves and sustains. This vision of human existence, in turn, informs a certain understanding of human goods, and of the purpose of human action. The portrayal of this vision will be a crucial accompaniment for lively ethical insight. Christian identity in ethical communication is marked by a commitment to this vision, the vision of the Kingdom of God, both in fidelity to the story of Jesus and in willingness to listen to the voice of the Spirit within the aspirations and conflicts of the world.

CHAPTER 5

Reconciling autonomy and community

The previous chapter was devoted to a general interpretation of the task of Christian ethical communication, in the light of the argument of this book as a whole. The purpose of this final chapter is to demonstrate the meaning and intention of this general interpretation by focussing – in a more concretely sociological context – on an ethical issue central to the concerns of this book, namely, the relationship between autonomy and ethical community. The importance of this issue was highlighted in chapter 1, in terms of the challenge facing liberal societies in reconciling the value of autonomy with ethical perspectives which could situate the worth of persons within community. This reconciliation of autonomy and community is at the heart of any communication of the Christian ethical vision – and its scope and meaning are urgently contested in normative debate.

The focus of disagreement in this normative debate is on the tension between conceptions of autonomy and of obligations to community. It is here that the liberal understanding of the public forum, and understandings which are informed by various traditions of the good, are in most direct conflict. It is important to note, however, that the source of the conflict is not in the importance that the liberal tradition gives to individual rights. The value of the individual is a truth that both liberal secular and Christian conceptions rightly cherish as fundamental to a humane polity. It is the ways in which individual rights and the autonomy of the individual are interpreted that are at the root of the conflict. Generally speaking, the contemporary secular liberal tradition rejects the notion of 'duties to oneself': ethics defines the realm of right action in relation to others. For this conception, the law can only be concerned with those actions which affect other agents, since only those actions can be judged to be of public ethical relevance. No traditions of the good, of human fulfilment, have any warrant to claim a public role in providing a normative scheme of individual fulfilment. The role of the law is to provide maximum freedom for autonomous individuals to realize their own private purposes and vision.

This understanding of ethical autonomy as independent of any particular vision of the good necessitates no argument between secular liberal ethics and Christian ethics in many spheres of life. In the area of judicial processes, for example, both approaches can insist on the crucial value of the presumption of innocence, or, in socio-economic life, on the value of equality of opportunity and the maintenance of decent standards of social assistance. It is in areas where the Christian vision understands the point and purpose of individual life as a freedom-in-relationship that a clash with liberal conceptions of autonomy often arises. The liberal conception of autonomy has as its highest value the free self-disposition of the self-aware individual agent. For the Christian tradition, the fullest expression of this free self-disposition is in the realization of the individual through relationships of mutual commitment: relationships to God as the source of human life and to other persons as the essential context for personal fulfilment. Freedom is understood as the possibility of fulfilment through relationships of community, rather than, as in the secular liberal conception, the absence of any warrantable and justified claims on the individual's autonomy.

Since any society, including a liberal pluralist society, is a fabric of relationships, and of legally sanctioned institutions that embody those relationships, this difference is one that is publicly relevant. There can be no legal stance that is impartial to these different understandings of freedom, since any legal decision must either judge certain relationships to be legitimate constraints on individual autonomy or to be subordinate to it.[1]

[1] For Ronald Dworkin, in his 'Liberalism', in *Public and Private Morality*, ed. S. Hampshire (Cambridge University Press, 1978), liberalism's 'constitutive morality

Critical argument between secular liberals and Christians tends to focus on those areas where these conceptions of freedom clash: for example, the nature and significance of marriage and the ethics of abortion and euthanasia. Secular liberalism and the Christian tradition are at variance over: the importance for society of the relationship between freedom and commitment in marital relationships; the status of the foetus in terms of the definition of an ethically relevant individual as a self-aware agent or as an individual human life in process of development; and the legitimacy of the agent's free self-disposition over her own life in contrast to conceptions of human existence as a calling whose end is not of our own choosing and as a web of relationships which we are not free to tear. The relevance of the Christian vision of creation and communion for ethical debate is that it implies an objective and fulfilling purpose for human life, a context of relationships within which human autonomy can be realized. The continuing contribution that Christian ethics can make to the normative deliberations of a liberal society is to draw attention to ethically relevant and intelligible forms of relationship and commitment which go beyond the bounds of conceptions of individual autonomy based exclusively in conceptions of freedom as self-disposition and self-fulfilment.

Recent decades have seen constant conflict between secular liberals and Christians over these questions, on a scale stemming from the significance of the difference between the understandings of freedom involved. The long-term character of this religious and social situation highlights the importance of theological reflection on the relationship between the church and liberal societies. Perhaps, most of all, it will involve reflection on and practical commitment to the meaning of communicating truth without resort to force or to structures of power. Christian ethics can continue to claim a legitimate role in

is a theory of equality that requires official neutrality amongst theories of what is valuable in life' (142). Dworkin's arguments point out the importance of basing a liberal society on the principle of equal concern and respect, rather than on varying conceptions of the fulfilled life, yet a liberal and pluralist society cannot remain neutral about questions concerning the scope and meaning of individual autonomy: it must make decisions concerning the relationship of this autonomy to various obligations of relational commitment.

contributing to the development of law, and to the institutions of constraint which necessarily accompany it, but if – as was argued in chapter 1 of this study – the genesis of the liberal state was in the chaos induced by Christians resorting to force to impose religious uniformity, then a truly self-aware and self-reforming Christian response to the vicissitudes of liberal societies must be one which focusses on the power of a truth which transcends both force and law. Such a response would be a prophetic critique of liberal agnosticism about the truths of the human condition, and at the same time would respect liberalism's emphasis on individual freedom from coercion. If Christians could communicate the Gospel they have been entrusted with in this way, it would be both a service to liberal and pluralist societies as well as a witness to essential Christian values.

The tension between autonomy and community in modern societies is at the same time a tension between autonomy and conceptions of the good, between private desires and purposes and conceptions of the good life that can found and bond communities.[2] In this sense, the development of resilient communities has everything to do with the development of shared meanings, which can draw on conceptions of the good life. Yet shared meanings that address the most profound and urgent issues of self and community – issues of solidarity, sacrifice, hope and survival – are properly religious meanings, concerned with questions of the point and purpose of human existence bounded by death. Because of this, the reconciliation of autonomy and community is vitally dependent on the communicative power of religious visions of the meaning of human existence. Just as the crisis of religious disunity in Western history led to fundamental conflicts between ideals of autonomy and community, so a new sense of religion's public role, based on an

[2] As Robert Wuthnow notes in his *Christianity and Civil Society: The Contemporary Debate* (Valley Forge, Pa.: Trinity Press International, 1996), from a sociological perspective, 'civil society' is a more well-defined term than 'community', particularly as talk of community or communities is often a misnomer for local neighbourhoods (7–8). However, the term 'community' is used in this discussion in the general sense of a morally significant interpersonal bond, with varying degrees of size and scope, such as marriage relationships, civil society itself or possible forms of global community.

affirmation of freedom of conscience, can help to create a new sense of human community in a global context.

Reacting against traditional conceptions of hierarchy and order in value and meaning, contemporary culture emphasizes the freedom of the self to discover its own meaning. Yet – if it is to avoid the perils of loneliness and alienation – the self's search for meaning must continue to come to terms with the imperative to form and to be faithful to community. Conceptions of self-identity are profoundly bound up with general conceptions of meaning and community. In particular, different religious perspectives form and are formed by different conceptions of the self in community. In contemporary culture, these religious perspectives have considerable influence on whether self-identity is understood in terms of an essentially self-contained autonomy or as necessarily bound up with communal relationships and obligations.

The evident vigour of the search for spiritual meaning in modern societies has put paid to those conceptions of secularization which saw religion in terminal decline. At the same time, it has heightened the challenge to those who seek to understand the true role and identity of Christian faith in the contemporary religious and ethical landscape. This book has argued for a conception of Christian identity which holds together particularity and universality, historicity and mystery, in the task of public ethical communication. This argument has involved a critique of other conceptions of Christian identity which – in my own judgement – do not do full justice to the relationship between particularity and universality, and therefore to the relationship between church and world.

These debates concerning Christian identity spring from profoundly serious, indeed agonizing, concerns: to avoid both the dissolution and alienation of tradition and the stifling of evangelization by rendering Christianity incommunicable. Yet these tensions within 'mainstream' Christianity are themselves situated within a contemporary religious landscape marked by much greater contrasts. The revival of religion in contemporary Western societies is marked by two newly powerful phenomena: fundamentalism and the religions of self-fulfilment and self-realization. As a global phenomenon of reaction to modernity, fundamentalism is of great significance. In stable liberal societies, however, its influence is limited, since fundamentalist communities are constrained to become yet one more element of 'difference' in the pluralist societies they are in such tension with.[3] For the purposes of the present study, the religions of self-fulfilment and self-realization are of much greater relevance, since they are a religious form within liberal societies which affirms individual autonomy but which tends to perpetuate the divergence between autonomy and community. Reflection on the role and identity of Christian faith within liberal societies must include a consideration of these vigorous and influential forms of religious life which are so characteristic of liberal modernity.

This chapter will briefly consider the key issues of this book from the perspective of a sociology of modernity, with particular reference to the work of Anthony Giddens and to the sociology of religion. Giddens' concepts of the 'pure relationship' and the 'sequestration of experience' can help to give a more concrete meaning to the tensions between autonomy and community in modern societies. These perspectives will then be related to the relationship between the search for community and the search for meaning in social thought, and to the character of the religions of self-realization. Finally, the chapter offers a response to the challenges posed by these sociological insights from the perspective of a Christian theology of communion and solidarity.

In his work *Modernity and Self-Identity: Self and Society in the Late*

---

[3] As Frank J. Lechner incisively points out in his 'Global Fundamentalism', in *A Future for Religion? New Paradigms for Social Analysis*, ed. W. H. Swatos, Jr. (Newbury Park, California: SAGE, 1993), fundamentalism is both quintessentially modern and self-compromising: 'where it does not take decisive control, it reproduces the dilemmas it sets out to resolve; as one active force among others, it affirms the depth of modern pluralism; it takes on the tensions produced by the clash between a universalizing global culture and particular local conditions; it expresses fundamental uncertainty in a crisis setting, not traditional confidence about taken-for-granted truths; by defending God, who formerly needed no defense, it creates and recreates difference as part of a global cultural struggle. So compromised, fundamentalism becomes part of the fabric of modernity' (30).

Modern Age,[4] Anthony Giddens emphasizes globalization and transformations of self-identity as the two poles of modernity. The dynamic of modernity is global: it involves various 'disembedding mechanisms' which lift social relationships out of local contexts and rearticulate them across indefinite expanses of space and time. Modern technology has created the conditions for global awareness, for humanity to identify itself as a unitary 'us'. Modernity is characterized by a number of specialized systems of technology, in communications, finance, production, etc., whose constant development gives modernity a 'run-away' or 'juggernaut' character, constantly increasing its power to 'disembed' local traditions.[5] The contrast between traditional existence and modernity centres on the doubt and reflexivity characteristic of modernity: modernity subjects knowledge and custom to doubt, constantly reflecting on its own beliefs and behaviour.

In the conditions of modernity, the autonomous self becomes a reflexive project. While past societies saw similar identities from generation to generation, in modernity 'the altered self has to be explored and constructed as part of a reflexive process of connecting personal and social change'.[6] Personal choice becomes an important element in the formation of identity, which has as its touchstone the maintenance of personal authenticity, the coherence of an individual biographical narrative, rather than fidelity to traditional canons of life and action.

The construction of the self in these conditions makes possible what Giddens calls the 'pure relationship', which is of fundamental importance for the reflexive project of the self. A 'pure relationship' is an interpersonal relationship no longer anchored in the external conditions of economic or social life, nor in the binding requirements of social tradition. Contempo-

---

[4] Cambridge: Polity Press, 1991. Giddens does not use the term 'post-modern' as an interpretive concept for contemporary society, arguing that the contemporary process of self-identity can be best understood as the expression of the continuing dynamics of modernity, or 'high modernity'. In his *The Consequences of Modernity* (Cambridge:Polity Press, 1990), Giddens reserves the term 'post-modernity' for a future stage in social development, beyond some of the structural tensions of contemporary life (163–73).
[5] *The Consequences of Modernity*, 139.
[6] *Modernity and Self-Identity*, 33.

rary marriage, for example, is structured less and less in terms of external circumstances and constraints, and more and more in terms of the personal fulfilment it can offer. The pure relationship must survive through the interpersonal strength of the relationship itself, rather than through the bonding power of traditional social norms. The pure relationship is reflexive, since it exists not as the fulfilment of a traditional order, but rather as a voluntary project whose success and viability is a matter of continuous reflection. It is based on mutual trust and commitment, and energized by the development of personal intimacy. The expectation of the fulfilment that personal intimacy can bring is what makes the pure relationship so important to self-identity. Commitment and reflexivity stand in an uneasy relationship, since reflection on the state of the relationship can lessen unconditional commitment. The maintenance of the pure relationship depends on a mutual commitment, that can only be maintained when both parties are reflexively aware of the relationship as personally fulfilling.[7]

Modern social life is constantly involved with abstract systems, based on specialized professional deployment of knowledge for the resolution of personal and social problems. These abstract systems remove many elements of insecurity and danger from individual existence, through their power to control nature and to provide goods and services. Professional specialization and training mean that many of the most threatening and intractable aspects of life are attended to by professionals, leaving ordinary life to pursue a relatively untroubled routine. Giddens calls this phenomenon the 'sequestration of experience': the removal from everyday life, through the efficacy of abstract systems, of such phenomena as death, sickness, madness, criminality, old age and even nature, in so far as technology can insulate everyday life from the elements to a considerable degree. This 'sequestration of experience', although providing relative everyday security, imposes the cost of 'repressing a cluster of basic moral and existential components of human life that are, as it were, squeezed to the

[7] Ibid., 89-98.

sidelines'.[8] One unintended consequence, then, of the development of modern professional institutions is the risk of moral impoverishment resulting from this 'sequestration of experience', so that the reflexive project of the self seeks even greater fulfilment in the sphere of 'pure relationships': 'the reflexive project of the self has to be undertaken in circumstances which limit personal engagement with some of the most fundamental issues that human existence poses for all of us. It follows that the project of the self has to be achieved in a technically competent but morally arid social environment.'[9]

The notions of the 'pure relationship' and the 'sequestration of experience', deployed by Giddens, are helpful tools for reflection on the task of reconciliation of autonomy and community. The increasing prevalence of the 'pure relationship' means that the fostering of community must pay attention to the characteristically modern forces which can tend to make or dissolve communities because of the autonomous self's expectations of a 'pure relationship'. Similarly, an attempt to ground the meaning of individual life within community must come to terms with the significance of this 'sequestration of experience' for contemporary human beings' personal search for meaning, and for their readiness to commit themselves to community. The writers of *Habits of the Heart* argue that most people in contemporary American society understand life in terms of the fulfilment of the autonomous self, a fulfilment expressed in varying relationships of utilitarianism and expressive individualism. The self is 'defined by its ability to choose its own values', but, characteristically, no grounds are offered for these choices themselves.[10] Expressive individualism emphasizes the growth and fulfilment of the self, but gives no guidance about 'the shape moral character should take, the limits it should respect, and the community it should serve'.[11] In the judgement of the authors, the emphasis on self-fulfilment means that modern Americans find it very difficult to achieve ways of understanding

---

[8] Ibid., 167. [9] Ibid., 201.
[10] R. Bellah, et al., *Habits of the Heart: Individualism and Commitment in American Life* (New York: Harper and Row, 1985), 75.
[11] Ibid., 79.

the world which can overcome the sharp distinction between self and other.[12] Love relationships tend to be understood as communication between two self-sufficient selves. Social groupings tend to become 'life style enclaves', gatherings of the similar oriented towards fulfilment of similar needs and desires, rather than communities, which involve some self-sacrifice and a common history and hope.[13] On this analysis, the crucial need of modernity is to complement self-fulfilment with communitarian ideals which can motivate self-sacrifice and make a genuinely public life possible.

In his *Sources of the Self* and *Ethics of Authenticity*, Charles Taylor presents a critique of modern individualism with similar implications. Modern culture, Taylor argues, has produced the notion of the 'punctual self', a self whose 'only constitutive property is self-awareness', who is defined in abstraction from any constitutive goals of human existence.[14] In opposition to naturalist moral philosophy, which understands a moral outlook as an 'optional extra', Taylor argues for the crucial role of an orientation to the good in the development of the self's identity.[15] We need this orientation to the good because 'the goods which define our spiritual orientation are the ones by which we will measure the worth of our lives'.[16] But this good must go beyond the good of self-realization, since the whole point of self-realization must be that there is something beyond the self that the self aspires to. Politically, a society of individuals focussed on self-realization cannot 'sustain the strong identification with the political community which public freedom needs'.[17] For Taylor, then, like the authors of *Habits of the Heart*, conceptions of the self focussing on self-realization and self-fulfilment pose serious obstacles to the development of community.

In his critique of *Habits of the Heart*, however, Taylor argues that the problems of the modern self are problems not only of *community*, but also of *meaning*. For Taylor, the modern lack of communal commitment and emphasis on self-realization is

[12] Ibid., 110.   [13] Ibid., 71–75.
[14] *Sources of the Self* (Cambridge University Press, 1989), 49.
[15] Ibid., 33–41.   [16] Ibid., 42.   [17] Ibid., 508.

linked in crucial ways to contemporary perceptions of the meaning of human existence. The authors of *Habits of the Heart* rightly search for ways to recover a language of commitment to a greater whole, 'but without ever saying so, they write as though there were not really an independent problem of the loss of meaning in our culture, as though the recovery of a Tocquevillian commitment would somehow also fully resolve our problems of meaning, of expressive unity, of the loss of substance and resonance in our man-made environment, of a disenchanted universe. A crucial area of modern search and concern has been elided'.[18] The modern lack of communal commitment and emphasis on self-realization are linked in crucial ways to contemporary perceptions of the meaning of human existence.[19]

For Taylor, if self-realization is to have any content it must consist in making non-trivial choices, choices informed by horizons of significance or conceptions of the good. Self-realization depends on a project of meaning which goes beyond the self and within which the self finds fulfilment. A sense of the self's own identity depends on personal and communal commitments which are not easily revocable: love relationships, for example, are the 'crucibles of inwardly generated identity'[20] and these relationships cannot be tentative if it is really identity that is being formed and not 'some modality of enjoyment'.[21]

The continuing urgency of the question of meaning is demonstrated in the resurgence of religion in the contemporary conditions of modernity, in ways that run counter to the predictions of Marx, Weber and Durkheim. While these classical sociologists developed theories of modern society which saw the decline of religion's social significance as an inevitable consequence of the process of industrialization and modernization, contemporary sociologists of religion are observing that,

---

[18] Ibid., 509.
[19] For an illuminating discussion of Taylor's reflections on meaning and transcendence in contemporary life, see Kerr, *Immortal Longings: Versions of Transcending Humanity* (University of Notre Dame Press, 1997), ch. 7: 'Charles Taylor's Moral Ontology of the Self'.
[20] *The Ethics of Authenticity* (Cambridge, Mass.: Harvard University Press, 1992), 49.
[21] Ibid., 53.

although religion can no longer play the role of providing a 'sacred canopy' in the differentiated and pluralist conditions of modern societies, it remains an influential social factor at the level of personal life, in the lives of voluntary communities and in debates within civil society.[22] For sociologist James Beckford, religion has come adrift from its former points of anchorage but is no less potentially powerful as a result. It remains a potent cultural force which may act as a vehicle of change, challenge, or conservation: 'it is nowadays better to conceptualize religion as a a cultural resource or form than as a social institution. As such, it is characterized by a greater degree of flexibility and unpredictability'.[23] Beckford notes that 'this deregulation of religion is one of the hidden ironies of secularization'.[24]

One of the most important 'ironies' of secularization is that the secularization of the state and of national identity has freed the Christian churches from the historical burdens of giving sacral legitimacy to political and national identity. This has enabled them to take up a new form of public role, which accepts freedom of conscience and the differentiated character of society but at the same time claims a hearing on matters of fundamental ethical concern. In this sense, as Jose Casanova has argued in his *Public Religions in the Modern World*,[25] the public ethical role of Christian faith is a form of 'deprivatization' of religion, which seeks to resist the unlimited claims to autonomy of particular elements of the social system, such as money and power, and to articulate a vision of human community as part of the ethical debates of civil society.

Yet much of the resurgence of religion in liberal societies is taking quite a different form, characterized especially by phenomena emphasizing self-realization and self-fulfilment, rather than the bonds of community life. The prevalence of such

---

[22] For discussions of the implications of the end of religion as 'sacred canopy', see Thomas Luckmann's *The Invisible Religion* (New York: Macmillan, 1967) and P. Berger's *The Social Reality of Religion* (Harmondsworth: Penguin, 1973).
[23] J. A. Beckford, *Religion and Advanced Industrial Society* (London:Unwin Hyman, 1989), 171.
[24] Ibid., 172. See also G. Bouma *Religion: Meaning, Transcendence and Community in Australia* (Melbourne: Longman Cheshire, 1992), ch. 9 'The future of religion'.
[25] University of Chicago Press, 1994.

religiosity in modern societies was predicted – and to some degree endorsed – by Ernst Troeltsch. For Troeltsch, 'mysticism' would be the future 'refuge for the religious life of the cultured classes', leading to the 'formation of groups on a purely personal basis, with no permanent form, which also tend to weaken the significance of forms of worship, doctrine and the historical element'.[26]

Sociologist Michael Hill identifies six features of this genus of contemporary religions, which are typically:

1 individualistic, characteristic of societies with an increasing division of labour;
2 characterized by an emphasis on an idealized human personality, with adherents pursuing the goal of self-perfection and a realization of their human potential;
3 tolerant, without intense primary group membership, with a free exchange of ideas and a relativistic acceptance of alternative views and visions;
4 syncretistic, with a range of ideas shaped into a relatively plastic amalgam;
5 monistic, rejecting any dichotomy of body and mind and seeing spiritual power as diffuse and all-pervasive;
6 characterized by an emphasis on a process whereby individuals are morally remade or empowered.[27]

What is the relationship of such religions to liberal modernity? In significant ways, they do offer a critique of aspects of secular modernity. Their monistic emphasis is highly critical of what is identified as the Cartesian strand in modern culture, with its

---

[26] *Social Teachings of the Christian Churches* (University of Chicago Press, 1960), vol. II, 993–4.
[27] Michael Hill, 'New Zealand's Cultic Milieu – Individualism and the Logic of Consumerism', in *Religion: Contemporary Issues*, ed. B. Wilson, The All Souls Seminars in the Sociology of Religion (London: Bellew Publishing, 1992), 224–5. Some variants of religions of self-realization have been studied in Rachael Kohn's 'Radical Subjectivity in "self religions" and the problem of authority', in *Religion in Australia: Sociological Perspectives*, ed. A. W. Black (Sydney: Allen and Unwin, 1991). In D. Millikan's and N. Drury's *Worlds Apart? Christianity and the New Age* (Crows Nest: Australian Broadcasting Corporation, 1991), Neville Drury identifies Theosophy, Transpersonal Psychology, Jung and the New England transcendentalists as some of the influences on contemporary religions of self-realization. For an analysis of the key characteristics of New Age religion, see A. Kelly, *An Expanding Theology* (Sydney: E. J. Dwyer, 1993), ch. 2, sects. 4, 5.

dualist and mechanistic consequences.[28] Their emphasis on the oneness and interdependence of all life is expressed in opposition to anti-ecological forms of technology. They are critical of many forms of reductive science, attempting to restore a holistic view of the psychosomatic unity of the human person. Their vision of the spiritual sources of human life – in affinity with primal religion – runs counter to the naturalistic philosophy characteristic of some major modern traditions. In terms of community, these contemporary movements put the global character of human community into high relief, as well as the community of the human species with all other forms of life. In terms of meaning, they understand the fulfilment of the self in terms of its union with the cosmic source of all life.

In all these ways, then, such religious movements do represent a strong and broadly based critique of the secularizing and naturalistic aspects of modernity. Yet their fundamental orientation to self-realization gives reason to think that this critique will be less influential than the affirmation that such religions give to some of modernity's deepest tendencies. As we have seen, these tendencies are towards the dissolution of communal bonds based on shared and public conceptions of meaning, towards the achievement of the 'pure relationship' as the encounter of free and fulfilled selves. Modernity emphasizes self-realization, but, at the same time, many characteristically modern philosophies deny the truth-claims of any theory of the good which will provide a realm of meaning within which the self can realize itself by going beyond itself. For modernity, personal autonomy tends to be understood in a way which makes the other inessential for my own identity and self-understanding: I am defined by my own autonomy as a free self, rather than by relationships with what is other than myself, with what calls me to give myself and offers a transformed self in

---

[28] In his *The Turning Point* (London: Flamingo, 1983), Fritjof Capra argues for an ecologically inspired 'systems view of life' (317) and a 'systems concept of God as the universal dynamics of self-organization' (332), which draws on Chinese religious and philosophical traditions. For Capra, new ecological technologies 'rather than being based on the principles of Cartesian science, will incorporate the principles observed in natural ecosystems and thus reflect systemic wisdom' (443).

return. Modernity's fear of authoritarian structures of the good tends to mean that a genuinely dialectical vision of self-realization in terms of a relationship between the self and the other is rejected as inimical to personal autonomy.

Religious movements which focus on self-realization cannot offer a critique of these fundamental aspects of modernity because their understanding of the relationship of the self to the cosmos gives no place to what is irreducibly other than the self. There is no need for a dialectic between self and other if self-knowledge is cosmic knowledge. The self can achieve full realization by journeying into its own interiority and rediscovering itself as a cosmic principle. Because of this, the self-religions emphasize gnosis as the path to self-realization: by self-knowledge, I can come to ultimate knowledge. The self-religions' critique of the attitude of religious faith is that it is less than knowledge, a critique depending on the premise that we can know the ultimate since it is within ourselves and therefore within the scope of our own reflexivity.[29] Faith, in contrast, implies that the other is irreducibly other and can only be known if it chooses to reveal itself. We cannot know the other purely through our own reflexivity: the other is known in faith as mystery, as the unknown which gives itself to us and invites us into relationship. Faith is knowledge born of love of what is other, rather than knowledge of what is ultimately myself. The self-religions' understanding of self-realization as a gnosis of cosmic oneness achieved through self-knowledge cannot offer a fundamental challenge to modernity's reduction of community to the 'pure relationships' of self-sufficient selves.

Giddens' deployment of the concept of the 'sequestration of

[29] Marilyn Ferguson, in her *The Aquarian Conspiracy* (Los Angeles: J. P. Tarcher, 1980), an influential statement of the religiosity of self-realization and cosmic oneness, expresses this attitude to faith as a lesser form of knowledge inevitably associated with spiritual authoritarianism: 'ironically, every organized religion has been based on the claims of direct experience of one or more persons, whose revelations are then handed down as articles of faith. Those who want direct knowledge, the mystics, have always been treated more or less as heretics, whether they were the medieval mystics within Christianity, the Sufis within the borders of Islam, or the Kabbalists within Judaism. Now the heretics are gaining ground, doctrine is losing its authority, and knowing is superseding belief' (370–1).

experience' suggested that the personal search for meaning within modernity can be emasculated by insulation from forms of experience characterized by suffering and existential crisis. For the self-religions, however, insight into cosmic meaning can be attained through various techniques of self-knowledge.[30] Since meaning is appropriated through the gnosis deriving from reflexivity, an encounter with various forms of marginalized human existence is not essential to it. The attainment of insight into cosmic meaning is a cognitive project within the control of the self, rather than something which essentially includes a dialectical encounter with the surds of suffering and evil in the lives of others. This is particularly clear in the emphasis on the doctrine of reincarnation characteristic of some of the self-religions: the advocacy of this doctrine suggests that suffering is perceived as an aspect of metaphysical order, rather than a challenge to any attempt to construct such order. If suffering is the logical result of previous existences, or the result of a lack of self-liberating gnosis, then the alleviation of the suffering of others cannot be considered to be constitutive of one's own self-realization, which is being enacted on another spiritual plane.[31] This means that the religions of self-realization are unlikely to offer any sustained or fundamental challenge to the 'sequestration of experience' characteristic of modernity.

It is of great importance to note that this analysis of some of the features of these contemporary Western religious phenomena cannot necessarily be applied to the Indian religions themselves. It is significant that the origins of Buddhism were precisely in Siddhārtha Gautama's overcoming of the 'sequestration of experience'. Buddhist legend reminds us that Siddhārtha Gautama was insulated from all experiences of sickness, old age and death, and that it was the encounter with these realities which led him to leave the securities of his

[30] See, for example, the various 'Approaches to Transpersonal States of Consciousness' discussed by Neville Drury in D. Millikan and N. Drury *Worlds Apart?*, 44–56.
[31] The biblical scholar John Drane, in his *What is the New Age saying to the Church?* (London: Marshall Pickering, 1991), 113, notes that the interpretation of the doctrine of reincarnation characteristic of Western religiosity of self-realization often neglects the moral element contained in traditional Hindu understandings of reincarnation in terms of the fulfilment of *dharma*.

luxurious home and to reflect on the meaning of suffering.[32] The 'four noble truths' of Buddhism emphasize that the experience of suffering is a constitutive part of human existence, and that it is the desire to cling to the self which is the origin of suffering. The overcoming of the 'burning thirst' of desire and the abandonment of the illusion of the self can lead to a compassion for all life, so that concern for the suffering of others is taken up into the spiritual project of overcoming of self.

The above argument has attempted to acknowledge the significant critique of modernity made by the contemporary religions of self-realization, but at the same time to contend that their core beliefs are readily assimilable to some of modernity's strongest socio-economic dynamics. Because of this, such religions are unlikely to fulfil their own millenarian aspirations, to fundamentally alter the civilization of modernity.[33] The new religious challenge to the mechanistic, dualistic and exploitative character of modernity cannot be sustained if at the same time modernity's emphasis on the supremacy of the autonomous and self-realizing self is magnified into a cosmic principle. The understanding of the self simply as a free agent characterized by needs and desires, characteristic of influential currents of modernity, is not fundamentally threatened by religious movements which believe ultimate reality to be attainable by reflection on

---

[32] As presented, for example, in *Buddhist Scriptures*, selected and translated by E. Conze (Harmondsworth: Penguin, 1959), Part 1, ch. 2, 'The Legend of the Buddha Shakyamuni'.

[33] Expectations expressed, for example, in the notion of the coming 'Age of Aquarius', or in the concluding part of Capra's *The Turning Point* entitled 'The Coming of the Solar Age' – ideas that, perhaps unwittingly, seem to draw on notions of a future age of the Spirit within terrestrial history that originate in the writings of the medieval monk Joachim of Fiore: see the discussion of the influence of Joachim's ideas in N. Cohn's *The Pursuit of the Millennium* (London: Paladin, 1970), 108–10. Bede Griffiths, in his *A New Vision of Reality* (Springfield: Templegate, 1989), shares this expectation of a new age which will transform the conditions of civilization (276–95). Griffiths' generous vision of a revival of the 'perennial philosophy' emphasizes the spiritual values common to the world religions and at the same time clearly differentiates between the monism characteristic of Shankara's *advaita vedanta* and Christian emphasis on the reality of personal and interpersonal life (153–7). His important critique of the reductionist and mechanical philosophy characteristic of much of contemporary Western culture does not, however, show much awareness of how contemporary emphasis on self-realization can, in fact, conform to rather than challenge some of the most powerful fragmenting forces of modernity.

our own interiority rather than by commitment to a good which is other and more than ourselves.

This critique of the religions of self-realization in their relationship to modernity must be complemented by a self-critical Christian theological reflection on the relationships of Christianity and the Christian community to modernity. In particular, a discussion of the significance for Christian faith of the 'pure relationship' and the 'sequestration of experience' should be attempted, since these concepts can shed light on the tensions Christians experience in attempting to reconcile autonomy and community in the conditions of modernity, as well as provide clues for the continuing development of Christian conceptions of existence in community.

The notion of the 'pure relationship' expresses the character of relationships as based on freely chosen interpersonal intimacy, rather than on the imperatives of traditional social structures. It expresses the conviction that personal affinity cannot be dictated or controlled by considerations outside the sphere of the relationship itself. The great value in this conception of personal relationships is in its affirmation of subjectivity, of personal relationships as a bond between free individuals who are committed to each other because of each other's uniqueness, rather than merely because each fulfils a role within a traditional social order. Yet, at the same time, the 'pure relationship' is inherently unstable, since the strength of the relationship depends on the degree of commitment to intimacy within it, although such commitment is given with the risk that the relationship will end because it ceases to be satisfying to both parties. Giddens is an advocate of the 'pure relationship' as a form of life which expresses the autonomy of the person and the optional character of particular ethical traditions in modern societies.[34] Yet he acknowledges that:

[34] Since modernity has 'disembedded' traditions, they can only be revived as a 'kind of lifestyle decision', quite different from the pre-modern role of tradition; 'Living in a Post-Traditional Society', in A. Giddens, *In Defence of Sociology: Essays, Interpretations and Rejoinders* (Cambridge: Polity Press, 1996), 32. At the same time, he notes 'that the defence of tradition has an important role' in a post-traditional society, if traditions are able to justify themselves in a dialogic and discursive way. Understood in this way, traditions may assist in resisting the 'compulsive' character of modernity (64).

there is a structural contradiction in the pure relationship, centring upon commitment . . . To generate commitment and develop a shared history, an individual must give of herself to the other. That is, she must provide, in word and deed, some kind of guarantees to the other that the relationship can be sustained for an indefinite period. Yet a present-day relationship is not, as marriage once was, a 'natural condition' whose durability can be taken for granted short of certain extreme circumstances. It is a feature of the pure relationship that it can be terminated, more or less at will, by either partner at any particular point. For a relationship to stand a chance of lasting, commitment is necessary; yet anyone who commits herself without reservations risks great hurt in the future, should the relationship become dissolved.[35]

This tension marked out by freedom and commitment, autonomy and community, is critically important both for personal relationships and for the lives of broader communities. A community based on 'pure relationships' is a community which prizes the uniqueness of its members and the affirmation and satisfaction which each member derives from freely given intimacy with others. The critical point for such 'pure relationships' is in those situations where one (or more) members no longer derive personal satisfaction from the relationship, and where further commitment to community may mean self-sacrifice. If the self is defined as an autonomous agent with needs and desires, and if there are no reasons external to the self why such commitment should be sustained, then it is difficult to see why such self-sacrifice should be accepted. If, however, communities cannot be sustained by individuals willing to risk self-sacrifice, then they will lack a crucial contribution to their own preservation in the face of adversity.

A Christian attempt to contribute to an understanding of community in the conditions of modernity must be critically

---

[35] *The Transformation of Intimacy: Sexuality, Love and Eroticism in Modern Societies*, (Cambridge: Polity Press, 1992), 137. See also *Consequences of Modernity* , 143–4. As Robert Wuthnow notes, an analogous tension exists at the level of civil society, which 'is always in jeopardy because individualism and associational ties are both needed and yet are at odds with each other'. Civil society is a 'precarious admixture of unity and diversity', because there is urgent need for a holistic moral community, yet the whole purpose of such a community is to permit free people to live together; *Christianity and Civil Society*, 40.

self-aware of the damage caused by Christians' endorsement of past societies based on enforced structures of order. For the religions of self-realization, it is the authoritarianism of Christianity, summed up in the image of a transcendent patriarchal deity, which is its characteristic most worthy of criticism.[36] Christians have also been guilty of promoting ideologies of self-sacrifice which have had little to do with individual welfare and much to do with preserving the hegemony of repressive and anachronistic forms of piety. Perhaps the most important insight that Christian faith can contribute to the contemporary search for community is a truly interpersonal understanding of the self, an understanding that recognizes both the values of individual subjectivity and the way in which this subjectivity depends on committed relationships to others for its full realization.[37] Such an understanding of the self would recognize the value of individual freedom which is enshrined in modernity, but at the same time attempt to show that this freedom is enhanced and fulfilled by understanding the human person in the context of communal, interpersonal relationships, rather than as a 'punctual self', an individual agent characterized by needs and desires.[38]

[36] For example, by Capra in *The Turning Point*: 'The view of man as dominating nature and woman, and the belief in the superior role of the rational mind, have been supported and encouraged by the Judaeo-Christian tradition, which adheres to the images of a male god, personification of supreme reason and source of ultimate power, which rules the world from above by imposing his divine law on it. The laws of nature searched for by the scientists were seen as reflections of this divine law, originating in the mind of God' (24).
[37] See, for example, Alistair McFadyen's expression of a Christian understanding of the nature of persons in community in *The Call to Personhood: A Christian Theory of the Individual in Social Relationships* (Cambridge University Press, 1990).
[38] In his *The One, the Three and the Many: God, Creation and the Culture of Modernity* (Cambridge University Press, 1993), Colin Gunton offers a philosophical and theological interpretation of the relationship between Christian faith, community and individuality. For Gunton, the crucial need of contemporary Christian theology is to develop understandings of the self, community and God which do justice to both unity and particularity. Gunton argues that it was the assertion of an overwhelming metaphysical unity by the Christian philosophical tradition that led to modernity's protest in the name of particularity, a protest that led to a loss of any sense of relationship between particulars – in Taylor's terms, to a loss of horizons of significance that could form the ultimate parameters for the self's search for authenticity. For Gunton, a true sense of particularity, conceived as particular existence lived in relationship with both God and others, can be achieved through a

This understanding of the self would affirm the value of the 'pure relationships' characteristic of modernity, relationships which celebrate subjectivity and intimacy rather than simply fulfilling social roles. Yet it would also draw attention to the ways in which the self's commitment to the other in relationship and community can go beyond what is perceived to be of direct benefit to the self's own realization. It would affirm that the self's realization cannot be achieved without the loss of self that commitment to relationship and community can demand. In both private and public life, an understanding of the self, that recognizes that self-fulfilment cannot be achieved without self-sacrificial commitment, can make a contribution to the problem of community. A key part of this understanding will be a reflection on those goods of interpersonal life, which can only be realized through fidelity, the depths of intimacy and communion, that have a voluntary relinquishing of various kinds of freedom as their prerequisite. Such an understanding can draw on the communication of the Christian vision of communion and solidarity.

In relation to the question of fundamental meaning, Christian faith can communicate a vision which can assist in addressing some of the effects of the contemporary 'sequestration of experience' resulting from the deployment of technological systems. The danger of this phenomenon is that those who are thereby relieved of the encounter with the suffering and the marginalized will construct systems of meaning which are not only based on a narrow field of experience, but which also purport to justify the privileges which have freed those concerned from exposure to the margins and crises of life. This is particularly evident when we consider that the 'sequestration of experience' is not only a phenomenon whereby existential crises within particular societies, such as criminality or mental illness, are removed from the experience of most members of those societies, but can also be a global process whereby members of

trinitarian theology which is truly relational and perichoretic. Since creation, and human existence, bear the marks of the Trinity, the meaning of human society must also be sought in a community constituted by the inherently interrelated quality of particularity.

modern societies, through the deployment of technological and economic advantage, remove themselves from encounter with the sheer physical want of much of the world. While modernity tends towards such a 'sequestration of experience', its technologies of communication also make an awareness of such problems possible, both on a global scale and within individual societies. Modernity provides both the means of becoming aware of the sufferings of the world and the means of effectively insulating ourselves from them.

The dangers of this 'sequestration of experience', as an impoverishment of the moral context within which we live our lives, are particularly evident when we consider how much Christian tradition has developed through the encounter with the pain of the exploited and oppressed. The discussion of the development of the church's social teaching, from the time of Lamennais to Vatican II, was intended to highlight one example of this broadening and purification of Christian tradition through the challenge posed by the encounter with the pain of those suffering the injustices that accompanied the development of modern capitalism in Europe. If the efficacy of modern technical systems is used as a means of escaping an encounter with the pain of others, then Christian communities will deprive themselves of the most powerful stimulus to a deeper understanding of their own faith.

What Christian faith seeks to communicate is that any vision or project of meaning is radically incomplete if it is constructed in abstraction from the reality of suffering. For Christianity, the discovery of ultimate meaning can never be a purely theoretical process, since any comprehensive theory of meaning is always refuted by the practical experience of meaninglessness in evil and suffering.[39] This is particularly true if the reality of my own

[39] See the discussion of the relationship between the problem of meaning and the problem of suffering in R. Haight's *An Alternative Vision: an Interpretation of Liberation Theology* (New York: Paulist Press, 1985). Haight emphasizes the need to grasp as a unity theology's attempt to answer the critiques of secular scepticism and its attempt to address the challenge of social suffering: the question of religious meaning is a question that can only be answered in a global context – 'Just as one cannot believe in one's own salvation without hope for the salvation of others, so one cannot affirm that there is meaning in my human existence, even though the human existence of half the race seems meaningless, pointless, valueless, leading nowhere, absurd'

self is defined in relation to other selves. If I am a self in isolation, then my own search for meaning need not be rendered null and void by others' experience of meaninglessness in suffering. If, however, the lives of others are in some way involved in the meaning of my own life, then their suffering negates any claim that I might make to have achieved meaning. On this basis, any claim to meaning must be based on an experience which has accepted and overcome suffering. Further, any claim to cosmic meaning must be one which is based on the faith that the meaning which is at the source and heart of the cosmos is also one which has endured and overcome suffering, the faith which Christians express as the Paschal mystery of Jesus of Nazareth, the incarnate Son of God.

In attempting to communicate this sense of solidarity with suffering, Christians should be aware that the meaning of their own lives must be one which is sought after in solidarity with the suffering, since any other claim to ultimate meaning runs counter to the meaning of Christianity itself. They will take advantage of the opportunities for global awareness that modernity offers, its great potential to develop the sense of the human race as a 'we', as a self-conscious community. At the same time, they will be critically aware of modernity's tendency to insulate everyday life from the experiences of the marginalized. They will applaud the development of professional systems that are devoted to serving those who are involved with the existential crises of life, but at the same time they will attempt to develop various practical means of encouraging and enhancing solidarity between those who suffer from such crises and those whose lives benefit from the tranquillity and security that modern technical systems can provide.[40] It is not only

---

(35–6). A similar position is taken by Edward Schillebeeckx in his *Church: The Human Story of God* (New York: Crossroad, 1991), in his discussion of 'The present "world context" of belief in God' (53–4).

[40] In his 'Solidarity with the Lowliest: Parish Growth through the Witness of Practical Service' in *Diakonia: Church for Others*, ed. N. Greinacher and N. Mette, *Concilium* (Edinburgh: T. and T. Clark, 1988), Norbert Mette warns of the dangers for the life of the church in separating parish-based pastoral work from large-scale church social-relief agencies. While he does not deny the commitment and effectiveness of such large-scale agencies, Mette argues that the interplay of *diakonia* and parish

those on the margins of society who will benefit from the solidarity attempted by the economically privileged citizens of modernity. The encounter with the marginalized will often bring new perspectives and new hope to those who act in community with them, whose economic security is no defence against the banalities of a civilization so deeply influenced by the image of the self as an ego confronting the world as nothing more than a passive terrain for the satisfaction of its own needs and desires.

The heart of any attempt to reconcile autonomy and community is, therefore, a theology of solidarity, a solidarity based in God's solidarity with humanity in the life and passion of Christ. Solidarity is the active expression of *communio*, a participation of all in the lives and destinies of others, through our common participation in the love of God. It is part of the character of solidarity to be an expression of freedom, a willing identification of the self with the plight and conditions of others. Because of this, an ethic of solidarity affirms the freedom of conscience and personal commitment fundamental to modern societies. At the same time, because it sees the fulfilment of human freedom in commitment to others, it overcomes notions of the self and of autonomy purely as freedom from unwarranted restraint. Finally, a theology of solidarity and communion provides the key to Christian identity: an identity grounded in the concrete, historical reality of God's love in Christ, and expressed in an engagement with the world motivated by the faith that the Spirit calls all humanity to participation in the communion of divine love.

sacramental life is crucial for the life of the church, so that a reduction of pastoral life to service of the 'abstract inwardness' (82) of individuals is overcome through a sense of solidarity in community.

Select bibliography

CHURCH DOCUMENTS

Mirari vos. (Gregory XVI) 1832.
Singulari nos. (Gregory XVI) 1834.
Dei Filius. (*On the Catholic Faith*) Vatican I, 1870.
Gaudium et spes. (*Pastoral Constitution on the Church in the Modern World*) Vatican II, 1965.
Dei Verbum. (*Dogmatic Constitution on Divine Revelation*) Vatican II, 1965.
The Challenge of Peace. National Conference of Catholic Bishops of the United States, 1983.
Economic Justice for All. National Conference of Catholic Bishops of the United States, 1986.
Sollicitudo Rei Socialis. (*On Social Concerns*) John Paul II, 1987.

OTHER WORKS

Ahlstrom, S. *A Religious History of the American People.* New Haven: Yale University Press, 1972.
Apel, K.-O. 'Die Apriori der Kommunikationsgemeinschaft und die Grundlagen der Ethik', in *Transformation der Philosophie*, volume II. Frankfurt: Suhrkamp, 1973.
  Sprachpragmatik und Philosophie. Frankfurt: Suhrkamp, 1976.
Auer, A. *Autonome Moral und christlicher Glaube.* Düsseldorf: Patmos Verlag, 2nd edn, 1984.
Bauman, Z. *Postmodern Ethics.* Oxford: Blackwell, 1993.
Beck, L. W. *A Commentary on Kant's Critique of Practical Reason.* University of Chicago Press, 1960.
Beckford, J. A. *Religion and Advanced Industrial Society.* London: Unwin Hyman, 1989.
Bellah, R., Madsen, R., Sullivan, W. M., Swidler, A. and Tipton, S. M. *Habits of the Heart: Individualism and Commitment in American Life.* New York: Harper and Row, 1985.

Select bibliography 237

Benhabib, S. *Situating the Self: Gender, Community and Postmodernism in Contemporary Ethics*. Cambridge: Polity Press, 1992.
Berger, P. *The Social Reality of Religion*. Harmondsworth: Penguin, 1973.
Black, A. W. *Religion in Australia: Sociological Perspectives*. Sydney: Allen and Unwin, 1991.
Böckle, F. *Fundamentalmoral*. Munich: Kösel, 1977.
Bouma, G. *Religion: Meaning, Transcendence and Community in Australia*. Melbourne: Longman Cheshire, 1992.
Bultmann, R. 'Der Begriff der Offenbarung im Neuen Testament', in *Glauben und Wissen*, III. Tübingen: J. C. B. Mohr, 1929.
Cady, L. 'Foundations vs. Scaffolding: The Possibility of Justification in an Historicist Approach to Ethics'. *Union Seminary Quarterly Review* 41 (1987): no. 2.
Casanova, J. *Public Religions in the Modern World*. University of Chicago Press, 1994.
Cavanaugh, William T. ' "A Fire Strong Enough to Consume the House": The Wars of Religion and the Rise of the State'. *Modern Theology* 11 (1995): 4.
Charlesworth, M. J. *Bioethics in a Liberal Society*. Melbourne: Cambridge University Press, 1993.
Cohn, N. *The Pursuit of the Millennium*. London: Paladin, 1970.
Commentary on the Documents of Vatican II, edited by H. Vorgrimler. London and New York: Burns and Oates, Herder and Herder, 1969.
Conze, E. *Buddhist Scriptures*. Harmondsworth: Penguin, 1959.
Cook, M. L. 'Revelation as Metaphoric Process'. *Theological Studies* 47 (1986): no. 3.
Copeland, M. Shawn 'Toward a Critical Christian Feminist Theology of Solidarity', in *Women and Theology*, edited by M. A. Hinsdale and P. H. Kaminski. Maryknoll, N.Y.: Orbis Books and College Theology Society, 1995.
Curran, C. and McCormick, R. A. *The Distinctiveness of Christian Ethics*. Readings in Moral Theology 2. New York: Paulist Press, 1980.
Daniels, N., ed. *Reading Rawls – Critical Studies on Rawls' 'A Theory of Justice'*. New York: Basic Books, 1975.
Davis, C. *Religion and the Making of Society: Essays in Social Theology*. Cambridge University Press, 1994.
Demmer, K. *Deuten und Handeln*. Freiburg im Breisgau: Herder, 1985.
Demmer, K. and Schüller, B., eds. *Christlich Glauben und Handeln*. Düsseldorf: Patmos, 1977.
De Dinechin, O. 'Catechesis in France'. *Lumen Vitae*, 34 (1984): no. 2, 226–230.

Donovan, P. 'Do Different Religions have Common Moral Ground?'. *Religious Studies* 22 (1986): 367–76.
Downing, F. G. *Has Christianity a Revelation?* London: SCM, 1962.
Drane, J. *What is the New Age saying to the Church?* London: Marshall Pickering, 1991.
Dulles, A. *Models of Revelation*. Dublin: Gill and Macmillan, 1983.
Dworkin, R. 'Liberalism', in *Public and Private Morality*, edited by S. Hampshire. Cambridge University Press, 1978.
Ebeling, G. 'Die Evidenz des Ethischen und die Theologie', in *Wort und Glaube*, volume II. Tübingen: J. C. B. Mohr, 1969.
Eicher, P. *Offenbarung: Prinzip Neuzeitlicher Theologie*. Munich: Kösel, 1977.
Engelhardt, H. T. *The Foundations of Bioethics*. New York: Oxford University Press, 1986.
Fahrenbach, H. *Existenzphilosophie und Ethik*. Tübingen: J. C. B. Mohr, 1972.
Ferguson, M. *The Aquarian Conspiracy*. Los Angeles: J. P. Tarcher, 1980.
Fergusson, D. *Community, Liberalism and Christian Ethics*. Cambridge University Press, 1998.
Fiorenza, F. S. 'The Church as a Community of Interpretation: Political Theology between Discourse Ethics and Hermeneutical Reconstruction', in *Habermas, Modernity and Public Theology*, edited by D. S. Browning and F. S. Fiorenza. New York: Crossroad, 1992.
Flannery, A. ed. OP. *Vatican Council II: The Basic Sixteen Documents*. Dublin: Dominican Publications, 1996.
Fuchs, J. *Natural Law: A Theological Approach*. Dublin: Gill and Son, 1965.
  'Gibt es eine spezifisch christliche Moral?', *Stimmen der Zeit*, 1970: 99–112.
  'Das Gottesbild und die Moral innerweltlichen Handelns'. *Stimmen der Zeit* 1984: 363–382.
  'Heil, Sittlichkeit, Richtiges Handeln'. *Stimmen der Zeit* 1987: 15–23.
  'Christliche Moral, biblische Orientierung und menschliche Wertung'. *Stimmen der Zeit* 1987: 671–83.
Gallagher, John A. *Time Past, Time Future: An Historical Study of Catholic Moral Theology*. Mahwah: Paulist Press, 1990.
Gascoigne, R. *Religion, Rationality and Community: Sacred and Secular in the Thought of Hegel and his Critics*. The Hague: Martinus Nijhoff, 1985.
Giddens, A. *The Consequences of Modernity*. Cambridge: Polity Press, 1990.

Modernity and Self-Identity: Self and Society in the Late Modern Age. Cambridge: Polity Press, 1991.
The Transformation of Intimacy: Sexuality, Love and Eroticism in Modern Societies. Cambridge: Polity Press, 1992.
'Living in a Post-Traditional Society', in *In Defence of Sociology: Essays, Interpretations and Rejoinders.* Cambridge: Polity Press, 1996.
Gill, R. 'Moral Communities and Christian Ethics', in *Moral Leadership in a Postmodern Age.* Edinburgh: T. and T. Clark, 1997.
Godlove, T. F. 'Two Kinds of Narrative Coherence: Transcendental and Religious'. *Journal of Religion* 67 (1987): no. 4.
Goldberg, M. *Theology and Narrative – A Critical Introduction.* Nashville: Abingdon Press, 1981.
Griffiths, B. *A New Vision of Reality.* Springfield: Templegate, 1989.
Gula, R. *Reason Informed by Faith.* Mahwah: Paulist Press, 1989.
Gunton, C. *The One, the Three and the Many: God, Creation and the Culture of Modernity.* Cambridge University Press, 1993.
Habermas, J. *Legitimationskrise im Spätkapitalismus.* Frankfurt: Suhrkamp, 1973.
Theory and Practice. London: Heinemann, 1974.
Moralbewusstsein und kommunikatives Handeln. Frankfurt: Suhrkamp, 1983.
'Transcendence from Within, Transcendence in this World', in *Habermas, Modernity and Public Theology,* edited by D. S. Browning and F. S. Fiorenza. New York: Crossroad, 1992.
Haight, R. *An Alternative Vision: an Interpretation of Liberation Theology.* New York: Paulist Press, 1985.
Hannon, P. *Church, State, Morality and Law.* Dublin: Gill and Macmillan, 1992.
Hare, R. M. *Freedom and Reason.* Oxford University Press, 1963.
Moral Thinking: Its Levels, Method and Point. Oxford: Clarendon Press, 1981.
Hart, R. L. *Unfinished Man and the Imagination.* New York: Seabury Press, 1968.
Hastings, A. 'Theology and Contemporary Reality', in *The Shaping of Prophecy.* London: Geoffrey Chapman, 1995.
Hauerwas, S. *A Community of Character: Towards a Contructive Christian Social Ethic.* University of Notre Dame Press, 1981.
The Peaceable Kingdom: A Primer in Christian Ethics. University of Notre Dame Press, 1983.
Against the Nations: War and Survival in a Liberal Society. Minneapolis: Winston Press, 1985.
'Positioning: In the Church and University but not of Either', in

Dispatches from the Front: Theological Engagements with the Secular. Durham and London: Duke University Press, 1994.
'The Democratic Policing of Christianity', in *Dispatches from the Front: Theological Engagements with the Secular.* Durham and London: Duke University Press, 1994.
Hauerwas, S. and Burrell, D. 'From System to Story: An Alternative Pattern for Rationality in Ethics', in *Why Narrative? Readings in Narrative Theology,* edited by S. Hauerwas and L. Gregory Jones. Grand Rapids: Eerdmans, 1989.
Hauerwas, S. and MacIntyre, A., eds. *Revisions – Changing Perspectives in Moral Philosophy.* University of Notre Dame Press, 1983.
Hegel, G. W. F. *Philosophy of Right,* trans. Knox, M. Oxford: Clarendon Press, 1952.
Werke in zwanzig Bänden. Frankfurt: Suhrkamp, 1970.
Hill, M. 'New Zealand's Cultic Milieu – Individualism and the Logic of Consumerism', in *Religion: Contemporary Issues,* The All Souls Seminars in the Sociology of Religion, edited by B. Wilson. London: Bellew Publishing, 1992.
Hilpert, K. *Ethik und Rationalität: Untersuchungen zum Autonomieproblem und zu seiner Bedeutung für die theologische Ethik.* Düsseldorf: Patmos Verlag, 1980.
Himes, M. J. and Himes, K. R. *Fullness of Faith: The Public Significance of Theology.* Mahwah: Paulist Press, 1993.
Hollenbach, D. *Claims in Conflict: Retrieving and Renewing the Catholic Human Rights Traditions.* New York: Paulist Press, 1979.
'A Communitarian Reconstruction of Human Rights: Contributions from Catholic Tradition', in *Catholicism and Liberalism: Contributions to American Public Philosophy,* edited by R. Bruce Douglass and D. Hollenbach. Cambridge University Press, 1994.
'Politically Active Churches: Some Empirical Prolegomena to a Normative Approach', in *Religion and Contemporary Liberalism,* edited by P. J. Weithman. University of Notre Dame Press, 1997.
Jedin, H., ed. *History of the Church.* Volume VII: *The Church between Revolution and Restoration.* New York: Crossroad, 1981.
Jones, L. Gregory. 'Alasdair MacIntyre on Narrative, Community and the Moral Life'. *Modern Theology* 4 (1987): no. 1.
'Should Christians Affirm Rawls' "Justice as Fairness"? A Response to Professor Beckley'. *Journal of Religious Ethics* 16 (1988): 251–71.
Kant, I. *Werkausgabe in XII Bänden.* Frankfurt: Suhrkamp, 1968.
Die Religion innerhalb der Grenzen der blossen Vernunft. Stuttgart: Reclam, 1974.
Kasper, W. *The God of Jesus Christ.* London: SCM, 1984.

Select bibliography 241

'Offenbarung Gottes in der Geschichte', in *Handbuch der Verkündigung*, volume II. Freiburg, Basel, Vienna: Herder, 1970.
'Autonomie und Theonomie: Zur Ortsbestimmung des Christentums in der modernen Welt', in *Anspruch der Wirklichkeit und christlicher Glaube*. Düsseldorf: Patmos Verlag, 1980.
'The Church as a Universal Sacrament of Salvation', in *Theology and Church*. New York: Crossroad, 1989.
'The Church as Communion: Reflections on the Guiding Ecclesiological Idea of the Second Vatican Council', in *Theology and Church*. New York: Crossroad, 1989.
'Revelation and Mystery: The Christian Understanding of God', in *Theology and Church*. New York: Crossroad, 1989.
Kelly, A. *An Expanding Theology: Faith in a World of Connections*. Sydney: E. J. Dwyer, 1993.
Kern, W. 'Der Beitrag des Christentums zu einer menschlicheren Welt', in *Handbuch der Fundamentaltheologie*, volume IV, edited by W. Kern, H. Pottmeyer, and M. Seckler. Freiburg im Breisgau: Herder, 1985.
Kerr, F. *Immortal Longings: Versions of Transcending Humanity*. University of Notre Dame Press, 1997.
Kolakowski, L. *Religion*. Glasgow: Fount, Collins, 1982.
Metaphysical Horror. Oxford: Blackwell, 1988.
Korff, W. *Norm und Sittlichkeit: Untersuchungen zur Logic der Normativen Vernunft*. Mainz: Matthias Grünewald, 1973.
Lakeland, P. *Postmodernity: Christian Identity in a Fragmented Age*, Minneapolis: Fortress Press, 1997.
Lamb, M. 'Solidarity', in *New Dictionary of Catholic Social Thought*, edited by J. A. Dwyer. Collegeville: Liturgical Press, Michael Glazier, 1994.
Lamennais, F. de *Paroles d'un croyant*. L. de Guillou, ed. Paris: Flammarion, 1973.
Latourelle, R. *Theology of Revelation*. London: Mercier Press, 1968.
Lauritzen, P. 'Is "Narrative" Really a Panacea? The Use of "Narrative" in the Works of Metz and Hauerwas'. *Journal of Religion* 67 (1987): no. 3.
Lechner, F. J. 'Global Fundamentalism', in *A Future for Religion? New Paradigms for Social Analysis*, edited by William H. Swatos, Jr. Newbury Park, Calif.: SAGE, 1993.
Lindbeck, G. *The Nature of Doctrine: Religion and Theology in a Post-Liberal Age*. Philadelphia: Westminster Press, 1984.
'Barth and Textuality', *Theology Today* 43 (1986): no. 3.
Löwith, K. *From Hegel to Nietzsche*. London: Constable, 1965.
Luckmann, T. *The Invisible Religion*. New York: Macmillan, 1967.

McCormick, R. *The Critical Calling*. Georgetown: Washington, 1989.
McFadyen, A. *The Call to Personhood: A Christian Theory of the Individual in Social Relationships*. Cambridge University Press, 1990.
MacIntyre, A. *After Virtue*. London: Duckworth, 1981.
Whose Justice? Which Rationality? University of Notre Dame Press, 1988.
Mackie, J. L. *Ethics – Inventing Right and Wrong*. Harmondsworth: Penguin, 1977.
MacNamara, V. *Faith and Ethics – Recent Roman Catholicism*. Dublin: Gill and Macmillan/Washington: Georgetown University Press, 1985.
Mahoney, J. *The Making of Moral Theology: A Study of the Roman Catholic Tradition*. Oxford: Clarendon Press, 1987.
Markham, I. S. *Plurality and Christian Ethics*. Cambridge University Press, 1994.
Marty, M. E., and Appleby, R. S., eds. *Fundamentalisms and the State: Remaking Polities, Economies and Militance*. University of Chicago Press, 1993.
Mette, N. 'Solidarity with the Lowliest: Parish Growth through the Witness of Practical Service' in *Diakonia: Church for Others*, edited by N. Greinacher and N. Mette. *Concilium*. Edinburgh: T. and T. Clark, 1988.
Metz, J. B. *Glaube in Geschichte und Gesellschaft*. Mainz: Matthias Grünewald, 1977.
Mieth, D. and Compagnoni, F. *Ethik im Kontext des Glaubens*. Freiburg: Universitätsverlag Freiburg, 1978.
Milbank, J. *Theology and Social Theory*. Oxford: Blackwell, 1990.
Millikan, D. and Drury, N. *Worlds Apart? Christianity and the New Age*. Crows Nest: Australian Broadcasting Corporation, 1991.
Misner, P. *Social Catholicism in Europe: From the Onset of Industrialization to the First World War*. New York: Crossroad, 1991.
Mitchell, B. *Law, Morality and Religion in a Secular Society*. Oxford University Press, 1970.
Morality: Religious and Secular. Oxford: Clarendon Press, 1980.
Moltmann, J. *Theology of Hope*. London: SCM, 1967.
Moran, G. *Theology of Revelation*. New York: Herder and Herder, 1966.
The Present Revelation. New York: Herder and Herder, 1972.
Nagel, T. 'Moral Conflict and Political Legitimacy'. *Philosophy and Public Affairs* 16 (1987): no. 3.
Nelson, P. *Narrative and Morality: A Theological Inquiry*. University Park and London: Pennsylvania State University Press, 1987.
Neuhaus, R. J. *The Naked Public Square: Religion and Democracy in America*. Eerdmans: Grand Rapids, 1984.

The Catholic Moment: The Paradox of the Church in the Postmodern World.
San Francisco: Harper and Row, 1987.
Newbigin, L. *The Gospel in a Pluralist Society.* Grand Rapids: Eerdmans, 1989.
Niebuhr, H. R. *The Meaning of Revelation.* London: Macmillan, 1941.
O'Connell, T. *Principles for a Catholic Morality.* (Revised edition) New York: Seabury Press, 1990.
Pannenberg, W. *Revelation as History.* London: Macmillan, 1968.
Theologie und Reich Gottes. Gütersloh: Gerd Mohn, 1971.
Ethik und Ekklesiologie. Göttingen: Vandenhoeck und Ruprecht, 1977.
Anthropology in Theological Perspective. Edinburgh: T. and T. Clark, 1985.
Systematische Theologie, volume 1. Göttingen: Vandenhoeck und Ruprecht, 1988.
'Die Offenbarung Gottes in Jesus von Nazareth', in *Theologie als Geschichte.* Zurich: Zwingli Verlag, 1967.
'Offenbarung und "Offenbarungen" im Zeugnis der Geschichte', in *Handbuch der Fundamentaltheologie,* volume II, edited by W. Kern, H. Pottmeyer and M. Seckler. Freiburg im Breisgau: Herder, 1985.
Peukert, H. *Science, Action and Fundamental Theology: Towards a Theology of Communicative Action.* Cambridge, Mass.: MIT Press, 1984.
Porter, J. *Moral Action and Christian Ethics.* Cambridge University Press, 1995.
Rahner, K. *Grundkurs des Glaubens.* Freiburg im Breisgau: Herder, 1976.
Rahner, K. and Ratzinger, J. *Offenbarung und Überlieferung,* Quaestiones Disputatae. Freiburg im Breisgau: Herder, 1965.
Ramsey, I. T., ed. *Christian Ethics and Contemporary Philosophy.* London: SCM, 1965.
Ratzinger, J. *Prinzipien Christlicher Moral.* Einsiedeln: Johannes Verlag, 1975.
'Sources and Transmission of the Faith'. *Communio* 10 (1983): no. 1.
Rawls, J. *A Theory of Justice.* Oxford University Press, 1972.
Political Liberalism. New York: Columbia University Press, 1993.
Reardon, B. *Liberalism and Tradition: Aspects of Catholic Thought in Nineteenth-Century France.* Cambridge University Press, 1975.
Rigali, N. 'The Uniqueness and Distinctiveness of Christian Ethics', in *Moral Theology: Challenges for the Future. Essays in honour of R. A. McCormick,* edited by C. Curran. Mahwah: Paulist Press, 1990.
Ringeling, H. 'Christliche Ethik im Dialog mit der Anthropologie: Das Problem der Identität', in *Handbuch Christlicher Ethik.* Freiburg im Breisgau: Herder, 1978.

Rorty, R. *Contingency, Irony and Solidarity*. Cambridge University Press, 1989.
Rotter, H. *Christliches Handeln: Seine Begründung und Eigenart*. Graz–Vienna–Cologne: Styria, 1977.
'Zwölf Thesen zur heilsgeschichtlichen Begründung der Moral', in *Heilsgeschichte und ethische Normen*, Quaestiones Disputatae, edited by H. Rotter. Freiburg im Breisgau: Herder, 1984.
Schillebeeckx, E. *Christ: The Christian Experience in the Modern World*. London: SCM, 1980.
Church: The Human Story of God. New York: Crossroad, 1991.
Schnackenburg, R. *The Epistle to the Ephesians*. Edinburgh: T. and T. Clark, 1991.
Seckler, M. 'Der Begriff der Offenbarung', in *Handbuch der Fundamentaltheologie*, volume II, edited by W. Kern, H. J. Pottmeyer and M. Seckler. Freiburg im Breisgau: Herder, 1985.
'Zur Interdependenz von Aufklärung und Offenbarung'. *Tübinger Theologische Quartalschrift*, 165 (1985): 161–73.
Shanks, A. *Civil Society, Civil Religion*. Oxford: Blackwell, 1995.
Singer, M. G. *Generalization in Ethics*. London: Eyre and Spottiswoode, 1963.
Stoeckle, B. *Grenzen der autonomen Moral*. Munich: Kösel, 1974.
Stout, J. *Ethics after Babel: The Languages of Morals and their Discontents*. Boston: Beacon Press, 1988.
Strawson, P. 'Social Morality and Individual Ideal', in *Christian Ethics and Contemporary Philosophy*, ed. I. Ramsey. London: SCM, 1965.
Stroup, G. W. *The Promise of Narrative Theology: Recovering the Gospel in the Church*. Atlanta: John Knox Press, 1981.
Taylor, C. *Hegel*. Cambridge: Cambridge University Press, 1975.
Sources of the Self. Cambridge, Mass.: Harvard University Press, 1989.
The Ethics of Authenticity. Cambridge, Mass.: Harvard University Press, 1992.
Theunissen, M. *Hegels Lehre vom absoluten Geist als theologisch-politischer Traktat*. Berlin: De Gruyter, 1970.
Thiemann, R. *Revelation and Theology: The Gospel as Narrated Promise*. University of Notre Dame Press, 1985.
Constructing a Public Theology: The Church in a Pluralistic Culture. Louisville: Westminister/John Knox Press, 1991.
Religion in Public Life: A Dilemma for Democracy. Washington, D.C.: Georgetown University Press (Twentieth-Century Fund), 1996.
'Response to George Lindbeck', *Theology Today* 43 (1986): no. 3.
Toews, J. E. *Hegelianism: The Path toward Dialectical Humanism 1805–1841*. Cambridge University Press, 1980.

Index

Hauerwas, Stanley, 99, 125 n.40, 174 n.8, 175–6, 183, 199 n.42, 206–8
Hegel, G. W. F., 31–5, 40, 86–7, 92–3, 142–4, 155–7
Hill, Michael, 224
Hilpert, K., 172 n.5
Himes, K. R. and M. J., 78 n.36
Hollenbach, David, 36 n.34, 89 n.44, 197 n.41
incarnation, 31, 92, 156–7
intersubjectivity, 58, 62, 64–5, 68, 75

Kant, Immanuel, 15, 17 n.8, 26–31, 48–50, 86, 164–5, 170; and the 'highest good' 29, 190; 'kingdom of ends', 15–16, 28, 46, 47, 49–51, 57–8, 61–2, 68, 75, 94, 161, 196
Kasper, Walter, 82 n.39, 112 n.18
Kern, Walter, 12 n.2
Kerr, Fergus, 151 n.76, 222 n.19
Kolakowski, Leszek, 123 n.36
Korff, W., 170 n.1, 201 n.44

Lakeland, Paul, 95 n.2, 137 n.55
Lamennais, F. de, 131–2
Lauritzen, P., 104 n.15
Lechner, Frank J., 217 n.3
Leo XIII, 36
Lindbeck, George, 102, 119–22, 125 n.40, 182–3

MacIntyre, Alasdair, 40 n.37, 41 n.39, 89–91, 121 n.33, 151–2
Mackie, J. L., 16 n.6, 192
MacNamara, Vincent, 170 n.1, 173 n.6
Mahoney, John, 141 n.57
Markham, Ian, 91 n.52, 146 n.67
Marxism, 38–9, 133, 136
metaphysics (as basis for ethics), 46, 86–8
Mette, Norbert, 234 n.40
Metz, J. B., 81 n.38, 99, 103
Milbank, John, 102, 142–53
Misner, Paul, 134 n.54
Mitchell, Basil, 85 n.42, 174 n.7
Moltmann, Jürgen, 119 n.29
Moran, Gabriel, 154 n.77
mystery, 84–5, 128–30, 141 n.57, 195

Nagel, Thomas, 20 n.12
narrative, 21, 23, 38, 42, 98–9, 106–10, 113–24, 197–8

natural law, 35–6, 38, 41–3, 86–7, 164–5, 169–70, 179, 194
Nelson, P., 104 n.15
Neo-Scholasticism, 41, 46, 87
Newbigin, Lesslie, 174 n.8
Niebuhr, H. Richard, 118 n.27

Pannenberg, Wolfhart, 11 n.1, 100–1, 118 n.27, 119 n.29
Peukert, Helmut, 78 n.36
Pius IX, 36, 132
Porter, Jean, 209 n.58
positivism, 39, 59, 63–4
postmodernity, 95, 146, 165, 179
praxis, 98–9, 104–5, 189

Rahner, Karl, 100, 148–51
Ratzinger, Joseph, 102–3, 133 n.53, 170 n.1
Rawls, John, 12 n.2, 15 n.5, 19 n.11, 54–7
reductionism, ethical, 37–44
Rorty, Richard, 16 n.6, 18 n.9

Schillebeeckx, Edward, 118 n.27, 233 n.39
Schnackenburg, Rudolf, 129 n.47
Schwemmer, O., 63 n.14
Seckler, M., 84 n.41
secularization, 216, 222–3
Shanks, Andrew, 153–60
Singer, M. G., 48 n.1
social contract, 11, 79, 173–4
solidarity, 45, 78 n.36, 83–4, 84 n.40, 154–6, 215, 234–5
Sollicitudo Rei Socialis (John Paul II), 84 n.40
Stoeckle, Bernhard, 170 n.1, 173 n.6
Stout, Jeffrey, 40 n.37
Strawson, Peter, 174 n.7
Stroup, George, 108 n.16
subjectivity, 34, 62–3, 78–82, 84

Taylor, Charles, 17 n.7, 95 n.2, 221–2
Thiemann, Ronald, 113–19, 122 n.34, 125–7, 193 n.39
Tracy, David, 23 n.13, 74 n.33, 91, 101, 123 n.35, 126–7, 151, 200 n.43, 202 n.45, 208 n.54
tradition, 20–4, 41–3, 73, 85, 89–91, 101–2, 104–5, 130–6, 229 n.34
transcendence, 123, 149–51, 171–2
Troeltsch, Ernst, 224

Vatican I, 35-7

wars of religion, 11, 19, 22, 215
will, subjective, 51-4, 58, 76, 79, 86

Williams, Bernard, 17 n.8
Wogaman, J. Philip, 201 n.44
Wolterstorff, Nicholas, 19 n.10
Wuthnow, Robert, 215 n.2, 230 n.35

DATE DUE

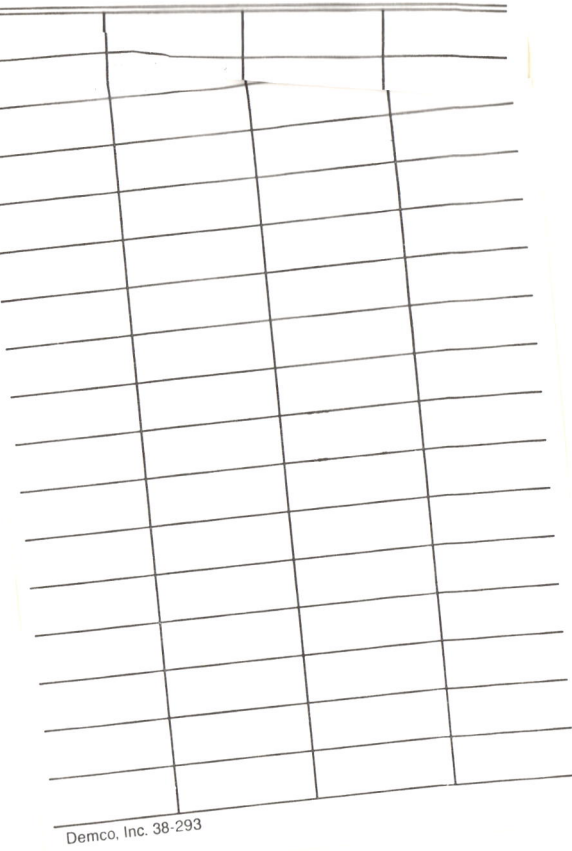

Demco, Inc. 38-293